Praise fo

A Box of Magick

"*A Box of Magick* does beautifully what brings most into the realm of the mystical best: it allows a slow building and a lure right from the beginning that is impossible to resist. A must for anyone who wants to light up their life and have a magickal adventure."

DAMIEN ECHOLS
author of *High Magick* and *Ritual*

"Jamie Della writes with deep dedication to mentoring the next genera-tions of witches. Her wisdom, practical knowledge, and guidance will help anyone who has an interest in deepening their craft, healing their heart, or even simply finding personal empowerment. It's a gift to our community that Jamie Della received the torch from her mentor, and has now chosen to pass that torch to us. Anyone who's ready to cast their own light will delight in this book."

AMANDA YATES GARCIA
author of *Initiated* and host of the *Between the Worlds* podcast

"*A Box of Magick* takes the reader on a magickal journey of healing, personal transformation, and empowerment. It illuminates a path of well-being and ceremonial living that connects one to the power of spirit within oneself and nature."

SANDRA INGERMAN
author of *Shamanic Journeying* and *The Book of Ceremony*

"Jamie Della is the real thing, a modern feminist witch whose creative down-to-earth spells and suggestions are fun, grounded, and helpful. Enjoy—as you deepen into your magic!"

VICKI NOBLE
cocreator of Motherpeace Tarot

"Jamie Della's comprehensive and inspiring book *A Box of Magick* will gift you with the wise teachings of two High Priestesses—the author and her elder mentor Connie DeMasters. You are invited to walk your own path, which is your unique expression of the Divine. The magick is already inside of you, and to access it you need only remember and reclaim what was never lost, only hidden. This tome will show you how."

SUSAN ILKA TUTTLE
author of *Green Witch Magick*

"Jamie Della's latest book, *A Box of Magick*, is a delightful combination of memoir and grimoire that takes the reader on a journey of remembrance and discovery. Nestled in between recollections of honest, down-to-earth conversations with her now-departed mentor Connie DeMasters, Jamie artfully delivers the details of Connie's wide variety of teachings for creating and growing a meaningful magical practice. Every person who's meant to walk a witchy path will find something within these pages that resonates with their own magic. Wherever Connie is now, she's beaming with pride, as her student has obviously become the teacher. Well done!"

CAIRELLE CROW
genealogist and author of *The Magic in Your Genes*

"Jamie Della's *A Box of Magick* is a generous book of magick drawn from her considerable experience and written directly from her heart. Her beloved mentor's teachings are present throughout, so you have two wise women guiding you for the price of one! Jamie writes, 'No Witch is like any other, because the connection we each make between nature and ourselves is as unique as a fingerprint.' Jamie's *Box of Magick* will guide you step by spiraling step in how to make your own magick come fully alive; this is a 'box' you'll want to open again and again!"

ROBIN ROSE BENNETT
author of *Healing Magic* and *The Gift of Healing Herbs*

A Box of Magick

ALSO BY JAMIE DELLA

(Also writing as Jamie Wood and Jamie Martinez Wood)

The Book of Spells: The Magick of Witchcraft

The Wicca Cookbook: Recipes, Ritual, and Lore

The Teen Spell Book: Magick for Young Witches

¿Como Te Llamas, Baby?: The Hispanic Baby Name Book

The Wicca Herbal: Recipes, Magick, and Abundance

The Enchanted Diary: A Teen's Guide to Magick and Life

Latino Writers and Journalists (A to Z of Latino Americans)

The Faerie's Guide to Green Magick in the Garden

Rogelia's House of Magic

Other publications in which Jamie's writing has appeared

Cakes and Ale for the Pagan Soul: Spells, Recipes, and Reflections from Neopagan Elders and Teachers, edited by Patricia Telesco

Brigid's Light: Tending the Ancestral Flame of the Beloved Celtic Goddess, edited by Cairelle Crow and Loura Louella

#MeToo: Essays About How and Why This Happened, What It Means and How to Make Sure It Never Happens Again, edited by Lori Perkins

A Box of Magick

Magick

A Guided Journey to Crafting a Magickal
Life Through Witchcraft,
Ritual Herbalism, and Spellcrafting

JAMIE DELLA

sounds true
BOULDER, COLORADO

Sounds True
Boulder, CO 80306

Sounds True is a trademark of Sounds True, Inc.

Published 2023

Cover design by Jennifer Miles
Book design by Meredith Jarrett
Illustrations © 2023 Katarina Samohin

Cover image by Katarina Samohin

A Box of Magick will highlight Connie DeMasters' contributions in the Acknowledgments
and storytelling excerpts throughout the book.

Printed in the United States of America

BK06631

Library of Congress Cataloging-in-Publication Data
Names: Della, Jamie, 1967- author.
Title: A box of magick : a guided journey to crafting a magickal life through witchcraft,
    ritual herbalism, and spellcrafting / by Jamie Della.
Description: Boulder, CO : Sounds True, 2023.
Identifiers: LCCN 2023000947 (print) | LCCN 2023000948 (ebook) | ISBN
    9781649630605 (trade paperback) | ISBN 9781649630612 (ebook)
Subjects: LCSH: Magic. | Mysticism. | Witchcraft.
Classification: LCC BF1611 .D355 2023 (print) | LCC BF1611 (ebook) |
    DDC 133.4/3--dc23/eng/20230503
LC record available at https://lccn.loc.gov/2023000947
LC ebook record available at https://lccn.loc.gov/2023000948

10 9 8 7 6 5 4 3 2 1

This book is dedicated
with love for the Crimson Dragon.

Contents

Introduction

Snow was still on the ground in May when my mentor's life's work arrived on my doorstep. I felt the presence of my teacher, Connie DeMasters, Wiccan Elder High Priestess, even though she had crossed over to the Spirit World fifteen years earlier. The air tingled with the buzzing density of Magick as I stared at the twenty-three-pound cardboard box containing fifty years' worth of Witchcraft spells, rituals, hymns, plays, and teaching curricula. My beloved teacher was standing in front of me again, with her mischievous, cat-like eyes and pixie haircut, asking me to pass on the torch of her collected wisdom to you.

I had sat at Connie's knee for years discovering how to craft a magickal life, and I want to give you the same gift—a mentor to help you live the craft of the wise and deepen your ability to manifest, intuit, and connect with the language of our alive world and its limitless possibilities.

You are essential to keeping the legacy of Magick alive. Your perspective and insight deepen the practice of Witchcraft because it is an evolving spirituality that has survived by teachers sharing their knowledge and students adding theirs.

Patience in the Craft has always been a must.

Sifting through the fragile sheets of Connie's magickal curricula, I felt overwhelmed by the sheer amount of information to impart. I was deeply honored, even as my skin prickled with trepidation, when I read the note from Connie's daughter, Alexa: "I hope that you can do something with this stuff."

I waited a year for inspiration. I barely dared to touch the pages, afraid of dishonoring Connie's memory by putting her information together "wrong." Finally, I heard Connie say: "Tell them about us." Her infectious giggle rippled through my mind as a wave of grief and release passed through me. Tears fell down my cheeks. Conversations with Connie had taught me how to apply magickal lessons to everyday tasks, like cooking dinner or discerning the wisdom in the changing seasons. Her teachings and support led to the personal development that would help me realize my biggest dreams for success. Now I knew how to give you, the reader, your very own box of Magick.

Within the pages of this book, there are twelve magickal lessons that correspond with the twelve steps that Joseph Campbell identified as the Hero's Journey, the pattern of personal discovery found in many myths and stories throughout the world. Stories of my meetings with Connie reinforce the teachings of *living* Magick. The spells and rituals give you the opportunity to practice paying attention to the seasonal, mystical, and ancestral wisdom that guides us in our everyday matters and inner life.

Throughout this book, Connie's curriculum will be shaded to indicate that you are indeed being taught by two priestesses. I recommend reading this book from beginning to end because the Magick intentionally builds upon itself and within ourselves. Over time, we all assign meaning to objects that are important to us.

A spell is a prayer in 3D.

My favorite, most visceral example of this is when Donna Reed, in the movie *It's a Wonderful Life*, offers a housewarming blessing with bread so the family will never know hunger, salt so they will always know flavor, and wine so they will always know joy and prosperity.

We exist in a swirling, alive universe where all of nature is conscious of itself and is in constant communication with us. You cannot "unknow" Magick once you accept it into your heart and life, and you cannot unring the bell of self-knowledge once you discover how to manifest or deepen your bond with the vibration of magickal energy and the language of nature and the cosmos. Living a truly magickal life begins with seeing everything and every place as alive and calling out to you. Let's make Magick together!

1

Call to Adventure

agick is created by aligning your will with the conscious world and universal influences. All of nature, from the wind to the crystals on an altar to the herbs in a kitchen cabinet, is trying to help us experience great joy and satisfaction through continual conversation. The river reminds us to go with the flow, the redwood forest reminds us of our ever-present ability to stand up tall, and the horse symbolizes wild-hearted freedom. This is animism, the belief that there is a consciousness in everything alive, whether it's animals, plants, weather systems, human handiwork, and even words and stories.

This supernatural aid is always available because the law of attraction, the belief that you attract what you focus on, is a two-way street. Universal spirits, whether they're plant allies, animal guides, crystals, or archetypes, are constantly drawing us into their worldview so we may gain insight on how to craft a more fulfilling life. When we drop lavender essential oil into a diffuser to create a calm environment, the basic belief is that we are reaching out to the lavender and drawing its power into our world. But what if the inspiration for relaxation came from the spirit of the lavender pulling *us* into its state of calm? What if the leaves that floated down onto your path really are a message to let it go?

We grow and evolve through a give-and-take conversation with living creatures, elemental spirits, and even our beloved friends and family who have crossed to the other side. This open dialogue with the supernatural and natural worlds is the essence of Witchcraft.

I truly hope that you find it peaceful and empowering that the animated world is sending personalized messages and lending its assistance so you can be your best self. The Divine, Creative Source, Great Spirit, God, or Goddess is the font of life, love, and intelligence for every living thing, from the rose quartz to the lamb to the pine tree. Each time you feel love, you are experiencing the unique expression or interpretation of the Divine Source that is you. From there, consider that another expression of the Great Spirit, whether it's a tree, herb, crystal, or animal, has the intelligence and ability to communicate with you through a cosmic language of energy and vibration.

In a magickal life, the lavender and the feather call out to us as much as we call upon them. Yes, the law of attraction is real; we will attract whatever we focus on. However, it is important to take a moment here to reject feelings of guilt, shame, or blame for "attracting" bad things or living a life of oppressive social situations and status. Born with original innocence, we are eternal spirits who are becoming more aware of our power in human form. Within every life there is a blessing, however hidden. Allow curiosity and a sense of adventure to replace the feelings of "getting it wrong."

We are more than this particular existence, yet this is where we can experience what it means to be viscerally alive, co-creating and communicating with an alive world. Diving into this conversation elevates our awareness and makes everywhere we step holy. This earth is where the Magick happens.

The poet Rumi said, "That which you seek is also seeking you." Submerse yourself in self-care, lean into the world, and pay attention to the messages that are everywhere. Feeling connected leads to a sense of belonging and less stress. When we belong and feel supported, we can reach for our biggest dreams and self-actualization. We are given permission to create our happiness when we truly love ourselves as a member of a community that is interwoven. Magick teaches us how to connect with the multilayered awareness and consciousness of animals, plants, trees, mountains, water, and forests.

In accordance with the Principles of Wiccan Belief adopted at the Spring 1974 Witchmeet in Minneapolis, Minnesota, "We acknowledge that it is the affirmation and fulfillment of life, in a continuation of evolution and development of consciousness, that gives meaning to the universe we know, and to our personal role within it."

Like intuition, mindfulness, or even a muscle, Magick grows with daily practice. For centuries, the Japanese have practiced shinrin-yoku, or forest bathing. Forest bathing is a simple act of being still and quiet in a forest of whatever size, perceiving nature through all of our senses. Listen to the birds singing and try to detect different sounds and feelings that support each trill. Look at the different leaves of the trees and the sunlight filtering through the branches. Allow nature to entice you with its fragrance and the natural aromatherapy of phytoncides, the volatile organic compounds (VOCs) or "essential oils" produced by trees that help them stave off bugs and boost our immune systems. Taste the dew in the air as you take deep breaths. Touch the trunks of trees, stems of leaves, and blades of grass. Lie on the ground and feel Mother Earth supporting you. Breathe with the trees and tap into the idea that you and the trees are breathing buddies. The living world is always calling us into its state of being, whether for healing, protection, love, or whatever else is needed at any given moment. Shinrin-yoku works as a bridge to close the gap between us and the natural world.

Our spirits also call out to each other, whether they are here on Earth or have crossed over. In Mexican families, such as mine, we create ofrendas for Día de los Muertos to keep the spirits of our beloved dead alive in our hearts. This is how we reach out to them. It is completely acknowledged that our beloved dead send signs to us, such as the scent of your grandmother's favorite flowers wafting in the air after her passing. Many people have experienced hearing a love song just as they thought of their beloved, picking up on snatches of strangers' conversations that seemed like they were meant just for them, or getting a phone call from their sibling just as they picked up the phone to call them. This is the Magick of Witchcraft, the art of listening and responding with intention.

In 2001, when I first met my mentor, Connie DeMasters, I had already published two Wiccan Witchcraft books and wanted to level up my magickal knowledge. Connie was in her fifties and was eager to share her wisdom with someone who could pass along her teachings and add their unique perspective and experience. After all, no Witch is like any other because the connection we each make between nature and ourselves is as unique as a fingerprint. As we practice our personalized version of the Craft, we walk a unique path toward becoming wise and knowledgeable in the areas we are attracted to or where we are most needed.

For three years, I sat at Connie's knee, taking in her wisdom and teachings on Wicca, lightwork (the meditative focus on positivity, love, and faith, regardless of spirituality or religion), and conscious personal development from one-on-one magickal instruction. She taught me in the tradition of the Druidic Craft of the Wise of America (DCWA). I would then apply the teachings in my life and make connections between Witchcraft and earth sciences, esoterica, mindfulness, and even my Christian Science upbringing. She gave me the scaffolding upon which to grow my spiritual practice.

Fifteen years after Connie's passing, when her daughter asked if she could send me all of her mother's magickal lessons, I accepted the responsibility and honor of creating something wonderful with her mother's collection. It was the onset of the 2020 pandemic, and I needed strong arms around me as I faced isolation in menopause. It had been a long time since I'd felt the support of an elder. When we're encouraged to embody the fullness of our Divine expression, our greatest potential and Magick often alight on our fingertips. Receiving Connie's treasure trove of Magick with her family's blessing confirmed that I was still on the right track. A mentor can often reflect back to you the inner wisdom you didn't realize you had. This reflection can even come from beyond the veil.

I remember the first day Connie and I spoke like it was yesterday.

✳

"The Spirits tell me that I am supposed to teach you," Connie said during our introductory phone call.

I stared at the phone in disbelief. I wondered if this was a joke, but my intuition told me that Connie was the answer for my recent spell for a new Witchcraft mentor. I felt a chill race through my body. In my mind's eye, I saw Connie, a full-figured woman of fifty-plus years, sitting at the Eye of the Cat booth at the 2001 Long Beach WomanSpirit Winter Solstice Faire. She had a glint in her eyes, Santa Claus peepers that crinkled in merriment as she watched the parades of pagans, Witches, and bohos dressed in velvet capes, jangling bracelets, and flowy goddess garb. Connie regarded the revelers as if each person was her own precious grandchild. She simply emanated pride and love.

Even though I was in a neighboring booth twenty feet away, I had a feeling that Connie was listening to me converse with people who bought signed copies of *The Wicca Cookbook* and *The Teen Spell Book*. I could feel her sending waves of support when festivalgoers paused uncertainly in front of my books and, within minutes, pulled out their credit cards or cash.

Call to Adventure

Two days after the fair, I stood in my son's bedroom with the phone in my hand, goosebumps rising across the backs of my arms. I could feel that Magick was afoot. From nowhere and everywhere, I sensed the aroma of temple incense and heard the tinkling of bells. I felt that destiny had drawn us both toward that moment, an exciting new mentor-mentee relationship.

As if she were reading my thoughts, Connie tittered like a bubbly schoolgirl. "Shall we meet at my house?" she asked.

I answered immediately. "What can I bring?"

It was time to own my power.

A few days later, I secured a babysitter for my toddler sons, picked up two caramel macchiatos and maple nut scones from Starbucks, and drove to Connie's eclectic neighborhood in Long Beach. Artful and not-so-artful graffiti on buildings and walls made me feel far too suburban as the discomfort from that raw depiction of life washed over me. At the same time, I felt exhilarated to be breaking free from the blandly familiar and meeting a new teacher.

I knocked on the screen door, and Connie called for me to enter. She had set a chair across from where she sat in a black leather recliner. On the wall behind her was a framed picture of a grey wolf in the woods. I scanned her bookshelf, which was crammed with mojo bags, crystals, statues of various gods and goddesses, a series of lit, colored advent candles, and many dusty books. We sipped our coffee and smiled at each other. I had the sensation that Connie was drinking in everything about me, from my eyes to my clothes and jewelry to my posture. It was as if she had been waiting for this day for a long time.

She lit a white taper candle and said, "I'm glad you're here." The flame rose as if it were stretching, licking the air, and testing the room's vibration. When the light settled, Connie smiled at the candle, then looked at me. "I realize it took trust to come today, and I admire you for that. Why did you decide to come?"

When did you answer the calling to your wildness? When did you decide to trust your inner knowing above all else? When did you hear the first whisperings of your most untamed nature?

REWILDING THROUGH MAGICK

When I met my mentor, I was on the other side of my Saturn's Return at thirty-three years old, the master year. Saturn, the planet of discipline, has a long orbit. Around the time when you turn twenty-seven, it returns to the position in the sky it was in when you were born. For approximately five years, this strict disciplinarian sits on you, taking away all that you relied upon for your identity and security. You melt like a caterpillar, and when you restructure, you are reborn as a butterfly with a stronger sense of self and knowledge of how to fly.

However, this "adulting" can cause us to disconnect from our wild side. Mistakes feel huge and irreparable when really they are Spirit Holes, metaphysical openings for life's greatest lessons to enter. I was in one of those Spirit Holes and beginning to lose my grip on my faith in the natural world that once had called me into its harmonized existence. Whether through the wind, birdsong, or sunshine, nature had usually filled me with the best feeling in the world. But now I felt like I had been deprived of my connection to the earth, this sentient world that I knew was so eager to share its ancestral knowledge. Motherhood, a sad marriage, and a mortgage were making it difficult for me to find my feral spirit. At the same time, I resisted being pulled into domesticity with every fiber of my passionate spirit.

Some people come into this world with an innate and inexplicable relationship with nature, and others have to cultivate it. Sometimes we get disconnected and strive to embolden the truest parts of ourselves and reunite with our inner essence. Some people grow up surrounded by unspoiled land and have childhood memories of nature's language, whether in the West Virginia woods where they built a fort that no one but them and Mother Earth knew about or near the quiet and stillness of mountain lakes. Others replenish their energy, also known as *chi* or *qi*, the vital force of all living entities, from the desert moon on sagebrush to the peaks so high they feel on top of the world to the blue oceans so vast the horizon becomes a friend. And some hear the animals speak. They know the cat's keen, strategic nature, the dog's greatest joy in being silly, and the horse's ability to heal with its eyes.

Witchcraft is essentially an earth spirituality in which we see ourselves as belonging to the Elements: air as breath, water as blood, fire as energy, and earth as body. Nature offers peace, harmony, and protection that can be experienced and felt by human beings, as we are part of nature. Our job is to conjure a childlike wonder and listen to the consciousness of the earth, trust our intuition, and allow ourselves to be inspired. We were all born pure, regardless of how we were treated as children or adults. Sometimes it's very difficult to see our original innocence, and we may need help from a professional. We may need to remove obstacles that prevent us from seeing or remembering our imaginative curiosity and boundless hope.

Teacher, artist, occultist, social reformer, and clairvoyant Rudolf Steiner expanded the concept of human potential by stating that humans are linked to the cosmos and nature for self-development and individuality as well as for societal evolution. His pedagogy holds that children are deeply connected to both the natural and spirit worlds, so it follows that surrounding the young child with natural materials is the best way to inspire their creativity, imagination, and free play. My children attended a Waldorf school, where their playthings were made solely of natural materials. I watched as they interacted with the spirit in their wooden block that was once a tree, the silkworm that wove the thread for their hero's cape, and the hum of the bees that created the wax for their crayons. Children, Steiner believed, know how to speak with seemingly inanimate objects by connecting to them in their alive forms.

This symbiotic relationship isn't only experienced by children, however. It's also experienced by those who are willing to suspend their disbelief long enough to make room for miracles. In the 1960s in northern Scotland, a family built a legendary garden from once barren soil by listening to specific requests of the deva, or conscious spirit, of the plants. The family gave the land what it needed, including their friendship. Word spread about forty-pound cabbages and ten-foot-tall foxgloves. Horticulture experts arrived and could determine no other factor for the creation of the huge garden beyond the attention and respect given to the spirits of the plants. Now known as the Findhorn Foundation, this eco-village and retreat center rests on three guiding principles for its work in the world: inner listening, work as love in action, and co-creation with the intelligence of nature.

Now more than ever, socio-ecology, the study of the relationship between organisms, animals, and plants with their environments, is at the front of our minds as we feel the impact of climate change. Aldo Leopold, considered the father of socio-ecology, advocated for a land ethic: care for people cannot be separated from care for the land. He believed that direct contact with the natural world was crucial in shaping our ability to extend our ethics beyond our own self-interests. In the foreword of his seminal book *A Sand County Almanac*, Leopold writes, "We abuse land because we regard it as a commodity belonging to us. When we see land as a community to which we belong, we may begin to use it with love and respect."

Today we are rediscovering an ancient wisdom that asserts that we cannot impose our will over the land. We must respect the earth's natural resources and listen deeply to create a fertile, sustainable environment. With this knowledge that the earth is alive and needs time to regenerate, just as we do, we must give the land time to rest from its productivity. Our symbiotic relationship with nature is based on love.

> "And forget not that the earth delights to feel your bare
> feet and the winds long to play with your hair."
> Khalil Gibran

As a child, it was natural for me to talk with spirits. My maternal grandmother passed on one month before my birth. Transitioning through the corridor between the spiritual and physical worlds at the same time as my Nana Della opened a doorway to the other side, through which I could ask questions and receive an answer. At Christian Science Sunday school, I discovered that I had the power to heal my body or solve a problem with a firm focus on physical or spiritual wholeness. Then Nana Mame, a psychic tarot reader, taught me how to read energy, recognize members of my soul family (evolving individual souls who travel with you through time and space as you learn karmic lessons), and access magickal portals (doorways into alternate realms). Mame lived with us when I was a teenager and taught me that the numbers zero through nine are as powerful as gods and goddesses. To this day, based on numerology, a suite number or street address can make or break a deal for me.

By my mid-thirties, I had attended many public sabbat (Pagan holiday) rituals, Wiccan ceremonies and classes, sweat lodges, drum circles, transcendental meditations, massage therapy trainings, and Pagan festivals. I had magickal mentors in nature, my nanas, and an eclectic fae Witch named Jeanette, and I was particularly interested in the Wiccan path. I took classes from the iconic Eye of the Cat, a Witch shop in Long Beach. I was searching for a mentor with whom I could learn how to apply magickal lessons to my life, and I was blessed with Connie, who wanted to teach me.

✳

During that first visit, I told Connie, "I am here because I followed my intuition. You are an answer to a spell for a mentor, but also I felt drawn by you to be here."

Connie giggled like she had just been caught doing something outrageous. "Yes, I have been waiting for someone to teach. What do you want to learn?" she asked. She wrapped her arms around her belly and hugged herself.

"I want to return to my wild self," I answered.

Connie smiled and leaned forward, closing the gap between us. "Let us begin. But first, you've got to set the table when you are inviting the spirits to lend their Magick to your wishes."

CONSECRATING SACRED SPACE

Witchcraft is a practice of trusting our intuition to address each moment as it arises. We improve our intuition through a daily routine of listening to our unique essence so we can respond effortlessly with clear intention.

Trusting your inner wisdom or intuition is the first step of Magick. Intuition helps you feel into your body and get in touch with your desires. The universe shifts and moves in accordance with our spoken wishes. When we surround ourselves with empowering messages, we begin to visualize exciting opportunities. In addition to words, we are constantly creating and shaping our world through the environment we set. Magick works best when you lovingly and intentionally prepare a place—whether it's a room or a corner—to study and practice the art of Magick. Merely entering this sacred space heightens your sense of possibilities, calms the mind, and awakens your spirit to your ability to co-create your desires with an active and animated world.

I suggest consecrating a room or space so positive thoughts flourish. We will talk more about negative thoughts in chapter eight when we talk about shadow work, but for now, let's focus on creating a sanctum for the most optimistic and warm-hearted energy. Ask yourself, "What is the very best feeling in the world?" Be still to listen for the answer; it will be different for each person and will most likely change as you move through your life. Once you have the word for that "very best feeling," consider items that represent this emotion. For example, if you prefer comfort, then you may want to fill your room with cozy blankets, squishy pillows, and scents that bring you ease. Engage all five senses, paying close attention to what catches the eye or elicits the other senses of scent, touch, taste, and sound. If you prefer order, then maybe the scent of pine incense or sparse décor will focus your mind. If you burst with joy with the love of family, then fill your sacred space with pictures, handcrafted items, and things that represent the hearth of home.

Get rid of all distracting things in the room or space that you have decided will be your sacred working place. If the item does not pertain to working Magick or interrupts your practice, get it out of the room or area as it may subtly work against your spells. This includes books, pictures, or anything else that is eye-catching, brilliant in color, or distracting from your intention.

Each of us will experience supernatural energy differently in our body, and we will all receive universal messages in unique ways. Some of us will hear the voice of Spirit whispering in our ear, others will feel the message like a deep knowing as strong as a mother's love, and others will have visions that they see in their mind's eye or on the shimmering landscape. Observing how our spirit or energy influences the world is how we master the ability to interpret and direct energy. Magick elicits the feeling of your desire. Make sure your room or space feels like *you*.

Much of spellcrafting relies upon visualization skills, or mental pictures, so you can imagine what you want and make that dream a reality in the physical world. If you would like to further develop your ability to see mental images, try this mind-body connection adopted from Rolfing bodywork to improve your manifestations through visualization.

Lie down on your back with your knees bent and your feet resting on the ground, or whatever is most comfortable for you. Take calming breaths. With each inhalation, imagine sending your breath to a body part that needs it, like an aching joint, a tense muscle, or a general buildup of energy. Exhale. Then inhale and direct your breath to the sides of your ribs. Touch your torso if this helps. Exhale. From here, you can touch your wrist, hips, heart, or any other body part as you continue to send your breath and healing oxygen to the areas that need extra attention and loving care. Once you feel complete with this, slowly roll your head from side to side, inhaling as you roll in one direction and exhaling as you roll your head the other way. Visualize your chin scraping the sky as the back of your head rolls over the earth. Do this several times, concentrating on the physical sensations of stretching your chin and neck toward the heavens and the pressure of your head meeting the ground. Imagine yourself as the sacred space between heaven and earth. In your very existence, you blend the ordinary with the otherworldly.

AN ALTAR IS AN AFFIRMATION

Our altars work like visual affirmations in ways similar to placing your favorite quotes where you'll see them often. Countless studies have demonstrated how we learn better with visual cues because our brains function mainly as image processors. An altar is composed of visual reminders, or symbols, that can represent the blessings of the seasons (flowers for spring) or the specific aspects of our spellwork (coins for prosperity, roses for love, etc.). Spells are prayers in 3D because they're based on the wisdom of using imagery to convey messages to our brains so that we can transform a thought into a third-dimensional reality. Images are powerful tools to evoke and get in touch with our emotional drivers because visual memory is encoded in the medial temporal lobe of the brain, the same place emotions are processed.

When you create your altar, try to incorporate a minimum of three symbols that represent qualities or feelings associated with the desire you want to manifest. Three is a magickal number because it takes the union of the Divine Feminine and the Divine Masculine to create the child. You can even choose the color of an altar cloth to represent the Magick you want to bring into your life. A list of color correspondences can be found in the appendix in the back of the book. When you lay an altar cloth down, it's like you're laying the tablecloth for a meal or setting the framework for an important conversation.

For example, if you want to attract love, you might use a red altar cloth or candle. If you want to tap into the energy of freedom, you can choose feathers to symbolize flight. If you need to expand your thinking, you might choose a seashell to represent the vastness of the ocean. After you have all your items ready, write your intention in bold letters on a piece of paper and place it in the center of your altar. Make sure your altar is in a place where you will see it every day. Stand in front of your altar and sing this time-honored chant that reminds us how we are part of this world and in no way separate:

"Earth my body
Water my blood
Air my breath and
Fire my spirit."

Anoint Yourself

You can grow your magickal practice alongside your self-care and wellness practices by anointing your entire body with oil. Oiling can mark the beginning of establishing the sacred time, moment, space, and experience for Magick.

Abhyanga is an Ayurvedic therapy that involves massaging good-quality, natural carrier oils, like olive, jojoba, coconut, grapeseed, or apricot kernel oil, into your skin for a wide range of benefits. When done often, abhyanga helps your skin retain its hydration and luster; reduces cellulite; tones skin, infuses your body, mind, and spirit with a grounding energy that soothes anxiety, stress, and tension; provides a physical layer of protection for the largest organ of your body; and offers psychic protection that allows you to hold onto your energy when situations or people drain you. This last benefit works especially well when herbs known for their protective properties are infused in the oils with an intention of preserving your energy. Each carrier oil has a different viscosity and emollience, so choose one that feels the best on your skin.

I suggest you begin this practice by taking a warm bath or shower. Our skin cells open with warm water, which permits the oil to penetrate the skin easier. Another method to make the most of your oiling practice is to pat yourself dry with a fresh towel and then oil your entire body while your skin is damp. The oils seal in the leftover moisture on the surface of the skin, slowing its evaporation, thus keeping the skin moisturized longer.

It is important to know that most essential oils cannot be applied "neat" or directly on the skin but must be diluted in a carrier oil. When I was new to herbalism, I dropped peppermint essential oil onto the shower floor. As the steam rose, the volatile oils stung every sensitive body part. Not only did water not wash off the oil, it had the opposite effect by causing the peppermint oil to absorb more into my skin. I quickly applied a carrier oil to my skin, which I then wiped off to extract the oil from my body. As long as you are learning as you go, be gentle with yourself as you make mistakes.

You can add to your oiling practice by applying heavier strokes toward your clavicles, the area of our bodies where we release all toxins. Our chest, just beneath the clavicles, is the exit point for our lymphatic system, also known as our immune system. As you massage the oil into your skin, imagine that you are directing anything that does not serve you to leave your body. When you are done, allow your skin to air dry; otherwise you will get oil on your clothes and possibly defeat the purpose of a calming practice.

If you would like to add to this ritual, after you have oiled your body, choose adornments, clothes, makeup, or jewelry that make you feel magickal, but don't put on shoes. Walking barefoot will help you feel more connected to the earth, the physical world, and it will make it easier for you to draw up energy from Mother Earth to help manifest your desires.

Take a moment to prepare your mind by going over the events of the day. Begin by counting your blessings, especially those you procured with magickal intention. This builds your faith and instills a sense of self-confidence. If the day or week has been particularly stressful, review your worries or fears as you squeeze your toes, then relax them. Move all the way up your body, imagining the tense emotions rising as you tighten your ankles, calves, knees, etc. Then, as you relax and release, feel the tension dissolving into nothingness. Alternatively, you can recall the day's blessings as you tighten and release.

Engage your five senses as if you were forest bathing. Visually, you will have placed items in your space that help evoke magickal possibilities for you. Light a bundle of incense or dried herbs, such as white sage or mugwort, to fill your sacred place with a pleasing scent. (Be certain that any herbs you use have been sustainably harvested; more information about this can be found in the appendix.) Create a sound that builds your power, whether that is bells, chimes, a singing bowl, meditative music, or silence. Taste and feel the Magick in the air.

You have now prepared your space, mind, body, and spirit for Magick.

Whether you oil every night or morning, whenever you remember, or for sex, the more you feel your body, the more aware you can be of your own greatness and how joyful life can be. Self-care proves that you matter. You might even add a dry brush session for a healthy, sensory experience for your immune system. You may call this oiling practice a self-massage, common sense, or abhyanga, or the ritual that creates sacred space for your physical, mental, and spiritual bodies.

✳

"Stillness resides at the center of Magick and manifestation," Connie said. "Patience is Elder Goddess wisdom, sometimes known as 'granny wisdom.'" Connie took a pinch of dried herbs from a red velvet bag on the glass end table. She dropped the dried leaves onto a piece of charcoal lying at the bottom of a mug-sized iron cauldron. Immediately, the herbs crackled and released the pungent scent of mugwort.

"Time spent practicing the Craft, learning its magickal language, teaches you how to trust the ebb as much as the flow. It is time for me to pass along my information, and the spirits tell me you are the one. Have you ever heard about the woman who trekked four days to meet the guru?" Connie looked at me expectantly.

I shook my head as I inhaled the incense smoke. I hadn't heard about the woman.

Connie smiled and settled into her chair. "The woman who sought out the guru traveled for ten hours by plane." Her tone was rich, warm, and lyrical, like that of all good storytellers. "Then she took a steamboat for three days. Next, she rode in a rickety train, a souped-up school bus, and finally she made a five-mile uphill climb." Connie spoke slowly to help me visualize the woman's arduous journey.

"At last, she reached the secluded mountaintop where the guru lived. There, she found a long line of people. She waited for hours, and at long last she was at the front of the line. The guru's assistant reminded the woman that she could only have one question. She nodded, then quietly entered the guru's cave. A shaft of light fell upon the woman's husband, who sat serenely in the lotus position. 'Maurice,' the woman asked, 'when are you coming home?'"

Connie leaned back in her chair and chuckled at her own joke for a solid minute. Then she sat up, wiped a tear from her sparkling eyes, and looked me directly in the eyes. The mood went from lighthearted to somber in seconds.

"It's one thing to teach from where I sit, and it's another thing to write about it and stand up against the prejudice coming from people who are not in the Craft as well as from other Witches. You will have critics responding to what you write and teach about Wicca or Witchcraft." She held my attention with the steady gaze of her brown eyes. "Do you know why?"

I could feel her testing me, yet I could also sense her confidence in me. "There are no two Witches who are the same," I responded. I looked out the window at the branches of the tree swaying in the breeze. I returned my gaze to Connie. "Experience makes us all our own best teachers, so we all see the Magick slightly differently."

"Exactly." Connie smiled. "One day, more people will awaken to the Witch within. It may take years; it may take decades. I want to share a meditation to help you let go of your concerns. You are a lightworker, and the road ahead is not easy."

"Yes!" I almost choked on my enthusiasm.

Connie smiled warmly at me. I felt a deep acceptance I had rarely known. I felt I could trust her with my secrets and my heart.

"I'm kind of a Tigger, always hyper-positive and charged up," I said with a shrug.

Connie winked and blew me a kiss. "I know, my sunshine. Now, close your eyes."

◇ The Cave Meditation

Imagine yourself at the entrance of a cave. The rocks on either side are smooth and hard. Inside, the cave has a damp, musty smell, and the light is dim, yet ahead, you can see steps leading down. Follow the steps slowly, going down, counting them as you go. Ten, nine, eight . . . going deeper . . . seven . . . going deeper still . . . six . . . going even deeper . . . five, four . . . going down . . . three . . . deeper . . . two . . . down . . . one. You are at the bottom step. Ahead there is a faint light. Move toward the light, and as it grows, you see the tunnel has another opening, this one leading into the sunshine. Beside the opening, a white robe lies folded and waiting. Put on the robe. Feel its softness against your skin, its gentle, flowing folds brushing against your legs. Step outside. Listen to the sounds of the breeze playing in the leaves of the trees overhead and the chirping of birds. Before you is a path that winds and curves through the trees. Ahead you hear the sound of water flowing. Follow the path toward the sound.

Suddenly you find yourself in a clearing, and in the center of the clearing lies a small pool of water. The light of the sun sparkles and dances across its surface, which is blue and green. And you know, within yourself, that this is a magickal pond, deep and wonderful. You slip off the white robe and, for an instant, feel the warm breeze again on your body as you dip one foot into the water and then the other. The bottom is soft yet firm. Feel the water move around your feet and your ankles and then your calves and your thighs, gently swirling around your hips and waist, warm and soothing, easing up around your chest and shoulders. Move your arms about in the water, feeling its slight resistance, and lay your head back, letting the water hold you, carry you, and wash you cleaner than you have ever been before. Any disease, any burden, any ill feeling is gently washed away by the water. You are at peace, utterly and completely at one with yourself and all of nature as you relax more and more in the soothing, healing waters.

The water cools slightly and tingles rush through your body as a feeling of new life flows into your blood. You rise—fresh, clean, new, and revitalized—and head toward the shore, letting the water drip off your body as you reach for the robe. Deeply breathe in the cool forest air and slip the robe on. You feel young, energetic, and vibrantly alive with every nerve in your being. You bound along the path beneath the trees. The twists and turns feel familiar now, and eventually you see the cave entrance ahead.

Slowly, the images in your mind begin to fade. As you drift up in consciousness and become aware of your physical body, squeeze your toes and then your fingers. Breathe slowly and allow the thoughts and ideas that you received in this cave meditation to sink into your awareness. Meditation is like an awake dream with messages, and as you transcend from the subconscious state of deep relaxation to your active mind, you want to hold onto the lessons. Intentionally bringing the messages across this bridge of subconscious to conscious awareness is how you deepen your magickal practice.

We all have the ability to listen to nature's conversations and feel into the wisdom of a sentient and alive universe. You choose the path and methods that resonate most with you and your sensory abilities and preferences. We have six senses: vision, sound, taste, touch, smell, and proprioception, also called *kinesthesia* or the body's ability to sense its location. I will explore *claires* or the senses we can work with to perceive spiritual information in chapter four.

As the author of this book, I am both the teacher and the student who listens to the voice of my elder as we share the teachings behind the spells, magickal correspondences, ancient traditions, and rites that tell us when to manifest and when to be still. *A Box of Magick* shows us how to turn seeds of knowledge into a magickal life. There is a little Witch in all of us and a sparkle of Magick at our fingertips that itch with the ability to cast spells, forge connections, and manifest desires. Water the vision with your unique spirit and watch it bloom. This book will help you hear and understand the cosmic language and foster a relationship with the sentient spirits that surround you every day of your life.

2

Ritual Herbalism

Each step of awakening to the call of your inner Witch is rife with excitement. The Path, as it is known, can feel electrifying upon your first steps as well as at every threshold you approach along the way. Your worldview expands as you see all things as alive and potential allies for this journey we call life. At this crossroads, the important question is not whether you can manifest but where you will place your extraordinary energy. Where will you direct your Divine Essence and love? The practice of Witchcraft is as individual as a yoga practice, a daily meditation, a garden, an exercise or self-care routine, a diet, a parenting technique, or a teaching practice. Magick, connection, and manifestation grow when you listen.

In time, Witches learn that Magick reveals itself in the slow and steady process of listening for answers to the questions you didn't know to ask. Witchcraft connects you to your inner Magick and opens the portal to a worldview where everything in nature and the cosmos is alive and speaking to you. Through the reciprocity of interacting with the Divine within you and the forces in the universe, you can craft a magickal life. The Witchcraft Path is a lifestyle where the emphasis is on the journey, not the destination or outcome of any one spell, ritual, or perfectly planned sabbat, the name we use for Pagan holidays. Magick is a journey of discovering the deepest part of you as you connect with the cycles of nature.

The connection you yearn for is already within you. You are the closest to God, Great Spirit, or Goddess that you will ever be. Your relationship to your own creative nature is the most magickal part of you. When you connect with the life that pulsates in everything, you expand the creative potential of the entire universe.

Whether you prefer to be barefoot upon an earthen forest floor, ankle deep in sand or living waters, or upon stone steps, you must walk your own path, which is your unique expression of the Divine Essence. Whether we are conscious of it or not, we are always expressing our soul light; sometimes it's radiant, but it's always in the same hue of our unique spirit. Answering the call of the Witch simply means you are ready to experience the Divine within. The word *witch* derives from the word *wise*. Witchcraft is the art and process of consciously becoming wise through emanating our Divine Essence, deeply connecting with the unique spirits and cosmic influences that cross our path, and living honorably within the web that connects us all.

Ritual herbalism, the art and craft of listening to the spirits of plant allies, can be a source of empowerment through healing the mind, body, and spirit. Plant medicine guides us to wholeness by radiating its devic (derived from *devas*) energy. In other words, the herb's spirit or deva calls out and entices us into its realm, whether for healing, nourishment, or restructuring.

Anyone can be a ritual herbalist, even if you simply enjoy being outside. Some of the Witchcraft traditions particularly known for their connection with nature may be called green, hedge, fae, folk, ritual, and by many other names that are blossoming at a rate that's difficult to keep up with. Witches are multiplying like a garden of mint with plenty of water and room to grow.

Nature teaches us to indulge in the present moment, for within a day (or maybe more) everything will change. The snow melts, the shoots reach for the sun, flowers blossom, and leaves fall, round and round. Change is the only constant. Nature shows us how to go with the flow of life's ever-evolving pattern; whether and how you choose to do this is up to you. You might grow your own herbs, prefer an herbalist's tincture, or use essential oils.

Ritual herbalism teaches the wisdom of empirical knowledge through a conscious conversation with plants. The elemental energy of the plant world is often called the *fae*, to indicate all spirits of nature. We can sit with plants or their products, listen to their vibrations, sense their smells, and discover how to feel their unique energy. Slowly, every day, we learn. When we engage with plants as conscious beings, they respond, and our Magick has more healing potential, more strength, and better direction. Our tending and pruning of the plants, in turn, increases their production.

When we employ a purposeful focus on the unique properties of a plant, that attention increases its ability to heal. Quantum physics is interwoven into Magick. Our focus and attention help manifest ideas and desires. When we recognize the sentience in the plant world, the energy of each herb, tree, and flower will respond in kind and send more energy and medicine to us. Witches heal, and we lead by example, living in harmony with the cycles and rhythms of nature.

Plants and humans draw from the same Divine Source. The poem "Desiderata" by Max Ehrmann says, "You are a child of the universe, no less than the trees or the stars." It is never appropriate to force our will upon another, including our sister and brother plants. Plants respond to our energy, requests, and attention from their own will and consciousness.

The Secret Life of Plants book gives detailed information about Cleve Backster's studies in the 1960s using lie detectors to record evidence of plants' emotional intelligence. In the experiment, plants were hooked up to a polygraph machine that measured three things: pulse, respiration rate, and galvanic skin response, otherwise known as perspiration. The plants responded with a surge of electrical activity when Backster burned or cut leaves or when he held violent thoughts toward the plants. Even though scientific evidence regarding the plants' responses wasn't consistent, the magickal idea that plants could be listening inspired many people to try talking to or playing music for their houseplants and gardens. To their delight, many people discovered that those interactions resulted in the plants becoming more robust and stronger. This empirical evidence of communicating with the plants' consciousness is the root of ritual herbalism.

Today, many people don't know about Backster's experiment, yet they still notice how talking with plants affects their vitality. If we can believe our pets respond to our affections, then why not extend the same level of conscious self-awareness to plants? After all, they nourish, feed, and mend our bodies.

When you recognize the sentience of the green world and humbly and respectfully ask for its help, you will receive energy, attention, and healing potential from the plants themselves because they hear you and are willing to respond.

"Paying attention is a form of reciprocity with the living
world, receiving the gifts with open eyes and open heart."
Robin Wall Kimmerer

CONSECRATING THE TOOL OF INTENTION

Plants are beings of nature that deserve our respect and consideration. Lettuce, daisies, a walnut tree, or a rosemary bush are living presences that would greatly appreciate your forewarning before they are plucked, pruned, or picked. First and foremost, it is a sign of respect to approach plants that you are harvesting with love and gratitude. The plant world perceives your intentions through your energetic field and always responds accordingly.

Your deference to the equality of the human and green worlds can inspire the plants to give you more of their energy. Some of the best gardeners have noticed that their tomatoes grow redder and plumper with verbal encouragement. We coax the bloom into fruit and taste the difference. Masaru Emoto demonstrated how human consciousness affects the molecular structure of water in his 2004 book *The Hidden Messages in Water*. His experiments showed beautiful water molecules forming in response to thoughts or spoken words of love and chaotic formations resulting from negativity. As a plant's healing potential grows with your loving attention, consider energetically cleansing your garden tools, kitchen scissors, and/or athame with salt water, your favorite smoking herbs, or even your breath before trimming or harvesting.

The athame is the Witch's ceremonial knife, which is the tool of intention. Typically, the athame is a black-hilted, steel-bladed knife used to cast circles and other diagrams. The athame represents the assertion of our will and helps us direct our energy. Of course, we can project our will with our mind, actions, or intention, but Witches tend to enlist magickal objects that help them remember how to call up the specific energy a tool represents. Each magickal tool represents the power within you to experience whatever you need, whether it's knowledge, passion, empathy, or security. Not every tradition views their magickal tools in the same way. For example, I work in the DCWA tradition, which states that the sword is a tool of fire and the wand is the symbol of air. Other traditions flip those correspondences.

New Witches, people who are new to Magick as a lifestyle, or those who are even mildly intrigued by Witchcraft can dip a toe into this mysterious world by designating a few everyday tools, such as scissors, knives, or bowls, as sacred objects. Your magickal tools for a spell, ritual, or ceremony are ingredients, just like vanilla extract is an ingredient for a cookie recipe. Witchcraft is alchemy. Magick is play, and tools help us remember to embody our divinity as we enjoy the whimsical ride on the cycles of life.

Crimson Dragon on the Athame

An athame is used to project the force of one's will. There are varying schools of thought with regard to this and other tools. The ceremonialists, the purists, feel that magickal tools should never be handled by others or used for anything but ritual purposes. They believe that objects can become reservoirs of psychic energy, which may be dissipated by using a tool for something other than its ritual purpose, like slicing fruit with your athame. If this point of view resonates with you, you can reserve a white-handled knife called a boline for kitchen and garden purposes.

Another school of thought, referred to as kitchen Magick, asserts that the Goddess is manifest in ordinary tasks as well as magickal circles, and since you are already filled with Magick, your tool, by extension, is also pulsating with Magick whether you slice fruit for breakfast or herbs for a spell with it. With your intention, a kitchen chore is as sacred a task as drawing a magickal circle for a full moon ceremony.

No matter the school of thought that most intrigues you or the one to which you belong, it is in very poor taste to handle another Witch's tools without asking permission first. The same etiquette should be applied to another's altar, crystals, jewelry, wand, framed pictures, or anything they have imbued with their personal Magick. It's like touching a woman's pregnant belly without asking.

EVERYDAY MAGICK

You can buy a special knife, or you can consecrate your garden clippers or the house scissors you already have on hand. Your sacred consecration imbues and blesses the blade with your intention to perform Magick with the tool. *You* make it special. The ceremony can be simple or elaborate. You can bless your athame or boline with one or all four Elements of air, fire, water, and earth.

Many spells and rituals throughout this book will include candle Magick. It's up to you whether you douse the candle's flame after your ritual is complete, even if it has only burned a little, or prefer to let magickal candles burn all the way out. You may feel like the spell's energy isn't released into the universe until the candle is completely burned. Or you may prefer to visit your altar, relight the candle, and sit with the fire of your desire over the course of a few days. You empower your Magick when you listen to your own inner wisdom and what feels most magickally charged for you.

The intention or method behind how you douse the flame is similar to whether or not you tell people your birthday wish, new dreams, or ideas, or keep them to yourself. Do you speak about your desires to feed them the energy of your words and positive vibes? Or do you cradle your desires like seeds in the earth, protecting them in their embryonic stage? Depending on what feels right, you might blow out your candle to disperse the energy of your intention or contain the energy by using a snuffer or pinching the flame at the end of the wick with wet fingertips. Follow your inner guidance and recognize that you might feel different for different spells or rituals.

Consecrating Your Athame

Wave your athame or boline through purified smoke of an incense stick or a lit, dried herb bundle or steam from an essential oil diffuser to represent air and intelligence.

Pass the athame or boline through a candle flame to invoke your passion and fire.

Plunge the athame or boline into a cup of water to fill your blade with your emotions and feelings.

Sprinkle salt on the athame or boline to ground your purest intention in earth energy.

Let the plants you are about to harvest know how you plan to use them and ask that they send their most healing energy. You can even add a request for specific energy that you know they possess, such as self-love from rose geranium or success from bay leaves. Provide a gratitude offering, such as a pinch of dried herbs, a strand of hair, a libation of water, or even saliva. Many earth spiritualities include the practice of giving to the plants before taking. Honor the plants, and they will honor you in return.

GARDEN OF SPIRITS

According to anthroposophy, the therapeutic and creative teaching system of Rudolf Steiner, around the ninth year of life, we become more aware of the veil that separates make-believe and reality, faerie and human, life and death. This is the first of life's thresholds and is when we form our beliefs about the world, a time when we can choose whether to believe in the tooth fairy, Santa Claus, and talking gardens.

Written in the Holy Grail tradition, the book *The Three Candles of Little Veronica* describes how we live our first seven to nine years in the Garden of Spirits. This is the time of our lives when we inherently believe in animism. We interact with the Magick of nature, entertain Elements of fire, air, water, and earth, and see with the Eyes of Heaven. Then comes the Twilight, or the loneliness and confusion that accompanies adolescence and the social pressure to give up "childish fanciful beliefs." In the Twilight, we may forget all that we know about the light that illuminates and connects everything on this planet, from people to rocks to rivers and dogs.

My Nana Mame, a psychic reader, spoke of metaphysical portals to other dimensions that can open our ears and hearts so we can send and receive messages to and from the Spirit World. These portals exist in time, such as the 11:11 phenomenon, which signifies intuition, insight, and enlightenment. According to numerology, the number eleven is a "master number," and when you see 11:11 on the clock or a sign, this is a clear message from the universe to become more conscious and aware of the opportunities in the moment. All duplicate numbers of time carry some significance and are sometimes known as angel numbers. Connie was particularly drawn to 12:12, the sign that good things are coming your way, and I'm a fan of 4:44, which I (along with others) view as the Witches' minute.

Sometimes a sacred site can be a portal, like a faerie mound that is filled with the power to transport you, because the place itself has become a doorway. Stone circles might do the same. Perhaps it's that the place itself holds the memory of centuries of rituals that have transformed the mundane hill into a magickal place. Special, sacred places on Earth are connected by ley lines, the geometric, energetic grid that lies over the entire planet. Sacred sites such as the Great Pyramid of Giza and psychic portals are often found where ley lines intersect. These doorways are also found in your mind in the form of paradigm shifts, which can evoke a radical change in perspective.

I extended my time in the Garden of Spirits in a simple yet pivotal "portal" moment when my Aunt Elaine suggested that I color a tree trunk purple in my coloring book. This small act solidified my belief that trees had a spirit, a personality that was unique to them. She gave me permission and a tool to practice creating and playing with a world that I already believed existed, and in that moment, a portal opened for Magick to enter my life and take up residence. It doesn't matter what the magickal tool is, whether it's a purple crayon or an athame; if it can help you focus and take you where you want to be, then it is magickal by definition.

Have you always kept the Eyes of Heaven, or did you also slip into the Twilight when the possibility of a tree hugging you back or a daisy saying hello seemed childish or naive? Do you remember the uncanny moments of faith—a rainbow or sudden snowfall when you needed it most? Something miraculous to remind you that nature was listening? What was your awakening to the energy of the plant kin-dom? How can you begin to trust in something you may have inherently known as a child but lost as you became an adult?

When we individuate ourselves from Divine Source for a human experience, we bring our unique essence with us. Our individuality is the Divine experiencing a unique aspect of itself while remaining connected to its source. For example, a ray of sunlight may ramble over the countryside, but it will remain connected to the sun. Human experience offers us an adventure to clearly seek and appreciate our Divine Essence. The next step in our evolution is to recognize and honor the reciprocities and channels of communication between ourselves and the natural and supernatural worlds.

Technology, industrialization, and consumer consumption have removed us from our natural rhythms and pace by encouraging instant gratification. Needs are met quickly, and we are pressured into process-ing our emotions and experiences at a dizzying rate. Convenience creates apathy and an insatiable appetite, as food, medicine, and water are over-sourced for a quick fix. This impatience and ease have put us out of sync with the natural order of the world and our own instincts.

Centuries before chemists began concocting drugs in laboratories, people went to Mother Earth in search of ingredients for health and ceremony. The Garden of Spirits held a rich supply of herbs and plants that comforted and healed the people. The living, breathing Mother Earth—who is often known as Gaia within the Wiccan faith—is quite literally supportive; we drink Her waters, walk upon Her, breathe oxygen from Her trees, and find our needs met through the curative powers of Her herbs and plants.

Cultivating an ongoing relationship with nature connects us with a higher order of intelligence and a rhythm that many of us have long for-gotten. Herbs teach us divine timing through their cycles of resting and blooming, providing guidance for our lives. We can maximize our potential by harmonizing with the cycles of the seasons: releasing unwanted habits or thoughts in autumn, diving deep into introspection during the winter months, birthing a new self with the onset of spring, and blooming into our greatest selves in summer.

Try this experiment to recall your original innocence and connection to the Garden of Spirits. Hold an open palm an inch from a tree, bush, flower, or whatever natural life you have in front of you. Close your eyes and move your hand slightly backward and forward like you are bouncing your hand on a balloon. Can you feel the sensation of your subtle body energy field (aura) meeting the plant's? Silently introduce yourself, then be still and listen.

✳

For our next visit, I brought Connie a bouquet of daffodils along with a caramel macchiato and a scone. I adjusted myself on the pillow I was seated upon and looked up at Connie sitting in her leather recliner. Her brown pixie haircut emphasized the fae-like energy of her cat-shaped eyes. She smiled at me, and I instantly opened up.

"I can't tell my Mexican grandfather about my Witchcraft books. I don't feel safe. I am tired of being afraid of losing my children, job, or family's love because I am a Witch. But then I get signs and messages to go forward. The push-pull drives me mad. Last summer, I shot a pilot to host my own cooking show called *The Cauldron* with the Syfy channel. I thought I was going to be free to live the life I want. Then 9/11 happened, and of course the show was cancelled." We stopped in a silent prayer for the lost souls.

"Believing in the spirit of nature is not an easy path," Connie said. "Not everyone will believe you."

I laughed with forced bravado. "I'm no stranger to being ostracized based on a misunderstood spirituality. I was raised as a Christian Scientist—no vaccines, never been on an antibiotic, and I believe in faith healing."

I paused, waiting to see if I had turned Connie off, but she brightened as if she had just discovered gold. She scrunched up her face in delight, making her features and wrinkles look like a sunburst. Connie exuded so much joy, I felt warm and cozy just being around her.

"Go on." She took a sip of her drink. Her eyes danced with merriment as she peered at me over the rim of the to-go cup.

"If you pluck the keystone idea, everything that rested on that foundation must collapse, even matter. During one Sunday school lesson, my teacher explained that all of matter is mostly an idea or energy. 'If ye have the faith of a grain of mustard seed, you can tell yonder mountain to move, and it will move' to quote the Bible! So, I closed my eyes and imagined the table as empty space, just a thought. I removed the idea that it had to be solid and passed my hand right through it. Mind over matter." I shrugged. "Never done it since."

"In my coven we call that Mental Magick," Connie said. She put down her cup on the side table and lit a white taper candle. She sprinkled golden nuggets of myrrh resin onto a red-hot charcoal resting at the bottom of her cup-sized iron cauldron. "Magickal tools, the physical objects we use in our Witchcraft, are tangible representations of the unseen forces and Elements. The mind works the Magick. The tools, like the athame, crystals, even incense, simply augment the power of a trained mind."

I sat in silence, absorbing her words and waiting for the myrrh to crack open and release its resin as spiraling smoke. I inhaled the heady, sweet, powerful Magick of the myrrh, an herbal ally native to the Arabian Peninsula and parts of Northeast Africa that purifies and elevates the vibration of meditative spaces.

"I love that," I said dreamily. "I have been defending my religious freedom since I first debated with a friend's mom when I was only eight years old. She was uber-Christian and very combative."

"Sunday fundies." Connie laughed. "People who go to church on Sunday to absolve a week of unkindness. Being a Witch is a 24/7 lifestyle."

I nodded. To me, Sunday fundies were like muggles, people who don't believe in Magick, from the *Harry Potter* series. "I live the Craft every day, and yet I'm a bit scared because, honestly, I would love nothing more than to be on my own with my sons, but I'm afraid to lose them in a custody battle." I shook my head to stop myself from saying too much. But it was too late and I could tell Connie wasn't going to let me off the hook that easily. "Recently, I watched an episode of the drama *Judging Amy* where a woman almost lost custody of her kid because she was Wiccan. The show was just made up, but too close for my comfort. Society reflects art and art reflects society, you know."

Connie raised an eyebrow to indicate she had recognized my fear and chose to focus on the solution. "But what do you want to create? Mental Magick connects our desires with natural allies, such as plants, trees, and herbs. I think you need some grounding and centering, my love. Let's work some Mental Magick to strengthen your core connection to yourself. We will visualize the Tree of Life, also known as *Yggdrasil*, which represents your individual growth and the ever-present connection to Oneness. It roots you to the ancestors and the earth while encouraging you to reach for your dreams or higher wisdom. Would you like to hear it?"

ᗡ Tree of Life Meditation

Find a quiet place where you will be undisturbed for about five minutes. Take three deep, calming breaths and bring your awareness to the present moment. You can choose to record this guided meditation, draw a picture of the images, or read it aloud or quietly to yourself.

Imagine your spine is like the trunk of a tree, and from its base, roots extend deep into the center of Mother Earth Herself. With this connection, you can draw up power from the earth with each breath. Feel the energy and power rise up your spine, like sap through a tree trunk. Feel yourself become more alive with each breath. From the crown of your head, branches reach up and sweep down to touch the earth. Feel the power burst from the crown of your head and flow down the branches until it touches the earth again, making a circle, a circuit, returning to its source. As you let this power flow into the earth, say:

Source to source, flow through me,
Above to Below, turn to return, clearly face to grow.
As I will it, so shall it be. Spell make it so.

I basked in the peace of the meditation for a few minutes, imagining myself as a tree, deeply rooted to the unconditional love of Mother Earth. Then I heard the snappish fighting of Connie's neighbors, and the pinched face of my next-door neighbor floated into my awareness.

"Yuck," I said aloud without meaning to.

"What is it?" Connie asked.

"My next-door neighbor is a bigot. Last night the couple behind our house had this raucous party. I drank wine in my backyard listening to their music. This morning, I was playing with my boys on the Slip 'N Slide in the front yard when my next-door neighbor asked me, as she backed out of the driveway, if I'd heard the party. With disgust, she asked whether I knew they were gay."

I paused to recall her judgment, her assumption that I would agree with her contempt, and my rising fury, then continued, "I told her that every neighborhood has to have at least one gay person and one Witch, and it was her karma to live next to both of us. She drove off and I laughed. After that, I wrote 'Witches Heal' in soap on the back window of my car." I sniffled.

"What is your definition of karma?" Connie asked, intrigued.

"The principle of karma says that whatever energy you send out to the world will return to you," I replied. "Of course, the universe has endless ways to bring the energy full circle, and karma doesn't always unfold as one would expect."

Connie added, "But the more you pay attention to energy, the more you will recognize the boomerang effect of karma at work."

"Yeah. The neighbor's narrow-mindedness came up as a karmic lesson, an opportunity to witness the pain caused by marginalizing others. And if I always expect to be judged poorly as a Witch, then that's exactly what I will find." I paused. "Why are so many people still afraid to test herbalism and our healing arts?"

Connie glanced down at my dirt-encrusted toenails and smiled broadly. That was one thing I loved about her: she accepted me exactly as I was, even when it had been another gardening day and I hadn't cleaned up before rushing over.

"This fear is encoded into our DNA," Connie said. "We have to work hard to reconnect with nature. Centuries ago, they burned women who knew about herbs, even when that meant murdering the only village healer during the plague. Empirical evidence and healing became synonymous with quackery, and old wives' tales were dismissed as the masses were encouraged by the churches to give up the people's medicine."

"Plants are the people's medicine," I defended, as if I wanted the world to hear this conversation.

"The centralization of power stole our collective confidence to heal ourselves," Connie said. "For several decades now, there has been a deep fear instilled in people to avoid ancient methods or herbal remedies."

"Even though nearly 70 percent of all prescription drugs are plant-based," I finished. "Unless they decide to eliminate nature's healing in the labs."

"We have to reclaim what we lost," Connie and I said simultaneously. Our eyes widened as we connected in purpose. Two Witches are stronger than one.

A large black cat suddenly jumped onto Connie's lap. She petted the velvet fur of the proud feline. "Well, hello," Connie greeted her cat familiar, her magickal companion. He purred, and she nodded as if she'd received an instruction and broke into a Scottish brogue: "This is Merlin McMerlin of Clan McMerlin, the Highlander Cat. Please meet my friend, Jamie." The black cat struck a royal pose, as if he was used to being formally introduced.

"Hello," I said. I reached out to pet him, and he looked at me like I was mad for trying to touch him. He jumped onto the bookshelf filled with magickal curios, walked the edge like it was a tightrope, and sprang shelf by shelf to the top—without disturbing a single thing. The magickal cat settled himself there and looked down upon me as if to say, "Don't touch me, you peasant."

"He likes to show off." Connie laughed.

My arms tingled, and it was hard to catch my breath. This whole house was a portal, and Connie was its queen. Being here heightened my desire for a deeper dive into Magick.

"Tell me what is on your mind, darling," Connie asked with such tenderness I felt she had read all my thoughts, as if they had rolled across my forehead like ticker tape.

"I am ready to own my power. I am prepared to learn from the past and no longer carry those burdens forward." I closed my eyes to roll the memories back to six years ago. "I was twenty-seven when I rented my grandfather's home. Just into my Saturn's Return, I sat in the backyard and peered into its darkness, asking to remember and rebuild my faith in faeries, in miracles, in animism. I pressed my pointer fingers together, tip to tip," I explained as I reenacted my movements of that night, "and slowly, I pulled them apart, also blurring my eyes, like when you gaze into a 3D hologram. I saw gossamer threads of light pulsating between my fingers. Then an emerald-green light sparked at the tip of my left pointer finger and shot over the top of my hand.

"I dropped my hands and felt the sudden and commanding presence of a large man, almost an angel in vibration, covered in dark-green leaves. Part man, part angel, part tree. In my mind's eye, his presence was firm, but the details were fuzzy, and I could not tell if he wore a cape or simply moved with sinewy grace, like branches in the wind. *Who are you?* I asked inside my mind, but I got no answer. Then the phone rang. It was a friend calling to ask me if I would dress up as the birthday faerie for her daughter's third birthday party."

"You met Pan." Connie was now sunk deep into her recliner as if to get a better look at me.

"I know!" I exclaimed and burst into giggles.

Connie giggled back, and our eyes locked. Somehow we remembered each other as what my Nana Mame would have called "a member of your soul family." Our giggling turned into huge guffaws at the reunion of our soul lights until my cheeks hurt and my belly became good and sore. In that moment, we made a silent pact: she would teach me the High Magick tradition of Witch-craft through the Druidic Craft of the Wise of America and the Wiccan Way. I would sit at her knee to reflect new ways of living the Magick. The torch had been passed; her knowledge would live on for another generation. We had conjured each other. Finally, the laughter subsided.

"I will teach you a magickal worldview of aligning your purest form of energy with the Divine Source that exists in every living thing, from a shaft of light to a drop of dew to a fox or your own mother." Connie spoke the last two words slowly, as if she knew about the battles between strong mothers and strong daughters. "We are spiritual beings in a human condition shining our Essence upon the world. There is no competition or hoops to jump through. And yet, here you are, talking about meeting Pan, the Spirit of the Seed, God of the Fae, as if it was nothing at all."

I took a sip of my caramel macchiato and winked at Connie, who pressed her hand to her heart in ecstasy.

"I didn't know who Pan was until the next day," I said. "I was about to get married, and I insisted we talk with a minister first. I hoped she could help me find a way to make it easier to be with someone who didn't believe in Magick," I said. "I felt such a rush when she told me about the Findhorn Foundation in Scotland and how they prayed to the devas, or nature spirits, and their attentions yielded astronomically grand results. They honored Pan, the wild spirit of the natural world, she said. And then I knew that Pan had materialized exactly when I needed to rely upon myself and not my relationships to restore my broken faith in my connection with nature and my wild self."

"Pan is Oneness," Connie said. Her voice reverberated around the room as visible bands of multicolored light that moved like fog. Everything around Connie pulsated with a vibrating energy—through the statue of pregnant Gaia, a perfectly clear crystal ball resting on a brass circlet, the mojo bags and books; even the wolf in the picture on the wall behind her chair seemed to come alive. Light shimmered from everything, her voice blowing life and animation into it all.

> The nature kingdoms need their champions to help redress the balance that has been upset by man. However, true balance is not a position of rigidity but one of great ease, a flowering with every moment, giving, taking and adjusting, constantly seeking oneness.

> *The Findhorn Garden:*
> *Pioneering a New Vision of Man and Nature in Cooperation,*
> by The Findhorn Community

What is wild in you that you could cultivate—a garden of your personal mystery and seed of your untamable spirit? Can you believe that your own wild nature is Divine?

When you are truest to your instincts and intuition, you are the closest you will ever be to God, the Great Spirit, or the Goddess. Nature carries and transmits the Magick that's inherent in the world.

Ritual herbalism rests on a reciprocal relationship with the plant world. Each plant should be approached as an individual spirit. An herbalist will call working with individual plants "working with simples." This is when you work with one plant, herb, tree, flower, or root at a time to better learn its unique personality and uses versus using a formula or combination of several herbs, like a tea blend of hawthorn, hibiscus, and lemon balm.

Take the time to get to know the energy and healing potential of each plant, and your Magick will deepen. For example, the next time you drop lavender essential oil into a diffuser or sprinkle oregano in your spaghetti sauce or sip chamomile tea, imagine the plant whose medicine you are taking. See the purple flowers atop thin lavender stalks swaying in a gentle breeze. Imagine the deep-green, heart-shaped oregano leaf. Visualize the white petals and bright yellow center of the chamomile flower. Or find images of the plants online if you don't know what they look like while growing in the earth. Acknowledge the plant, this one, right in front of you. Say hello. Listen. Give your gratitude, and you'll complete the cycle of giving and receiving, which raises your consciousness and, in turn, lifts the consciousness of the entire world.

3

Elemental Magick

Magick is the skill and art of remembering that you are a child of the Divine, a ray of unique energy from the Creative Source. There is nothing new you need to learn to awaken the Magick within; you can simply allow your inner wisdom to bubble to the surface. Then you can reclaim what was never lost but, rather, hidden in plain sight: you were born with original innocence, innate lovability, and the ability to co-create with the Divine. We are all individual, fabulously unique spirits who left the embrace of the Great Spirit to grow and learn in human form.

As discussed in the previous chapter, when we were little, the Garden of Spirits spoke directly to us. The wind tickled your neck, the roses brightened with your encouragement, and crystals made rainbows just for you. As you grew older, the people in your life may have encouraged you to distance yourself from nature and Magick. But the time has come for us to remember imagination, Magick, and play as our birthrights by integrating the wisdom of Elemental Magick into our lives.

According to the teachings of Witchcraft in the Wiccan Way, creation was founded upon four forces or Elements—earth, air, fire, and water—that were joined together by a fifth Element, known as Spirit, which is represented in the pentagram. These Elements are the primordial forces that make up our world. To say that any life-affirming philosophy, lifestyle, spirituality, or religion simply honors the elementals is a gross understatement. Our reverence is far more than a passive appreciation for the creative forces upon which our very lives depend. We seek to connect with the elemental forces in the world, in our own bodies, and in our own lives.

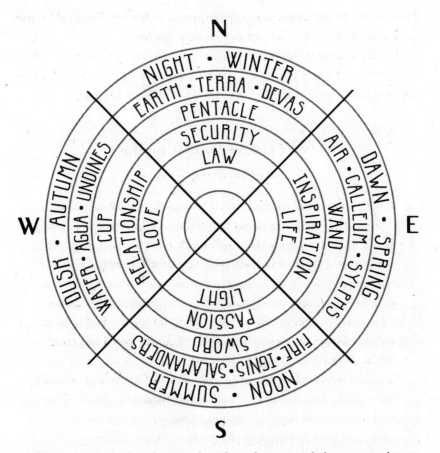

We can tap into the Elements based on their magickal correspondences. Earth may be thought of as your body or the ground, representing form and stability. Fire is the enthusiasm, spirit, or energy that generates activity. Water represents feelings, relationships, healing, and dreams. Air is the mind and represents intellect, ideas, objectivity, thought, and adaptability. You are encouraged to think of more ways to connect with the Elements, such as other areas of influence, the season of your life, animals, colors or the elementals—the fantastical, spiritual beings associated with each Element. You may even decide to assign the cardinal points (north, south, east, and west) to different Elements. When we speak of these Elements, it is important to think expansively. Water can mean any form of a liquid, frozen or thawed. Air could be any gaseous substance, including the sky or smoke.

Earth might be the mountains, crystals, trees, or flowers. Fire could range from a candle flame to a bonfire to your digestive fire.

The Elements are often associated with astrological signs, as in the following humorous curriculum from Connie's treasure trove. It's up to you how you decide to engage with the Elements, and even with this story.

🔥 Crimson Dragon on the Elements at the Movies

People who are influenced by the Element of air (Gemini, Libra, and Aquarius) are more detached, intellectual, logical, and abstract. They'd rather solve a problem with a slide rule than see a mushy movie with a person heavily influenced by the Element of water. If they did go, they'd offer a running commentary through the show, criticizing the dialogue and analyzing the characters. A fire person (Aries, Leo, or Sagittarius) will most likely leave a movie if it doesn't enthrall them right away. Fire people are quickly bored and must be fed the passion that sparks their interest.

Those who are influenced by water (Pisces, Cancer, and Scorpio) are ruled by their emotions. They cry and fall in love quickly. They do whatever their heart tells them and relate to everything on an emotional level. Earth people (Capricorn, Taurus, and Virgo) are more concerned with how much it costs to get into the theater, how comfortable the seats are, and if they got their money's worth. These folks are practical and materialistic. Someone influenced by earth energy would sit through the whole movie, even if they didn't like it, simply because they paid for the seat.

SUPERNATURAL AID

Supernatural aid comes when you allow Magick to weave effortlessly through your days. You are not a Witch because of how many crystals you own, your heredity, or even the initiations you hold. Being a Witch is a worldview, a philosophy, a lifestyle of observing, recognizing, and responding to the signs and communications from the universe. These signs could be when a friend calls exactly when you need them or when the sun breaks through the clouds just when you asked for inspiration. Your faith can redouble when you feel the response from an alive world. Raising your consciousness depends upon your ability to listen for the still, quiet voice of your personal truth and put your new knowledge into action.

The Elements and all of the universe reflect back to you the energy you put forth. They answer the questions of your heart. Witchcraft is the art of listening for these signs in snatches of conversations, looking for patterns in chaos, recognizing visits from spirit animals, gleaning directions from crystals, accepting guidance from the universe, support from the ancestors, comfort from herbal teas, and maybe even lessons from our children.

*

I grabbed the full cauldron from the bathroom and walked down the hallway to the kitchen, where I scooped up the defrosted package lying on the counter. I carried it all to the front courtyard, called to my sons, and sat down on the ground next to two hand shovels and a potted aloe vera plant with thick, spear-like leaves and a single orange flower. We had just bought our first home, and it was time to plant Kobe's placenta, which I'd kept in the freezer for the last few years. My tanned, tow-headed sons, Skyler, five years old, and Kobe, three, came running out to the courtyard.

"Sit here," I said, patting the warm adobe tiles, and the boys plopped down. I looked into Skyler's brown eyes that were so like my own, my mother's, and my grandfather's. Kobe's labradorite eyes were simply otherworldly in their compassion, as if he came straight from an advanced civilization who knew how to love without fear.

"Boys, this is an aloe vera plant." I held up a thick aloe leaf, careful to avoid the spines running along the edge. "And this is a placenta," I said, holding up the package. "It's kind of like a balloon that nourished and protected you, Kobe, while you grew in my belly. We'll plant the placenta under the aloe to give the plant extra nourishment to grow."

I caressed Kobe's pudgy cheek. "This aloe will be your very own plant ally, your buddy in the green world. It will be able to heal you of burns and other things." I kissed the top of Skyler's head. "I didn't know a mama could ask for the placenta when you were born, my love. But this will be good medicine for you, too."

Skyler smiled. "That's okay, Mama. I know you love me."

I winked at my eldest son. We dug a hole and I placed the placenta in it. I extracted the aloe vera from its container and massaged the roots so they dislodged from the clump they had formed in the pot. Once the roots hung loosely, I placed the plant on top of the placenta. The boys scooped the earth around the plant to support it; then I tipped the cauldron to pour water that held my menses blood from my last period on the base of the plant. Kobe patted the top of the flower affectionately.

I held up a bag of garlic bulbs. "Garlic is for protection, and it will guard us and our home." I placed the bulbs in a straight row on top of the soil like a line of defense under my bedroom window, which faced the street. A few weeks prior, members of the KKK had distributed flyers in our new neighborhood. I wasn't sure if they would be more offended by me being a Witch or Mexican.

The phone rang, and I ran inside to grab it. By the time I got back to my sons, they had happily planted the bulbs in three clumps, not the rows I had intended. They looked up with proud smiles and the dirty faces of gardening cherubs. "Great job, boys."

Later that afternoon, I blew into Connie's small living room like a tornado and handed her a caramel macchiato. I dropped onto the flattened beanbag in front of her recliner.

"I want to capture this feeling forever!" I said, wiggling my fingers. "I love teaching my sons Magick!" I relayed the gardening story.

"Did you place a single bulb in each hole?" Connie asked. "That's not—"

"Some garlic varieties like to be planted in clumps!" I laughed. "I just found out. I am so glad I didn't undo their work. We have such a strong sense of the Divine when we're young. And then we forget."

"Our light and purity are the best protection any of us could ever have," Connie said with her fingers intertwined and resting on her belly.

"What would life be like if we all trusted our inner light, Divine Essence, and original innocence? Would we feel safer, more lovable?" I mused.

Connie put on a rather pained smile, "What if, indeed." Then she shook it off and smiled warmly at me. She lit a white taper candle, and the shadows in the wolf painting behind her chair flickered. "What if we never forgot that the Elements all live within us? What would change if we really knew how close to the wild we truly are?"

"You were wild once. Don't let them tame you."

Isadora Duncan

EARTH

Most meditations begin and end with grounding, a process by which you bring yourself to stillness in mind, body, and spirit. Serenity and belonging are in the teachings of the earth Element of the north. Grounding leads to a centering or aligning of your physical, intellectual, and etheric energies. Your heartbeat is the path back to being grounded and secure on this earthly rock. The heartbeat of the earth can be your tuning fork for balance and inner strength. When we can go into nature and synchronize our heartbeat with that of Mother Earth, we will feel more grounded and centered.

In the earth we find another ally: the members of the mineral realm, our sentient ancestors who have watched humanity evolve through the centuries. The devas of the mineral realm are constantly seeking connection with us, their human neighbors and family, to help us once again perceive and listen to their energy's vibrational language.

Crystals are great transmitters of energy. They're used in watches, cell phones, microscopes, cars, and countless technological devices. They do for us what we cannot do alone. Working with the consciousness of crystals, stones, and earth by giving them basic care and feedings is a form of conversing with the universe. It's just like when you clean your windows to allow light to shine through and give you energy or messages from the outside world. It's also a good idea to cleanse any new crystal you buy of its former energy: from the earth where it was mined, to the conditions or attitude of the person who harvested it, to the shop owner from whom you bought it, and all the people who may have touched it.

⸙ Basic Care and Feeding of Crystals

All crystals emerge from the earth in a pure state. They have grown in an environment permeated with earth energy and are great storehouses and conductors. Crystals are very sensitive to energetic fields and "remember" the vibratory forces to which they are exposed, including human energy fields.

CLEANING

Quartz crystals in particular discharge negative ions. In exchange, they attract and store positive ions. For this reason, it's necessary to remove the positive ions periodically because if we don't, the crystal will become clogged and less effective for healing work. To cleanse a crystal, bathe it in clean well, spring, or sea water or a solution of 1/8 teaspoon of sea salt or kosher salt to a quart of water. The salt should be non-iodized, and the water should not be chlorinated or polluted in any way. If you feel the crystal is carrying the energy of others, you may also use a special solution of hyssop-infused water (1/5 plant matter to 4/5 water) that will draw off the positive ions and remove any former intentions placed in the crystal, to provide you with personal guidance.

As you place your crystal in the water, say:

> "Orb of light
> I charge this night
> With Luna's potent glow
> Infuse, magnify, and flow
> Divine for me
> The future to see
> In the name of the Goddess
> Blessed be."

When crystals are being cleansed for the first time, they should remain in the salt bath for seven days and seven nights to neutralize any energies that they have acquired. If the water becomes cloudy during this time, refresh the bath. Otherwise, the salt solution will be "good" for about seven days. After the first cleansing, the following guidelines apply:

- Personal crystals (those worn for protection) should be cleaned or sprinkled with water every day. This can be done in the time it takes to have a bath or shower.

- Crystals used for healing work should be cleansed between clients. A short bath is usually fine. If the crystal has been working very hard, try a longer bath.

- Crystals used for meditation or those kept in a room for their beauty and presence should be cleaned when they become cloudy or congested to the touch. Your intention and observations are the best guides here.

HANDLING AND CARE

Although quartz crystals are hard, they are very fragile and can crack, chip, or fracture if they are dropped or knocked into other objects or surfaces, exposed to sudden temperature changes, or left in very cold (freezing) environments. Crystals that are stored together should always be wrapped separately to prevent accidental knocks. Only natural fibers should be used for wrapping your crystals; otherwise, they cannot breathe and will become clogged with former energy. Use red fabrics to repel energies that may accidentally become attached during the transport of a crystal.

Crystals appreciate being taken to moving waters for an occasional bath. Because running waters are a source of renewal and can recharge energy, crystals emerge from these waters with greater vitality. Be sure to place your crystals carefully in a safe nook for these baths. Crystals can also be bathed in the ocean, rivers, lakes, or other natural bodies of water, but be careful: they could be carried away by the Goddess in one of Her guises.

Choose a beautiful piece of cloth or a silken pouch to wrap your most personal stones and crystals. Consecrate a scarf with the hyssop-water solution. You can bless a crystal wrap with incense, bells, or even your menses.

Feel into Earth Magick

You do not need to bathe your crystals in moonlight every esbat, which is the name for the full and the new moon. There will always be significant celestial moments and auspicious opportunities to channel the power of the cosmos. You can decide when and if you need help from the universe. If you are paying attention to the ebb and flow of your own energy and tapping into your intuition, then you will know when it is time to cleanse your crystals, plant or harvest herbs, adorn a new altar, or indulge in self-care.

The more aware you become of the Elements active within you and all around you, the better and more often you will see that the universe responds to your internal state. If we carry fear, then dogs, bees, and other potential predators (humans included) will sense the fear-based chemistry we are emitting and attack. Fear attracts, but so do love and light. If we focus on shining our brilliant spirit, we will attract the positive, life-affirming power we want to receive. If we hold firm boundaries, others will be forced to comply with how well we protect ourselves. We lead by example and teach through our actions. When we listen to the language of nature and our own wisdom, the Magick grows stronger.

In Witchcraft, we direct our mind precisely toward the outcome we want to experience—not the way it will look, but how our manifestations will make us *feel* when they have materialized. Mental Magick is not simply about visualization; it's a conscious, vibrational meditation you undergo as you walk through this world. It's about looking for lessons hidden behind veils—and sometimes in plain sight.

✳

A frightening thought passed through me as I watched the shadows dance against the wall where the framed poster hung. Behind the glass, the wolf seemed to pace back and forth through the mist, like Connie's personal guardian.

Several thoughts came into my mind. *What if I never make it as an author? What if the dream to be independent never materializes into doing what I really love?* I shook my head, erasing the thoughts like an Etch A Sketch, and blurted, "Have you ever refused anyone a reading?"

"Depends on the situation," Connie replied. She paused to take a sip of her caramel macchiato, purposely slowing the pace of the conversation and calming my frenetic energy. "Sometimes people ask the wrong question," she said after a long, silent moment. "I try to guide them to look at the situation from another perspective." She picked up a five-inch, pointed, clear quartz crystal from her side table. Her fingers did not reach around the crystal's girth as she held it under the light of her lamp. "Crystals teach us that we are fractals of light, always moving and changing." Rainbow light danced around the small living room with its low ceilings and walls covered in magickal art.

"Tools are like training wheels that can help you practice feeling into the innate power of the Elements," Connie continued. "Eventually, after you have amassed experience through magickal practice, you will want to ask yourself, 'Can I do my Magick on a deserted island?' It takes time and sometimes the help of others to see the Magick that lives within ourselves. Who refused you a reading?"

"Last year," I said, "when I was in Sedona, I asked for a past life reading. As soon as I sat down, the reader, an Indigenous man with long black braids, said he would not give me the reading I wanted because I had too much going on in my present life to worry about any karmic debts or Akashic records or vows I made five hundred years ago. Instead of the reading I wanted, he gave me a large black tourmaline crystal and some wise counsel on how to stand in my integrity in the present moment."

"What did you think of the gift exchange?" she asked.

"I was mad at first. I really wanted some distraction from the anxiety I felt in my marriage and career. But the more I held the black tourmaline, and especially after I cleansed it for myself, I felt the strength of the crystal protecting me like a guard dog—or wolf." I laughed at the analogy even though it felt so true.

Connie nodded. "He matched your vibration with what would help stabilize the frenetic energy of being in pain. He gave you protection instead of adding to your plate." She raised her left eyebrow, as if challenging me to reflect deeper. "And black tourmaline . . . such a powerful crystal to cleanse negativity. What a blessing!"

"I never thought of it that way." I chewed on my lip.

When she raised both eyebrows as if to say she didn't believe me, I couldn't stop the grin from spreading across my face. We both started laughing uncontrollably, and my fear and anxiety vanished as if they couldn't stand to be in a room filled with so much joy and love.

AIR

The Element of air corresponds with the direction of the east, new beginnings, awakening, inspiration, and dawning awareness. Air is represented by your breath and voice, which offer not only a unique way of putting words together, but also a unique sensibility, a distinctive worldview, and an outlook that can only come from you. Each voice offers different notes to the same song. We are the Uni-verse, one song, but each phrase is important. Each voice has a cadence, a rhythm, a sound. Your voice is the magickal tool that you use to speak with the Divine and turn your ideas into manifestation. Give your voice wings and become more familiar with the Element of air through this ritual.

Air Meditation and Candle Dressing

Gather the following supplies:

- Yellow candle

- Essential oils of bergamot, frankincense, myrrh (one or all three)

- A pinch each of the following dried or fresh herbs: lavender, thyme, and mugwort

- Crystals in any combination of amethyst, sodalite, blue celestite, or blue lace agate

- Wand

- Feather

- Athame

- Incense: jasmine, lavender, or sandalwood (stick or cones)

- Carving tool (optional; to carve a symbol for air on the candle)

A Box of Magick

This ritual and meditation were designed to help you connect with the Element of air in a visceral way, so it is best performed at dawn on a Wednesday as you face the east (see page 156 for the significance of the days of the week). Prepare an altar with all your supplies. Place your candle in the center of your ritual altar space (or carve the symbol for air on your candle). Anoint a taper candle with your essential oil. If using a candle tin, place a few drops of the oil on the top of the candle. Sprinkle each herb on and around the candle, stating its purpose as you do so. Lavender aids in divination and communication, thyme awakens the mind and increases psychic ability, and mugwort provides protection and is a visionary aid. Place the crystals around the candle in any way your intuition guides you. Then place your incense to the right of the candle and lay the feather close to it, being careful to not set it on fire. On the left side of the candle, lay your wand, and in front of the candle, lay your athame. Be creative here: you can use a found stick for your wand and a kitchen knife or a pen for your athame.

Take deep, calm breaths, or do whatever will help you mindfully focus on the present moment. Light your incense. Focus your mind on the knowledge or wisdom you intend to obtain from completing the ritual, and in that space, light your air Element candle. Imagine a circle of protection all around you. Raise your arms and say,

"Welcome, ancestors and spirit guides. [Name them if you choose.] Welcome, Element of air, the Keeper of Knowledge, Spirit of the Raven, Eagle, Dragon, or Sphinx. [You may choose any animal or deity that you prefer, or none at all.] Welcome, Gods and Goddesses associated with air, such as Hermes, Mercury, Odin, Athena, and Nut."

Light your candle. Focus your mind on your intention to commune with the spirits/guides/gods in the air realm and gain the knowledge you seek. Chant the following several times while focusing on your intention:

"Wisdom from above
Wisdom from the wind
Wisdom come inside
Wisdom come within."

You may want to record this meditation before you begin. Focus on your breath and begin calming your mind. Breathe in love and compassion, then breathe out any unwanted thoughts and negative feelings. Count down from thirteen to one.

Envision Yggdrasil—the World Tree, the Witches' Tree, the Tree of Life—with its roots planted deep into Mother Earth's soil. Its branches reach all the way up through the skies and clouds, up through the starry heavens, and into the upper world. Its trunk is planted in the middle realm, our physical space.

Approach the tree and request to travel on it to the upper world, to the realm of air. Begin to climb the tree higher and higher until you reach the stars, then climb higher still, until you find yourself at the summit, the upper world. Here, you see a door. This is the door to the realm of air. On it, you may see the symbol for air or a color you associate with air. Open the door.

You enter a tunnel and feel the wind swirl around you. Take notice of your surroundings. In the distance, you see two figures. As you get closer, you realize they are the Goddess, the Divine Feminine, and the God, the Divine Masculine. They are dancing, singing, and playing instruments. Soon, others join the party. Take this time to explore and commune with the God and Goddess, or whoever or whatever you're drawn to. When you feel ready, begin to return to "normal" life. Ask yourself if there are gifts for you to give or receive. Pause. Breathe. Try to sense somewhere within your mind, body, or spirit if this meditation is complete.

When you are ready to leave, give thanks to all and return to the air tunnel in the branches of the World Tree. Go back through the door, and be certain to close it behind you—this is important. Climb back down the branches through the stars, climbing lower and lower until you reach the base of the trunk. Give thanks to the World Tree for your journey. Begin bringing your awareness back to your physical body as you count from one to thirteen. Start to feel your feet and hands, and notice your breath. Slowly open your eyes, releasing any unwanted energies from your travels by simply touching the floor with the palms of your hands.

Journal any findings, messages, or revelations you received. Enjoy cakes (any bread-like treat) to honor the God and wine (any liquid) to honor the Goddess. Take your time. When you are ready to end this ritual, raise your arms, and say,

> "Merry meet and farewell, [name the gods, goddesses, or animal spirits you have invited to the ceremony]. Thank you for your presence. The circle is cleared. So mote it be! Merry meet and farewell, the weavers of the wind, the breezes that blow from the east, blessing us with wisdom and knowledge. Merry did I meet, merry do I part, and merry will I meet again! The circle is cleared. So mote it be! Merry meet and farewell, spirit guides and ancestors. Depart in peace. You aid and bless me from the Otherworld. Thank you. The circle is cleared. So mote it be!"

Bring your hands in a prayer position at your heart and say, "The ceremony is ended. Blessings have been given. Blessings have been received." Ground yourself by laying your hands or walking barefoot on Mother Earth and releasing any excess energy. Put away your magickal tools and clear the altar.

FIRE

Fire, the Element of the south, is composed of three things: passion, purpose, and play. Our passions are unique because the essence we emit is exclusive to us. Tapping into the Element of fire allows your passion to be a tool that cuts away what no longer serves you or your community and defends what you most fervently desire. In accord with my teachings, the Element of fire is represented by the sword. No one takes up a sword unless they must. Whether for the safety of your children or others, the warmth of a community, or the political rights of marginalized groups, where do you stand and firmly hold your sword?

It is purpose that fuels the spirit and gives us the drive to get up in the morning and tackle the day. What inspires you? What drives your passion? Develop the inner compass that will direct you to your innate wisdom, the light of your passion. "Know thyself." Watch an open fire or perhaps a video of fire and consider verbs or phrases that define the action or state of being that is fire. What does fire invoke in you?

Many of the words used to describe the movement of fire and its flames, like "lick," "flicker," and "dance," indicate evocative and playful states.

Engaging in playfulness is an essential practice for invoking the Element of fire. In her book *The Artist's Way*, author Julia Cameron recommends you have a weekly "playdate" as a means of inspiring creativity. As Cameron writes, "Perfection is not a quest for the best. It is a pursuit of the worst in us." When we are playful, our passion is ignited. We see the joy in the creative process itself, and any errors or imperfections can be interpreted as inspiration and insights to explore. We engage with our best qualities, and our purpose naturally rises to the surface.

Fire Ritual

Gather the following supplies:

- One lemon

- Water (about two cups)

- Salt (just a pinch, and sustainably harvested, if possible)

- Tamale husks, 5-8 depending on preference

- Mortar and pestle

- String (three or four inches)

- Sheet of paper

- Red, orange, or purple writing utensil (pen, pencil, or marker)

- Red, orange, or purple candle

Fire draws you in with the passion of Ares, the god of war, and allows you to be enticed as if Bacchus, the god of wine, were the host of the party. Fire's magnetism is in its dancing flames. Passion, purpose, and play can bring you to the brink of raucous delight. What can you learn about pleasure while watching flames dance? What gifts of delight can you give yourself?

Prepare the sacred fire tender's drink, known as a solé, by quartering a lemon. Grind the lemon slices in the bottom of a mason jar using a pestle. Sprinkle in sustainably harvested salt to taste. Chant while you add pure water and continue to grind in the lemons.

> "Oh, my children born of the flame,
> Come to me and dance with me again
> Oh, my passions, how I love your light
> Won't you tempt me this very night
> Let me play and my spirit will soar,
> You bring me such joy that I want more.
> Fire within fire without
> Fire within fire without
> I release to the fire what I no longer desire
> I ask of the fire what I most desire
> Blessed be to Element of Fire!"

Take frequent sips of the solé to keep your body hydrated. The heat of fire tending will cause you to lose electrolytes more quickly, but the solé will work to keep the water in your body as you tend the fire or gaze into a candle flame. Consider what feeds your passion, purpose, and play as you watch the flames. Listen for guidance from the elemental wisdom of fire.

Next, create a corn dolly from the tamale husks following the steps below. As you do so, focus on your intention to experience the purpose, passion, and play of fire, infusing the doll with the power to transform and release what no longer serves your highest good.

1. Soak the husks in a shallow pan of water for a couple of hours.

2. Select four husks and lay them flat on top of each other.

3. Bend the husks in half and tie them together with string about an inch from the crease. This will be the doll's torso.

4. Ball up a soaked piece of husk and cover it with another husk to create the head. Tie off the ball with a piece of string.

5. Braid three thin strands of husk to make an arm. Tie both ends (to stop the braid from unraveling). Make another arm and tie it off. Slip each arm in between the husks of the torso and tie them into place.

Repeat the final lines of the chant as you toss your corn dolly onto the flames. If you do not have a wood-burning oven or firepit, then you can burn your dolly in a fire-safe iron cauldron or cast-iron pot. Make sure the dolly is smaller than your container. Alternatively, if it is safer, you can simply write messages on a single corn husk, set it on fire, and drop it into a bowl of water. Toss the ash-filled water on the earth or flush it down the toilet.

"I release to the fire what I no longer desire
I ask of the fire what I most desire
Blessed be to Element of Fire!"

WATER

Water is life. We were each created in water inside our mother, where light filtered through blood and skin. We floated before we ever walked the earth. Some of us even swam while in our mother's womb. Our first sense of movement in the world is that of buoyancy and being in the flow of life. We had no worries as we were suspended and held by water, the Element of the west, of love, emotions, music, and the moon.

For those of you who have a menses cycle, you may choose to experiment with bleeding directly on the ground or onto a special cloth that you can later use to wrap your most precious crystals. You might also frame the cloth as artwork. You can soak your pads or tampons in a cauldron of water for at least twenty minutes, then pour the liquid in your garden. You can bury your child's placenta under a healing plant, like aloe, whose juice soothes burns just as water quenches fire. The blood mysteries are some of the most sacred, deeply ritualistic, and intensely private Magick we can do. Consider the pacts you might have made with blood sisters and brothers as a child.

Wherever you are on your path to better know the Element of water, it's important to stay hydrated and juicy so we can feed our creative fire and vibrancy.

Hydration is the genesis of our drive and fuel for all our Magick. To know an element, it helps to take it into your physical experience, literally as well as spiritually. Try adding a pinch of good magnesium salt or a squeeze of lemon to your drinking water to help your body hold onto important minerals (electrolytes). You can replenish and restore yourself with a footbath or by submersing in a bathtub, lake, ocean, river, hot spring, or whatever is available to you. Of all the Elements, water has the greatest ability to soothe us when we have become frayed in our sacred work. After all, we are made up of mostly water. By staying juicy and hydrated, we can achieve balance and know and respect our emotional motivators instead of indulging in their deluge.

Water Witch Ritual

Gather the following supplies:

- Seashells, sand, or sea glass

- Blue or green crystals

- Blue or green vessels of water (think watery colors)

- Motherwort tincture

- Hawthorn tea

- Jasmine flowers and/or any flowers that grow near water

- Moonstone and/or any other crystals associated with water

- Optional: pictures of water Orishas (such as Oshun or Yemoja), water gods (like Neptune), or river nymphs (such as Menthe)

Prepare an altar with whatever watery things you have on hand, such as vessels of water, blue or green crystals, flowers, seashells, hearts, or mermaid figurines. If you can do this ritual near a waterway (or maybe on the beach), that will add to the Magick. However, remember not to worry about getting it wrong. Of all the elementals, water is the most fluid and adaptable. The Elements teach us who they are through direct experience.

First, drink a large glass of pure water. Chant three times: "Water, water, come to me. Fill my cup with your entity."

Take a dropperful of motherwort tincture to evoke your fierce lion heart. Place your hand on your chest and feel for your heartbeat. Move your awareness from the palm of your hand through the epidermis (the top layer of skin) to the space just around your heart. Send and receive energy from your hand to your heart until you feel hypnotized by your own heartbeat.

When you are ready, begin to send that pulsing energy up and down your spine. Visualize the source where your everyday drinking water originated, perhaps a mountain stream or a well. Breathe slowly. Drink some water as you imagine that the water's source is sending you energy to encourage the positive potential of your growth. Perhaps record any thoughts, images, or music that come into your mind.

Alternatively, you can play recordings of rain, ocean waves, or bubbling brooks. Drink hawthorn tea, a plant ally for the heart that works as a tonic on physical, emotional, and magickal levels. Pause as you feel into the Magick of the waters. You will know when your thirst has been slaked.

The Elements are your guides and teachers, both within and outside of your body. You can stoke the flames of your passions and desires, causing heat to consume the body and redness to tinge the skin. You can beat a drum to call the ancestors or sit on the earth, dig your fingers and toes into the dirt, and feel grounded and secure. You can submerse yourself in a bath, the ocean, a river, or a lake, or allow rain, a shower, or a waterfall to quench your thirst for going with the flow and diving into your emotions and relationships.

Each Element brings a gift: earth is to be still, air is to know, fire is to will, and water is to feel. Follow your intuition and listen to the spirit that speaks from deep within your heart. Trust your voice, feed your passion, dare to feel, and know that you belong and always have. Follow your bliss and your inner knowing because that is the path of a truly magickal life. *You* are the Magick.

4

Divination

You can tap into the wisdom of the Great Spirit through divination. This act of aligning your energy with the Divine can help you sense the voice of Source. Also known as telepathy or extrasensory perception (ESP), this innate ability to perceive communication from another frequency was beaten, shamed, and burned out of many of us throughout the ages. Hearing voices is taboo in many cultures, and in some religions, even hearing the voice of the Divine is blasphemous if you have not been ordained.

So, why do you think divination is considered taboo? Who might benefit from such an idea? If we cannot access the Creator, then all meaning is handed to us until we understand or "stand under" someone else's opinion. Blocking the connection to our own Divine Source allows others to interpret meaning for us. Now the time has come to openly reclaim our ability to draw upon the power that lives within us all. The inspiration you'll find inside will help you feel encouraged, bolstered, and "on the right path."

Divination is achieved through quieting your internal chatter, opening a door to the Spirit World, and being receptive to the symbols it communicates. Opening this channel of communication is the threshold moment in your journey. Will you choose to develop your skills of deep listening to the voice of Spirit?

Divination is a major component of Witchcraft because it relies upon the Witch's clear communication with the Divine Self and Creative Source. How you interpret the results of divination will vary depending on how you perceive or receive information. We each have the ability to perceive Divine wisdom through our unique style of communication. Some people know exactly how they receive guidance, while others have to work on developing intuition and learning the language of the divination style that most appeals to them. There are several methods of intuition, all of which begin with the prefix "clair-" meaning clear: clairvoyance, clairaudience, claircognizance, clairsentience, clairgustance, and clairsalience. You may find that you resonate with one or more methods. All of these methods can be increased by trusting in the information you receive and by following its guidance so that you gain confidence in this mode of perception.

Clairvoyance means "clear seeing" and often manifests like a movie that plays inside your mind or images that display in your third eye. Some people are born with the Sight, the inner seeing that allows us to perceive images of faraway places, whether in time or place. To expand this ability and your confidence, write down what you see and track how your vision compares to what actually occurs.

Clairaudience means "clear hearing" and often reveals wisdom through dialogue. People with this kind of intuition may hear sounds that others do not, feel drawn by certain words or lyrics, or process situations by talking aloud or playing music. Often the sounds of bells or ringing tones accompany a powerful psychic "hit" or feeling. If this is you, be sensitive to your gift and surround yourself with pleasing sounds.

Claircognizance means "clear knowing," which can originate in your heart, gut, or somewhere unique in your body. With this kind of intuition, people suddenly know something completely. They may have déjà vu more often than others or feel a level of secure confidence in a knowing that is unemotional and factual. This perception can be referred to as a "mother's intuition." Practice following your inner guidance to build this muscle of knowing.

Clairsentience means "clear feeling" and is often associated with empathy because these people intuitively sense the feelings of others, a room, or a place. With this gift, your emotional intelligence is high, and feelings are typically expansive and difficult to contain in words. Clairsentience may require you to set firm boundaries so you don't become a satellite for the world's emotions. You can hone this talent by learning to ride the emotions like a surfer rides waves. Enjoy the connection without getting tumbled in the surf.

Clairgustance means "clear tasting" and is extrasensory perception through taste, flavor, and your palate. It may manifest as a taste of metal when someone discusses a car accident or the flavor of your grandmother's cooking when her name is mentioned. This sense is often used in mediumship to connect with the Spirit World. To improve this sensory perception, be mindful of messages that are sensed through your mouth and tongue when you eat or drink.

Clairsalience means "clear smelling" and utilizes scents and aromas to detect psychic information. The olfactory part of our brain is one of the brain's oldest structures, and our sense of smell is often tied to memory, which will include your own memories as well as the DNA memory that has been stored in your cells. To expand this sensory perception, focus on the life force and consciousness of floral and herbal scents. For example, you can ask for a message on how best to utilize eucalyptus while smelling its essential oil.

"The more you trust your intuition, the more empowered you become, the stronger you become, and the happier you become."

Gisele Bündchen

An Introduction to Divination

The word *divination* is derived from the Latin word *divinare*, meaning "prophet." It is also associated with the Sanskrit word *deva*, which means "gods." It has descended into English as the root stem *div*, which also means "god," and can be found in such words as *divine* and *divan*, which, in its literal interpretation, means "a seat for the gods." Our most common derivative of the root is the word *divine*, which means "of, or pertaining to, gods" or "god-like." Divination, in short, is the process of asking the gods for advice or guidance, and it is in this context that we use the word *divination* in the Craft.

THE THEORY BEHIND DIVINATION

Divination, also known as prophesy, is often divided into four broad methods or kinds of mental processes. The first form occurs through the observation and control of random happenings, where something occurs in a specific, divinatory way for you. The second method involves symbolic interpretation from a variety of sources, including dreams, visions from various scrying techniques, tarot, tasseomancy (tea leaf reading), or even astrological glyphs for planets and zodiac signs. The third area is purely intuition-based and occurs when, all of a sudden, you just know, and you know you know. The final form of divination is one in which you may receive direct communication from the spiritual world through your superconscious mind. This is the prophecy that comes from meeting your own spirit. All methods of divination utilize one of these four techniques in order for the spiritual world to communicate with us.

THE CONTROL OF RANDOM HAPPENINGS

When divining with this method, any activity that generates seemingly random happenings can be used, such as the shuffling of cards, the throwing of dice, the casting of rune sticks, or the tossing of a rock. When, for instance, you throw dice, the numbers that come up occur without rhyme or reason. In other words, the throws fall at random.

The theory behind using such phenomena for divination is that the Divine designed the universe with omnipotence (all-power) and omniscience (all-knowing). As its designer, the Divine Source has control of the universe and can determine everything and anything in it. Therefore, it is reasonable that the Divine can communicate with us through any random happenings, including a set of dancing dice or rune sticks. This is the rationale behind all forms of divination.

DIVINATORY VALUES

Much that we have read, heard, or perhaps even studied about divinatory systems may have led us to believe that divination depends upon fixed values or symbolic meanings. For instance, an authority who has written a book on card reading may have assigned a value to the ten of spades that says, "You will dig a ditch." Sometimes we are expected to understand this meaning as immutable or fixed, that the ten of spades has always meant one thing and that is what it must mean forever.

When a divination meaning becomes traditional or fixed, it does gain strength within the collective consciousness based on its popular use—just as an often-repeated prayer or national anthem becomes stronger the more often it is spoken or sung. However, Magick is always evolving and symbols can morph and change as humanity evolves. The possible meanings of values used or assigned in divination are endless, with as many interpretations as there are people, grains of sand, or stars in the sky. It is only necessary for you to know what meaning *you* assign to which card; then Divine Source will also know it and will reveal the divinatory message according to your personalized interpretations.

You should also keep in mind that the cards, or whatever you use, have no powers of their own. They are not magickally endowed in any way. They are merely a tool for divination. They mean whatever you decide they mean. Therefore, it is vital that you are clear about their meanings.

HUNCHES AND PROPHESY

You were born a prophet. You have already had hunches and dreams. If you have had even one dream that you understood as prophecy and it came to pass or clarified a problem, then you have to admit you are a prophet. The name of the game is to increase the frequency and accuracy of your precognition (literally "before knowing") whether it be for the events of your own life or somebody else's. So much of our daily routine could be easier and more fun if we paid attention to the precognitive faculty that is quietly working all the time.

Accuracy fades when there is too much emotional attachment. If you are worried about getting it "right," then you are in the way of the reading. When you are close to the situation or person for whom you are divining, then you can cloud the vision with your concern. Practice being an observer in your daily life by imagining that your consciousness has been perched in the corner of the room behind your left shoulder. Observe your divination insights without judging or assigning any kind of qualifying adjectives to the perceived outcome, especially those polar opposites of "good and bad."

INSTINCT AND INTUITION

The word *inspiration* is derived from the Latin word *spirare*, which means "to breathe." When we are inspired, the material—an idea or a solution—is "breathed into us" from a source outside of our human perception. Inspiration is related to mediumship, in which we channel information from other people, weather patterns, plants, or animals. The information from inspiration feels as if it's been suddenly downloaded, whereas intuition is more of a remembering of your inner wisdom, almost like a feeling of déjà vu or stepping back into yourself again. Intuition is the inner wisdom that just knows and illuminates your path.

The correlations and differences between inspiration and intuition can be clarified through the example of writing this book. I felt inspired to read through Connie's curricula, shape it, and bring this material to the reader. And, as I went through those steps, I intuitively blended in my own material to create a guided journey led by two priestesses.

Here are some things to keep in mind when you are divining so you can give an appropriate, accurate reading:

1. Have clearly assigned values in mind. Know what values you have given to or interpretations you associate with each symbol or tool you use.

2. Be mindful of the relationships among symbols, archetypes, tarot cards, sigils, runes, bones, or any two or more divinatory tools. The symbols affect each other in a reading, and their relationship may morph depending on the given situation or need. For example, if you pull the Strength card followed by the High Priestess card, you can deduce that you need to access your inner strength or compassion to reach the mysteries held by the High Priestess.

3. Be sincere, humble, and reverent about what you are doing. Divination is communication with Divine Source and your highest self.

4. Trust your ability to divine. To doubt divination is to doubt the ability of the Divine Source to perform such a tiny miracle as communication with you.

INNER WISDOM

The art of divining and hearing your spirit's message depends upon the development of a keen ear for your own inner wisdom. You have assigned meanings to words, imagery, and symbols that represent a unique sensibility, a distinct way of looking at the world, an outlook that could only come from you because there will only be one of you in all of time. You can develop a stronger connection to your inner voice by listening and responding. Practice following your instinct and recognize that your connection to the innate knowledge you possess within your soul will grow, like a muscle, with frequent use.

Another way to access the wisdom or the Witch within is through creative writing. Consider responding to the following writing prompts, approaching each one with curiosity and an open mind, and be willing to be surprised. When you respond to these questions, try free or automatic writing, where you don't stop to think, edit, or judge, but rather allow the words to flow from your fingertips to the keyboard or from pencil to paper. You could also try responding with your less dominant hand to reach a deeper level of your inner life. Don't worry about spelling, punctuation, or grammar. Write for yourself. Listen and record. This is for you.

• What does my inner wisdom want me to know?

• What are we really doing when we engage in divination?

• If I made room for my intuitive associations with tarot cards as well as the deck maker's meanings, I could . . .

• What would happen if I followed my inner guidance?

• If I sang in the shower and heard voices . . .

- If I smelled roses at a funeral, even if they weren't there . . .

- If I tasted flavors when I read cookbooks . . .

- If I had insight into possible futures, I could . . .

- What would I be able to accomplish if I trusted my feelings?

✳

"What was your introduction to divination?" Connie asked during our next meeting.

I settled my tush on the beanbag next to Connie's recliner, hesitating as I glanced over at a dark-haired kid wearing all black and covered by a blanket on the couch.

"Who's that?" I whispered.

"That's Nick," Connie answered. "He's sleeping. Don't worry about him. Who was your first teacher?"

I tore my attention away from the curious fellow. "My Nana Mame," I answered. "She was a psychic reader who worked with the tarot, psychometry, and palm reading. Every family gathering, we lined up for a reading from Mame. She always told us that whatever she perceived existed in a field of potentiality." I smiled, recalling Mame's southern drawl. "She would say, 'If things continue along this way, then your outcome is settled. But a change in attitude or the slightest shift in your actions could set up an entirely different scenario.'"

Connie smiled. "That is how I see divination—not as something locked in time but as your Nana said, 'a field of potentiality.'"

"Sometimes she did a reading with regular ol' playing cards." I sighed deeply. "I wish I had paid attention."

Connie smiled in that way that didn't let me off the hook for ignoring the banquet of knowledge my Nana had provided, but she also didn't judge.

"Once, Nana gave me a lesson I will never forget. I told Nana that I was hearing loud voices when I lay in bed at night and could not go to sleep. I was nine and we had just moved to the same hill where our ancestors built an adobe structure in 1806 that turned into a huge Spanish rancho the size of seven Orange County cities. The last ten generations still live in the area." I shook my head, "I didn't know the voices were my ancestors. I was just scared."

"Even our ancestors don't have the right to disturb a child's sleep."

"Nana said that we have the right, as human beings occupying a body, to tell a spirit to leave, and they have to go away. We choose whether or not we will listen to the spirits. We have autonomy over our human experience."

Connie nodded. "Oh, you were raised by a Wise One." She lit a white candle and sprinkled resin into an iron cauldron.

I inhaled the sweet copal incense smoke. "I thought I was losing it, but she told me that spirits are attracted to people who shine their brightness. Nana said that people who are spiritually awake are like a metaphorical porch light that indicates to the spirits, who want to communicate, that someone is listening and can hear them." I smiled and shrugged my shoulders. "But that doesn't mean we have to listen or serve every spirit that comes around. We get to choose because being alive gives us authority over this physical realm."

Connie waived a worn Rider-Waite-Smith tarot deck through the smoke. "You woke up to your skills at an early age."

"Yeah, when I was fourteen, some friends were messing around with a loaded gun that went off and killed one of the guys. Joey used to visit me when I was babysitting and alone and would ask me to deliver his messages to our friends and his family. I didn't have the confidence to do it." I smiled wryly. "I wanted to shut off my light, and I did for a long time."

"Some people turn off their light forever," Connie said as she looked over at the dark-haired goth kid asleep on her couch. "They remain devoted to the goodness." Connie turned her attention back to me. "Even when they can't see it in themselves."

As she spoke, I followed her glance to the sleeping kid, then held her gaze. I looked deep into her dark brown eyes, and I trusted her completely.

"I blocked the channel for years, and I got mean. I was scared and felt dead inside. I'm listening now, but more than ever, I need to speak with my younger self, love her completely, and bring her home." I swallowed hard. "When I was a teenager, I decided life hurt too much, and I refused to care. Then my bedroom got frigid cold. As soon as you passed through the door, the temperature dropped at least ten degrees."

Connie nodded. "Whenever a room gets strangely cold, that's where the spirits are."

"That's what Mame used to say. I don't remember how it came up. I just remember Mame smelling of Jean Nate perfume and wearing one of her animal-print silk muumuus and chunky crystal and brass necklaces and huge rings when she turned to me and said, 'Well, honey, the reason you're such a bitch is because you have all those spirits living in that room with you.'"

Connie cocked her head to the side and blew me a kiss. "She called you out. Best kind of teachers." Connie noticed my hurt look. "But she could have told you how to protect yourself."

"She did, in a way." I smiled. "She taught me that I could draw the boundaries with the Spirit World, and I eventually learned how to hold my own so I could listen to one ancestor at a time. I chose to focus on my mom's mom, who had died the month before I was born. Her name was Della. I learned how to not just accept the gift, but to hone it. I'm glad that Mame led me to find my way to listening to the spirit and my intuition, but she didn't do it for me."

"And today?" Connie asked. "How do you work on your divination?"

"I prefer oracle decks, like Jamie Sams's Animal Medicine cards. I like giving readings that provide insight for a more empowered path." I scratched my cheek as a way of stalling because I wasn't sure how Connie would take what I had to say next. "A few weeks ago, I was pretty sure the teenage kid who lives across the street was vandalizing my sons' preschool. Nobody messes with my babies," I added with a sassy headshake. "After school, while his parents are hard at work, he and his buddies roll trash cans down the roof of the house to crash on the driveway while blasting heavy metal."

A snicker came from the kid on the couch. He reminded me of a bat. Like how some people have loyal dogs, and Witches have loyal bats.

"I decided to see if I could redirect the guys' energy. I brought them homemade chocolate chip cookies infused with love and invited them to an animal spirit card reading. They were shocked, but they came over and had some real breakthroughs, especially my neighbor, who pulled the bat card, whose message is of rebirth. I felt that he got the memo that you could hit bottom but still find redemption and start again. That was so cool." I smiled, remembering the feeling of helping someone see another way.

"Then I told them my sons' preschool was being violated by someone who was turning over slides and tangling swings. I also told them that this Witch had moved into the neighborhood and she was not happy about it."

"That is exactly what a Witch would do," Connie replied with a chuckle. "Turn a difficult moment into an opportunity to help others who need it the most."

"The vandalism stopped immediately," I said with a wide grin and a little celebratory shimmy of my shoulders.

"Of course it did," Connie said with a shake of her head, her enigmatic smile conveying wonder and delight. She held up her deck of cards. "Would you like a reading?"

TRUSTING YOUR INNER GUIDANCE

You will experience more Magick every day by aligning with healing modalities designed to reconnect you to the natural and supernatural worlds. The art of divination involves learning to strengthen your inner guidance, then following its directive. Watch for the omens that you are on the right track. For example, since I am clairaudient, I've recently asked the universe to send me a bell or a chime when I'm following my spiritual guidance. Ever since, I've begun hearing a ringing tone from the universe when I need to pay special attention to the moment.

Different card layouts have been developed over the years to help diviners pinpoint or highlight specific questions, such as the seven-pointed star for a weekly forecast, the six-card spread to focus on harmony, the astrological spread to hone other divinatory skills and aspects, or the simple, two-card question-and-answer spread. You could also place three cards down to represent the past, present, and future (left to right).

Learning to read playing cards as messages from the Minor Arcana of the tarot is a fun way to explore your divination talents. Your reading will be based on a combination of the suit's significance and the card's number or court. Court cards typically relate to a person, usually yourself or someone significant. You can write these interpretations on the playing cards with a Sharpie. Remember, you can choose whether to follow the tradition that states wands are tools of fire and swords are the symbol of air or vice versa. Work with whatever feels right for you.

Suits

Spades = wands: east, air, thoughts, ideas, beginnings

Clubs = swords: south, fire, passion, drive, purpose, play

Hearts = cups: west, water, emotions, feelings, dreams, intuition

Diamonds = pentacles: north, earth, grounded, abundance, ancestors

Numbers

1. Centeredness, inner strength, protection, kindness

2. Duality, imagination, dreaming, sensitivity, conception

3. Manifestation, expansion, education, travel, creativity

4. Balance, individuality, originality, tolerance

5. Teaching, communication, flexibility, movement

6. Love, nurturing, compassion, romance

7. Spirituality, mystery, sensitivity, faith

8. Infinity, wisdom, patience, stability

9. Endings, courage, conflict, initiative

10. New beginnings, perspective, manifestation

Court Cards

King: order, status, wisdom, strategy, authority, masculinity, responsibility, discernment

Queen: presence, support, intuition, reliability, femininity, knowledge, refinement

Knight: action, vitality, passion, impulse, determination, initiation, enthusiasm, advantage

Page: youth, feeling, service, creativity, devotion, sensitivity, inspiration, contemplation

🔥 Magick 8-Ball Spread

I love the Magick 8-ball spread because it reminds me of the black globe that many of us have asked questions of, shaking it over and over until we got the answers we wanted. For this spread, focus on a yes-or-no question, shuffle the cards, then pull one card at a time and lay them face up in a pile until an ace comes up or until you pull thirteen cards. Then create a second and third pile following the same directions. When you are done, you should have three piles in front of you. Use the following key to interpret your reading.

MEANINGS

Three aces upright: Yes! More than you expected

Three aces with one reversed: Yes

Three aces with two reversed: May not be what you expected

Three aces reversed: Not how you expected, if at all

Two aces upright: Situation is favorable

Two aces with one reversed: 50/50 chance

Two aces reversed: Probably not

One or no aces: No

OR MORE BASIC

Three aces: Yes

Two aces: Maybe yes

One or no aces: No

HOW TO DISTINGUISH GUIDANCE FROM FEAR

(From the ESP Institute newsletter, dated 1971)

It is important to be able to distinguish divine guidance from fear, anxiety, or wishful thinking. Certainly, your discerning mind will improve with practice. Whenever you clearly recognize a symbol (whether you hear a voice in your ear or a billboard message offers the guidance you need), there is always a feeling that comes with it. Pay attention to that feeling. Sometimes it says loud and clear, "This is real," and other times, there is just static. When you get static as opposed to a clear feeling, it's saying, "Hey, tilt. There's an Element of wishful thinking or fear here. This one is not real."

Nobody can tell you exactly how to recognize a feeling. You have to practice as often as possible. Once you've taken time to pay attention to the feelings that come with each message, you'll gain a good handle on the difference. Fear typically screams anxiety, whereas guidance is a calm, still voice. Discernment between the two will be of greater importance in your prophetic work than anywhere else. When you receive a real, clear, good symbol, you'll get a solid feeling. Your thinking cap may try to talk you out of it, but stay with it.

Know that, afterward, your front mind will try to take it away from you. It's been trained by the world to do that. But when you really get comfortable with your feelings, you'll know.

✳

Connie placed three cards on her lap and looked at them carefully.

"What happened recently to make you question your integrity?"

The answer was immediately clear. "I did a spell to receive a request from a New York editor to write a book for them. My spell came true, but not as I had intended. At a literary conference that I had just attended, an editor from Simon and Schuster asked me to write a book about Santería. But I don't know any Orisha initiates, and I am not one. There's nowhere for me to learn about Santería authentically, and its traditions are not something you can write about by simply collecting information from others."

Connie nodded her approval. "Santería is an initiatory tradition."

"I really wanted to accept the offer, but it would've taken me out of my integrity." I shook my head. "Still, I was tempted. A few days ago, I performed a protection ritual from Luisah Teish's book *Jambalaya* that involved mopping the floor with my urine and brown sugar. As I mopped, I was trying to convince myself that I could write this book. Then, I heard a booming voice say to me, 'You are not our daughter. Yet.' After that, I refused the offer because I knew the consequences could be harsh if I had moved forward after I had been warned and without proper protection or guidance. I know I did the right thing. But it sucks."

"You listened to your wisdom. That's always the right decision."

I sighed deeply, mostly unconvinced.

Connie continued, "Our wisdom comes, in part, from our willingness to be playful with the information that arrives. Play allows for inspiration or intuition to bubble up naturally. You cannot stare at your tarot deck or runes and, by the mere force of your will, insist that the muse appear. Sometimes you need to take a break from trying to force an answer and allow the information to visit you on its own terms. Enjoy the process of divination without self-criticism, which can block the information you seek."

5

Archetypes

The tarot is one of many Witches' most relied upon forms of divination. The Major Arcana of the tarot consists of twenty-two archetypes. Archetypes are guiding forces or universal patterns that exist in every culture throughout time. Their themes feel bigger than life. At the same time, archetypes can feel tangible and real, as close and intimate as they live and breathe within us. Your sense of each archetypal pattern will differ from that of others. Ever-evolving, archetypes remain silent until you need their assistance or they need yours, and then they'll speak in a subtle yet universally known language of energy, vibration, symbols, and images.

Archetypal myths play out in the constellations, within our family dynamics and stories, big and small. Divine Mother can nurture by giving hugs, tending to the home garden, or setting up strong boundaries. Warrior may be a slight, highly strategic woman or a behemoth man of immense strength. Although appearances will differ, you can recognize the carefree laughter of the Wild Child and the influence of the quintessential Trickster, who plays his games on an unsuspecting crowd. Archetypes can also embody overarching concepts, such as love, power, success, faith, compassion, gratitude, and more.

Archetypes resist containment and can be elusive as they guide our attention, actions, and desires. They are so broad and encompassing, it takes time and processing to incorporate their lessons into our lives. The point of Magick is not to memorize the words others may have assigned to an archetype. Rather, it is up to you to discover what the symbols and energies mean to you so you can seek, honor, and revel in the synergy between the self and the world.

*

"I still get confused trying to understand the tarot. I feel like an imposter, like I am supposed to just know. Shouldn't every Witch or goddess in human form understand the archetypes?" I had just returned from a book signing tour in Salem, Massachusetts, for the Halloween or Samhain (pronounced SOW-when) season and was feeling an intense pressure to know everything that I "should" have already known.

"Not necessarily," Connie replied. She crossed her arms over her large belly and peered at me through squinty eyes.

"Will you teach me?" I leaned forward, unable to suppress my eagerness. "If I could, I'd download all the cards' meanings into my brain and just work on trusting my divination skills."

"An immediate download?" Connie mused, continuing to scrutinize me. Then she asked slowly, "Are you sure?"

"Oh, yes." I exhaled the mounting excitement. "Please."

"All right." Connie sat up straight in her chair. She lit a white taper candle, shuffled through her tarot deck, and pulled out the first three Major Arcana cards. "Beginning with the Fool," she held up the card of a man dressed like a jester stepping blithely off a cliff into open space while juggling, "in numerical order, place a Major Arcana card under your pillow every night. In the morning, write down your dreams or any messages you received."

I clasped my hands together under my chin. My heart fluttered in excitement. The candle flame had shot straight up as soon as Connie began to teach, and the tea light candles on each magickal bookshelf and altar around the room rose and flickered. I felt a rush of the flame against my skin, like a warm breeze. I breathed in the Magick.

Connie placed the Fool card face up and picked up a card of a man wearing red robes. His right arm extended toward a blue sky, and his left arm extended toward the green earth.

"On the following night, place the Magician card under your pillow and record any dreams or messages the next morning." She placed the Magician card face up and picked up the High Priestess, who was robed in blue with a half-moon crown and stood secure in the dark night, holding a single light. "Next will be the High Priestess, and so on, increasing in the numbered Major Arcana."

I did as Connie instructed starting that very night. The following morning, I wrote down the messages from the Fool about an inflated ego and the trickster energy that reminds us not to take ourselves so seriously. The next night, I dreamed about the Magician's deep, esoteric knowledge of the phrase "As above, so below." The following night, my dreams took on an otherworldly lyricism as I explored lucid dreams and imagery related to the mysteries of the High Priestess. Then came the nurturing, fertile Empress, the pragmatic and fair Emperor, and the teacher or Hierophant and all that comes with the mentor-mentee relationship.

Toward the end of the week, I was listening to the Lovers, the Chariot, Strength, and the Hermit. By the tenth day, I was overwhelmed with deeply significant messages of the Major Arcana. They piled on top of each other, calling for my attention, until I made a beeline for Long Beach and the refuge of Connie's cave.

I closed the screen door carefully behind me, in case Nick was still sleeping, but noticed that he wasn't on the couch.

"Well, that was like trying to take a sip of water from a firehose," I said.

"What was?" Connie took the scone and caramel macchiato with double whipped cream I'd brought her. Her look of utter faked surprise didn't fool me. "Thank you," she said demurely.

"Dreaming about a new archetype every night. I couldn't sleep. They all wanted to talk to me." I put my hands on my hips.

"I believe it. What did you learn?" Connie asked as she lit the white taper candle.

"Pacing and integration are how you learn Magick so that one lesson can breathe and speak to the next organically, or you may miss something along the way," I answered. I had a feeling Connie was going to ask me that question since the multiple-choice tests at the end of her Wiccan class at Eye of the Cat always included an essay section. I had written out several versions of my lesson takeaway before our meeting.

"Well put. I'm glad you stuck with it as long as you did. Which archetype called to you the most?"

"High Priestess, as I am sure you could have predicted, since I'm here asking about the mystery every week." I paused to giggle along with Connie. Unconditional mentor love is its own intoxication. "But also the Emperor because that's my guide in numerology when you add up all the numbers of my birthdate, and I feel so compelled to lead and shelter others, whether they ask for it or not." I chuckled. I usually took my bossy, pedantic nature way too seriously and was relieved that I was able to laugh about it. A warmth spread throughout my body that felt like home. "And the Empress because of Mother Earth and being so deep into motherhood with toddler sons."

"Ah, the Mother archetype. The Goddess is the Great Mother. With her nurturing guidance, we discover all that love can be." Connie sighed.

We sat in a moment's silence before the candle sputtered like an impatient audience member. I smiled at the flame.

"I really lost the thread by the time I got to the Strength card, and then the loneliness of the Hermit scared the shit out of me, so when I ended on the 'choose your own perspective' message of the Wheel of Fortune, I decided it was time for a break. Besides, I'm taking off for a book signing in Northern California in the morning. I love a solo road trip, but I don't know how I'm going to talk straight with all these deep thoughts crisscrossing my brain."

"I warned you," Connie said with a smile. Then she burst out laughing, rocking back and forth, until she got the hiccups.

TAROT DECKS

There has been much debate about whether or not your first tarot deck should be gifted to you or if it's "okay" to buy your own. First and foremost, the archetypes in the deck belong to everyone, and there is no gatekeeper between you and this particular channel of communication. You can make your own cards through any art medium you can imagine or choose decks based on the storytelling of their meanings, the colors, the art design, or any other indication that these cards are aligned with the specific path under your feet. In other words, go with what feels right, whether it's mermaids, herbalism, Celtic, or Thoth. Tarot cards are so abundant now as artists and writers come up with new symbols to represent this ancient pictorial language. We are evolving as we welcome new interpretations.

The Major Arcana definitions that follow are but brief sketches of the archetypes because of the confines of this book. There could be an entire chapter, or even a whole book, written on each of these archetypes. I recommend reading several books that describe the meaning of the tarot cards and piecing together the meanings that speak the most to you. Time and practice with the tarot will be your best teachers. Remember, words are also symbols that represent feelings and energy. My words are only meant to be guideposts or lanterns pointing you closer to your inner wisdom, unique corporeal experience, and mystical connection with these archetypes. I encourage you to sleep with a Major Arcana card under your pillow at night, as long as you are mindful of the pacing of working through the cards, giving yourself time between your sojourns with each archetype. The next day, with the archetype's wisdom tucked inside your heart and soul, journal and/or create. Just be aware of your energy level and ability to integrate the cards' symbolic messages into your everyday life.

"Pictures are like doors which open into unexpected chambers."

A. E. Waite, poet, mystic, co-creator of the
Rider-Waite-Smith tarot deck

TAROT ARCHETYPES

0. THE FOOL

The Fool archetype is called by many names, including Trickster and Jester. With a puckish smile and a strong sense of adventure, the Fool points to childlike wonder. This archetype teaches us not to take ourselves so seriously. The world is our playground, and laughter is essential to a healthy mind, body, and spirit.

1. THE MAGICIAN/MAGUS

The Magician represents the channel or instrument for bringing heaven's wisdom, light, and love to earth, demonstrating how to create a sense of mystery and Magick from ordinary Elements. Often the Magician is illustrated with one arm extended to the skies and one pointing to the earth, representing the phrase "As above, so below," which indicates the infinity of Magick that occurs in the channel that is you.

2. THE HIGH PRIESTESS

The High Priestess is the guardian of the Great Mystery, the moon, the unconscious, the dark womb of creation, and the underworld of dreams and symbols. She sits at the threshold between the conscious and unconscious, able to see both sides of the veil. She represents internal, spiritual listening and is often shown in a posture of welcoming inner guidance and enlightenment from within. She is the symbol of the mysterious Divine Feminine.

3. THE EMPRESS

The Empress represents verdant Mother Earth energy, full pregnancy, nurturing Divine Feminine, and shared abundance. She is the power of creation that is constantly growing and evolving. Her symbols evoke a sense of caregiving, compassion, receptivity, fertility, creativity, and unconditional love.

4. THE EMPEROR

The Emperor is the good and fair king and represents the Divine Masculine. A kindly father figure, he is courageous, discerning, sensitive, and a responsible and capable leader. His posture indicates balance and higher wisdom. He is guided by the sun, valor, and integrity.

5. THE HIEROPHANT

The Hierophant is the teacher and mentor who evolves by sharing wisdom and spiritual consciousness in a reciprocal pattern with the student, both learning from each other. The Hierophant stands for wisdom out in the world and is associated with structured spiritual organizations, books, learning, and hierarchy. This card's symbols represent faith, knowledge, reason, and reciprocity.

6. THE LOVERS

The Lovers represent the ultimate integration of heaven and earth reaching out to each other. The card's symbols may point to the nexus where consciousness and expression manifest as well as deep inner peace and comfort in beauty. The Lovers' message centers on elevating one's energy and consciousness to be more loving, feel more lovable, and experience what it means to express love in daily life, both toward others and oneself.

7. THE CHARIOT

The Chariot represents the synergy between the mind's intelligence and one's visceral, bodily knowledge, bringing together both instinct and strength. It is the metaphysical vehicle through which we move to the next step on our journey, often a public one, with armor or protection. This archetype represents the power we possess when we synergize the ego with the empirical wisdom of instinct.

8. STRENGTH

Strength represents the marriage between beauty and brawn, grace and confidence, and all its symbols point to this collaboration in everlasting infinity. Strength has the power of combining our animal instincts with other forms of knowing. Representing gut and intuition, the power to move without overthinking, this archetype is the symbol of the alpha and omega, beginnings and endings, life's enduring will to go on. With Strength, we have the ability to be aware, accept, and move into action.

9. THE HERMIT

The Hermit archetype relies upon one's own experiences for guidance. Its symbols often include imagery of solitude, reintegration, and the six-pointed star, which can represent one's unique light. When the Hermit emerges from seclusion, their gained knowledge can be brought forward for the benefit of others. The Hermit teaches us how to be self-reliant and recognize when it's time for quiet in the natural world.

10. WHEEL OF FORTUNE

Wheel of Fortune is the observer who accepts the turning of the wheel of life with all its highs and lows as they are, without judgment. Imagery associated with this archetype includes a single eye of perception, the four Elements, and a circle, which symbolizes the continuity of life. The Wheel of Fortune reminds us to enjoy the moment and speaks to the freedom gained from trusting Spirit and living in the moment.

11. JUSTICE

Justice points to the power of truth, fairness, and harmony. This archetype represents the process of reckoning to bring balance to one's energy. Its symbols include the sword of truth, a scale, the middle road, equitability between light and dark, and wisdom. This archetype points to logic and a well-ordered mind.

12. THE HANGED MAN

The Hanged Man archetype represents humanity and all of its perfect imperfections. The Hanged Man helps one simplify, prioritize, relax, and let go of attachments to outcomes by surrendering to Divine omniscience. Insights can be gained during a period of stillness or being held "upside down" so one's perspective flips. Its symbols include unknown paths, halos, a cheerful countenance, and, most often, a person hanging upside down.

13. DEATH

Death represents the middle stage of the birth, death, and rebirth cycle. This archetype requires you to release old ways of being or thinking that no longer serve your higher good, allowing for the alchemy of your life and clearing the way for new learning, growth, and changes. Symbols may include a crown, which represents your consciousness; a dead person, often a king or queen; skulls and other symbols of renewal, like a rising sun; and water.

14. TEMPERANCE

The Temperance archetype represents the balanced integration of the higher self with the human self. This archetype can be viewed metaphorically as a sword being tempered by fire or art that's created at the meeting point of more than one force or energy. It symbolizes the ability to embody the value of the middle path that helps bring peace to polarized situations. Its imagery conveys balance, peace of mind, cups of water, triangles, and a clear path.

15. THE DEVIL

The Devil often represents the ego or our unhealthy attachments, obsessions, addictions, or "bedevilments" that we can break free from if and when we accept and deal with them. This archetype points out obstacles that are

Archetypes

hidden from view and helps interpret external signs as messages that reveal our internal reality. Its symbols often include chains, a depiction of the devil, confusion, despair, or an inverted pentacle.

16. THE TOWER

The Tower archetype represents the crisis that provokes you to decide what is most important. It is time to sift through the chaos to find the lesson. Under the guidance of the Tower, the things you cling to most desperately and believe you must keep will fall away. These challenges eventually move you closer to your personal evolution. Its imagery may include a tower, lightning, people falling, fire, despair, or confusion.

17. THE STAR

The Star archetype represents your inner light, inviting you to dream big, let your light shine, and live your fullest potential. This archetype points to a time for meditation and inner reflection and symbolizes vulnerability and being willing to examine yourself. It asks that you look deep within in such a way that you can radiate your star self and shine for yourself and others. Its imagery may include one or many stars, water, water jugs, fertile land, or a naked (i.e., vulnerable/courageous) person.

18. THE MOON

The Moon archetype represents the subconscious dream world, emotions, illusions, or undercurrents that affect your daily life. This archetype helps bring clarity to confusion by separating fact from fiction so you will know when fears or doubts are clouding your vision. Its symbols may include the moon, two towers, dogs, a crab, reflective water, and a path.

19. THE SUN

The Sun archetype symbolizes creative force, bounty, abundance, and a deep connection to the healing power of the universe. The Sun teaches that happiness and joyful enthusiasm are always available, and a positive attitude can improve any situation. Its imagery may include the sun, a joyful countenance, fertile lands, and abundance.

20. JUDGMENT

The Judgment archetype suggests that we reach for a higher level of consciousness. It invites you to hone your clarity and discernment so you can be free to experience life without the limitations of anyone's opinion but your own. This is your wake-up call to rise up. Its symbols may include an angel, horns, a single eye, and exaltation.

21. THE WORLD

The World represents victory and celebration in the knowledge that there is no separation between your higher self and your worldly self. This is the moment of finding one's place in community, in the circle of giving, and knowing what one has to offer. You are in touch with all that is, and you see Spirit in all that you create. This archetype's symbols may include a globe, a wreath, a circle, arrows, a lion, a bull, or an eagle.

> "The privilege of a lifetime is being who you are."
> Joseph Campbell

WITCH AS AN ARCHETYPE

The Witch could be an amalgam of one or several of the Major Arcana archetypes, depending on how you experience it in your own somatic, mental, and spiritual ways. I see the Witch as a combination of the Magician, High Priestess, and Empress.

As the Magician, the Witch lives in the liminal space indicated by the saying "As above, so below." The Witch has a foot in both the etheric realm of the Divine Masculine's thought and action (symbolized by an apex triangle) and the Divine Feminine's knowing and rest (symbolized by a vortex triangle). In between heaven and earth is where the Magick is.

As the High Priestess, the Witch is the mystery, exploring the untapped power of the unknown that surrounds us. In this nebulous space, the Witch crystalizes and manifests ideas and thoughts. Witches answer to no one but inner wisdom and seek to know and dispense knowledge when the timing is right. The High Priestess knows these internal clocks as the Empress knows her seasons.

As the Empress, the Witch personifies a deep connection to nature's cycles. She protects, serves, and embodies Mother Earth, the divinely nurturing Feminine and Goddess. We experience her by imbuing the sacred into our sensual, visceral human existence. A Witch celebrates life with joy and enthusiasm at every turn of the Wheel of the Year, the Mandala of Nature.

No two Witches will appear alike, but all will be wise in their striving to be the truest versions of their unique essence and heart. Witches recognize each other from the commitment to their inner theos or Divine Self. Wisdom teaches us that when you learn to love yourself, you will not want to be anyone else. We must reclaim our ability to feel the Divine within.

Witches have been misunderstood and maligned because they own their power to heal and manifest desires. This threatens the toxic status quo of society, which attempts to control individuality. Now more than ever, the Witch is needed to express her knowledge for the benefit of all, shift the collective consciousness, and heal the polar energies. Because there are now so many people willing to claim their power, the Witch is rising.

✳

The Barnes & Noble event organizer plopped twenty copies of *The Wicca Cookbook* and *The Teen Spell Book* on a table covered by a black linen cloth. She introduced herself to me, then announced through the microphone that I would be speaking in five minutes. It was a week before Halloween, which made the timing right for a mainstream book chain to feature an actual Witch author. But still, I was nervous. The month before had been the one-year anniversary of 9/11, and I felt distinctly on the margins of the currently powerful Christian Coalition. My mouth went dry and my hands began to sweat as I started to count the people watching me. I froze after thirty and stopped counting.

Then, from a side door I hadn't noticed, *she* stumped into the room, the thwack of her staff hitting the ground with every step.

A large woman dressed in a tie-dyed muumuu limped on a bad hip into the room. She leaned heavily on her ornate wooden staff encrusted with crystals. The clunk of her staff hitting the floor resonated in my chest like a vibrating gong. I stared at her as if she had just walked out of a children's book illustration of a Witch. She had a grizzled, gray mane and moles on her cheek and chin that sported a few wily, silver hairs. This woman didn't give two fucks about the people swiveling in their seats to get a better look at her. She walked to the back row of chairs, stood like a sentinel, and nodded to me as if we had prearranged this. She reminded me of Connie, but wilder, freer.

The organizer took the mic and introduced me to the crowd. Hearing my name and witchy book titles ring out into the sprawling bookstore sent goosebumps up my arms. I felt the familiar sense of apprehension that often accompanied taking a public stand as a Witch in the early 2000s, but I held onto my determination.

The themes I shared in *The Wicca Cookbook*—particularly connecting with nature and living seasonally—aligned with the burgeoning farm-to-table movement, and this felt like a powerful opportunity to share Magick with a wider audience. I felt an obligation to bridge Wicca teachings and mainstream culture, to help people realize that Witchcraft is based on living attuned to nature as the basis of all Magick. I steadied myself as I prepared to speak.

"Wicca is a religion that follows the seasons as a guide, which allows us to flow with the natural rhythms of life," I began. "As Witches, we follow the wisdom of resting in the dark of winter. In spring, we birth ideas; during summer's light, we celebrate; and in fall, we release."

A few conservatively dressed book buyers within earshot squirmed as I presented information that contradicted their beliefs about Witches. But as I spoke, I was gaining the kind of passion and momentum reserved for church sermons. This was my podium, my moment.

"Witches heal because we trust the ebb as much as the flow."

Just beyond the group of people who had settled down to listen to me, I saw a mother cover her daughter's ears at the mention of the word *Witches*.

"To know the dark is to know the light." I heard the waver in my voice and instinctively made eye contact with the large woman in the back. "The Witch is willing to be in either realm, depending on what is needed."

She winked at me and pounded her staff on the ground, startling me into silence.

"What Jamie says is the truth." She pointed her staff at me. "I'm here today because this young woman before you is very brave."

I swallowed hard and smiled nervously, feeling the tension in the room rise as the audience looked back and forth between the outspoken woman and me. I gripped the sides of the podium, as entranced by this wild woman as everyone else.

"We Witches have been persecuted for years," she said, "and I'm not going to let anyone hurt this Witch." She paused to make eye contact with anyone who had turned to look at her. "Or say one thing disparaging to her." She glanced at the woman who had covered her child's ears.

I was stunned. I'd had no idea I would need protection. I'd thought I was safe because I believed Northern California, so close to my hippie town of San Francisco, to be more open-minded than the conservative, uptight people back in Orange County.

First thing the next day, I secured a babysitter to watch my sons so I could visit Connie. When I told her about the woman who commandeered my book signing, she laughed. "Sounds like something I would do."

"Did you send her?" I whispered. The possibility of Connie sending Magick hundreds of miles away crackled like a fire in the grate.

"You drew her in," Connie smiled. "And I always send protection when you are speaking in public."

Connie's presence steadied my heart, and I felt stronger. Even her name, short for Constance I'm pretty sure, infused me with confidence. Helping me strengthen the connection to my true self, the bond with my mentor was growing stronger with each of our sessions. She was the constant in my whirlpool of change.

"I assumed NorCal was safe for Witches," I said.

"You are ahead of the curve, Jamie. The Witches will rise. You're clearing the path by standing up in mainstream places as a Witch who emanates so much enthusiasm and light."

I chewed on a fingernail. "Next year, my son Skyler will graduate from our hippie preschool co-op and enter the mainstream kindergarten. I am afraid that my children will be ostracized because of my Witchcraft. What am I going to do if or when that day comes?"

"Why do you care what people might say?" Connie asked. "You are not what they say, *and* you are protected," Connie said in the deadpan manner she reserved for her most important lessons. "You are on a path of knowing, the path of the Witch. You see beyond what others see, which is how you will stitch together community around you wherever you go. Be who you are, and remember what I said: you are not what they say you are. You are a Goddess."

I smiled weakly, wanting to believe this more than I was willing to express out loud. "In Sunday school, they taught me that fear is an acronym for 'False Evidence Appearing Real.'"

"Witches would have died out centuries ago if we had stopped practicing our Magick based on society's fears and misunderstandings. Nothing can teach you that 'you are not what they say' more than being a Witch, Jamie." Laughing, Connie rocked back so far in her leather recliner that I thought she would topple backward. She was in a deep flow of joy, immersed in her laughter. I watched her ride the emotions like a wave, rocking herself deeply as the belly laughs filled her with light.

With just as much ease as she had reclined, Connie swung herself forward, wiping tears from her eyes. She looked at me as if I were her own child.

"All you have to do is trust yourself like I trust in you. Stare at this flame," she gestured to the candle, "and I'll give you a protection ritual for whenever you need it. The full power of this spell depends on the sacrifice or sacred offering that you will give to be blessed by the Goddess's boon. What will you sacrifice?"

I felt my heart drop as I heard the voice of Spirit say in my most inner ear, *drop the victim mindset.*

"Once inside the Goddess's cocoon," Connie continued, "dream and give birth to a new you. Protection is something you give yourself. Listen for the High Priestess to speak to you of your inner strength. She is coming."

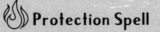# Protection Spell

As with any magickal practice or ritual, it is important that you find a place where you will not be disturbed so you can focus your mind on the spell you are casting. Check in with every part of yourself and make sure you are fully present so you can draw upon all of your available energy and channel it into this spell.

Imagine a silver light rising from your toes to encase your full body in an egg-shaped layer of protection. Feel the tingle of the lunar light's protection. This light represents your personal spirit, your unique reflection.

Then visualize a golden light rising up from your toes. This is the solar light that reflects outward. As the golden light covers you, it blends with the silver light, and the synergy between the two creates a force field to protect you.

The final protection is a pale, ice-blue light, like a glacier. This is light from the angelic realm, your higher spirit, and absolutely nothing can penetrate it.

Your ability to listen to your inner wisdom and follow its guidance is your sacrifice or offering of thanksgiving. So, take some time in this Goddess cocoon. Maybe you'll decide to take a nap, play meditative music, release an old story that is holding you back, or simply sit in nature.

MAGICKAL MENTORS

Clearly the Mentor archetype plays a key role in *A Box of Magick*, and therefore I would be remiss if I didn't discuss it further. When healthy, the synergy between mentor and mentee is reciprocal and equal in nature. The best teachers are perpetual students. The mentee is the audience and benefactor of earned wisdom, and the mentor augments, rather than drains, the student's energy. The positive exchange between mentor and student allows for the mentor's experiences to be safeguarded against time and forgetfulness. Sharing wisdom keeps society evolving as we broaden our perceptions with fresh insight, and avoiding the repetition of past mistakes saves time, which can prevent injury or harm.

Like with any intimate relationship, be certain that your mentor guides you with a generally loving hand. Sometimes they will share advice or give instructions that are difficult to hear or follow, and it will take your discernment and intuition to determine how best to heed their instruction. Personal transformation isn't always easy or comfortable because you are being asked to grow and welcome the blessings and the teachings.

You may have more than one mentor to reflect and guide the different aspects of yourself. Sometimes we have learned all we can from one person, and it's time for a new mentor to help us reach the next level. Whether you have several mentors or one special teacher, many of us, including yours truly, need to observe someone who has walked the path before us. Listening to someone else's story helps us to kinesthetically feel the lesson in our bones, so that the information can truly sink in. Enter the Mentor.

FIVE REASONS TO WORK WITH A MENTOR

1. Mentors reflect your true merit. They meet your success with praise and your failures with hope—in whatever form suits their personality, of course. This builds your self-confidence to take risks and explore the next levels.

2. Mentors hold you accountable. The very best mentors will astutely ascertain your abilities and help you integrate the lesson in a way that's designed for you to best absorb the information of their skill, craft, or art.

3. Mentors know the value of passing it on. To keep the circle of energy flowing, we must each find someone with whom we can share our gifts, talents, and knowledge. Magick and abundance are always found in the act of reciprocity.

4. Mentors teach spiritual flexibility and test the range of your humanity by teaching through parables, through their unique wit and wisdom, or by personal example, which deeply imprint us with a diverse perspective.

5. Mentors help their students find and establish boundaries. With a truly heartfelt connection with your mentor, you can break old relationships and forge new ones with authority and inner wisdom.

Requesting a Magickal Mentor

These are basic guidelines for a very simple and personalized ritual. You must first begin by considering the attributes you would like your mentor to have. You could utilize the power of Elemental Magick to attract the mentor that's best suited for your needs by creating an altar with symbols that represent the energy you need in a mentor. For example, you may want a mentor who sparks your wit with air energy, so you could include a pen, a feather, or incense. Perhaps you need someone to fuel your passion like fire, so your altar could be decorated with many candles. You may want a motherly mentor, in which case you can use bowls of sweet-smelling water or seashells. Or you may want an elder or crone, in which case you can use symbols corresponding to earth, like stones, bones, or crystals.

Choose a day when you feel most receptive to request a magickal mentor. You may choose to cast a magickal circle as shown on page 178. Take three deep breaths at your altar and carefully consider the significance of your altar items. Light a white candle and say,

> "I call to my mentor, please come to me.
> Fill me with the wisdom of antiquity.
> Show me how to face the dark.
> Discernment over a lark.
> Help me shine my inner light.
> Help me find my magickal might."

THE ONE AND THE MANY

Aside from tarot decks, you can find archetypes woven into our books, movies, myths, constellations, psychology, lotería, dreams, marriages, and offices. Each archetype represents one of the many expressions or energy patterns of the Divine. You may find that an archetype lives with and through you for much of your life. Perhaps the Fixer or Savior archetypes, or themes such as forgiveness and security, play a strong role for you. Or perhaps there is a phase in your life when you channel the Narcissist or the Nurturer. Archetypes are amorphous and do not have to be fixed identities that remain with you forever.

When a new archetype enters your life, you may find yourself consumed with new behaviors or solutions you had not considered before. Archetypes evolve through humanity, playing out their messages in daily life. They arise out of a desire to raise our consciousness, and when we resist, the Fool steps in.

Known as Coyote, Jester, Kokopelli, Interrupter, Trickster, and the Heyoka, among many other names, the Fool archetype is present in almost every culture. The Fool disrupts our complacency when we have become too cocky, ungrateful, proud, lazy, or, most especially, when we have gotten off track of our soul's journey. When we are born, we possess all the possible paths to a specific calling that only we can fulfill by remaining true to our unique essence. We are like an acorn that has the blueprint to become a magnificent oak tree, yet we don't know how it will grow to such grandeur. Over time, wind, rain, and sun will determine which branches, leaves, and acorns grow. Our personal evolution grows in a similar pattern of being influenced by our circumstances, attitudes, and choices that work together to determine our life.

The Fool shows up when we need direction. Its message is often confusing because the goal is to surprise you into a new perspective. The Fool is unpredictable, and with its sly humor, it will knock you off your self-created pedestal and remind you to not take yourself so seriously. The ironic chaos created by the Fool is intended to shake up the perfectionist and remind you that there are no mistakes, only blessings disguised as lessons. The Fool will test you until you learn to laugh at yourself and remember that you are one of many, a blessed and needed member of the grand community that is life.

You are the hands and the feet of the archetypes. When you pay attention to their energy as they move through you, your life will become richer in its multidimensional experience.

6

God and Goddess Energy

Within Wicca, the concepts of the Divine Masculine and Divine Feminine are also referred to as the Lord and Lady or God and Goddess. This duality is known by a multitude of names and concepts across many cultures, such as yin and yang, day and night, light and dark, action and rest, sun and moon, anima and animus, and right and left. These energies are not stuck in duality. Rather, they are mutable within our lives, bodies, and the cosmos. You can reference their massive energy, but they can never be trapped or imprisoned by the "right words"; they can only be experienced.

The Divine Feminine, or Goddess, is the Great Mother and the source of fertility, life, love, and the wisdom of the mysteries. The power of the Goddess can be felt in a multitude of ways, from spring flowers and tornadoes to a mother's gentle touch and healing abilities. The Divine Masculine, or God, is represented by the sun and the seed. The sun provides warmth, without which we could not grow and thrive, and the seed is the spirit of growth itself. Like wild animals and places, these offer a connection to God's verdant power.

Most experts agree that Wicca was introduced to America by Gerald Gardner in the 1950s. His tradition of Witchcraft, known as Gardnerian, took on a very structured approach, with specifically designed methods of opening circles, casting spells, and performing rituals. The Druidic Craft of the Wise of America also reverently held onto a highly organized approach. Both traditions of the Craft believe that a strict adherence to the process created a groove, or pattern, on the collective consciousness.

The repetition of incantations with a "buttoned-up" routine helped the Wiccan path make inroads into the minds and hearts of a society hardened against Magick. This reiteration of communication with the Great Spirit, who is both God and Goddess, built confidence for its practitioners. Muscle memory builds through repetitive movements, which further embeds the message: hands clasped means prayer, on your knees means supplication, holding hands means unity, etc. Repeated words also have an effect on our thoughts, whether they are sermons, affirmations, stereotypes, or propaganda. Consistent rivulets of water create channels in dirt; likewise, when spells, rituals, and messaging are repeated, they gain a footing in the collective consciousness.

The rise of Wiccan rituals helped inspire the return of balanced power between God and Goddess. At the time of Wicca's introduction to American society—during the height of white masculine power, oppressive patriarchy, hierarchy, and limited privilege—it was considered blasphemous to some and controversial to others to call the divine a woman. But Wicca as a religion views the masculine and feminine on equal terms with each other. The very presence of this new, equitable view of the Creator elevated the Divine Feminine.

The rising power of the Divine Feminine consciousness was fueled by many factors that are beyond the scope of this book; suffice it to say that each step was vital to bring the powers of masculine and feminine back into balance. UCLA professor and internationally renowned archaeologist Marija Gimbutas found hard evidence of goddesses and peaceful goddess-worshipping cultures. In 1956, Gimbutas introduced the Kurgan hypothesis, which asserted that Proto-Indo-European–speaking people upended the existing matriarchal traditions when they arrived in central and southern Europe. Between 1967 and 1980, Gimbutas directed major excavations of Neolithic sites in southeastern Europe, unearthing thousands of goddess figurines, cave paintings, and carvings in the shape of vulvas and women's bodies that dated as far back as 35,000 BCE. Based on her knowledge of linguistics, ethnology, and the history of religions, she reinterpreted assumptions about the beginnings of European civilization. Gimbutas's evidence proved that there had been thousands of centuries of civilizations that venerated feminine powers. This perspective challenged many traditional scholarly researchers, who often ignored or overlooked prehistoric cultures in which women held power and the divine was considered a woman. Now the information was available and feeding the rise of the feminine.

God and Goddess Energy

During the Women's Liberation Movement in the 1960s and 70s, women began to reject men's choices for their careers and bodies, and collectively, we began to reject the single male god and its patriarchal judgments of feminine power, instead seeking the warm embrace of a mother goddess.

The focus on goddess worship and Gaia theory gave rise and energy to the environmental and women's movements at the early onset of the Aquarian Age in the 1960s. Those brave souls willing to fight for progress paved the way for other human rights movements at the time. The Human Potential Movement arose out of the counterculture and formed around the concept of humanity's extraordinary potential to elevate our consciousness. Yoga, meditation, Indigenous women-honoring spiritualities, and various forms of Eastern philosophy and spirituality began to take hold in Western civilization as a result.

In 1978, Shakti Gawain wrote *Creative Visualization*, teaching readers worldwide about our ability to manifest with our thoughts. In 1984, Louise Hay's *You Can Heal Your Life* was published, inspiring many to recognize that we have the power to heal our bodies. And in 1998, positive thinking entered the mainstream when Martin Seligman chose it as the theme for his term as president of the American Psychological Association.

As humanity has evolved to be more inclusive, we have invested in studying empathy, language, social studies, memory, and creativity in universities, conferences, symposiums, and workshops. The reintroduction of the Goddess arose at the peak of toxic masculinity, and has been gaining in strength, diversity, and beauty ever since.

Ultimately, Spirit has no gender. Within the tradition I practice, the focus on the Goddess exists to bring balance and restore the equanimity of power. It has been a long, hard battle to reclaim the Divine aspect of the feminine. History has suppressed and ruled women's bodies because we hold the immense power to create life through our menses. But whether or not we identify as a woman or menstruate, and no matter the body we were born in, we can tap into the power of the inner Goddess. When we sing the praises of the Goddess, this is not merely for women, but also a callout to the Divine Feminine within us all. The Goddess is considered to have a thousand faces, and there are a myriad of ways She is expressed in the world. She can be a fierce, young, and agile huntress like Artemis, or She can confront both her darkness and light like the goddess of the Witches, the great Hecate.

Biologically, when we experience the cycles of life in our own bodies through menstruation, we are connected to the Spiral Dance, the seasonal Magick of the Goddess Earth Mother. When we grow a human baby within our body, we are connected to the life force that the Goddess brings into this world. These two gifts of life and power provide direct access to the Goddess. I want to deter people from referring to their menses, the gift of life itself, as a "curse." If, instead, we embraced that we are at our most powerful when we bleed, there would be a lot less anxiety and fear regarding PMS. We could then recognize the sacredness of the Goddess cycle when our menses subsides and menopause quenches our fire, we settle into the dark rest of the crone or elder years.

Within Witchcraft circles and other transformative practices, the term "dark" is often connected with the Goddess's realm and directives for rest, integration, womb space, the void before creation, and insight. While we sit in the quiet, anticipation can be painful. But in the dark, we are still dreaming potentiality into form. In this cauldron of hope before manifestation, we are free to explore the endless possibilities of our imagination and decide how much abundance we will receive. We can visualize a plethora of ways to see oneself in a life worth living. The dark helps us focus our Mental Magick on the feeling we want to attain most.

Dark can also represent the hidden parts of our soul that unknowingly affect our self-image and actions. It may represent unwanted energy that has been corrupted by a lack of light. Harmony comes when dark and light are in balance. We spend far too much time *doing* in the light of day and not enough time being still in the dark cover of night. When we sit in the dark and quiet, we can more easily integrate the blessings and lessons of our lives.

"We are witnessing the re-emergence of the archetypal feminine wisdom long underrated in the world but now rising up to balance the heroic and individualistic and logical masculine wisdom. It's time for both/and, not either/or."

Seena Frost, Founder of SoulCollage®

✳

"He was drunk before Thanksgiving even started. And it started at noon!" I practically shouted as I recounted a family party to Connie. I dropped down on the cushion in front of her recliner.

Connie gave me a consoling smile. "I am sorry, my love."

Sounds of dishes being put away came from her kitchen. I hadn't realized anyone else was in her home before I arrived. I was worried whoever was here might judge me, but I was desperate for my mentor's advice and couldn't stop my choleric energy or tears if I tried.

I swiped at my wet eyes and lowered my voice. "I'm no angel when it comes to drinking. I love my beer. But seriously?" I said, talking with my hands. "I did everything for us to host a family party for twenty people, and then he embarrassed me by braying like Rodney Dangerfield. 'I get no respect,' he kept saying."

"You want a consort. A god for your goddess," Connie answered in the words I had not even formed yet. "You may not be able to fashion him into your perfect partner."

"Why can't he be more like Ian?" I complained.

"Who's Ian?" Connie asked. Merlin the Highlander Cat jumped onto Connie's lap, nested himself into a seated position, and faced me as if he was also curious. Connie petted the back of Merlin's head, and they both waited for my reply.

"The guy from my writer friend's Scottish historical romance book," I admitted.

Bursts of laughter erupted from the kitchen. Connie smiled. "Fantasy men." Merlin jumped down to the floor and walked away.

"Not exactly," I defended. "Ian is the main character from the book *Kilgannon*. I bought it from the author, Kathleen Givens. She and I signed our books next to each other at the Tea & Sympathy booth at the Scottish Highland games and—"

"If you want a consort, then you'll have to stop manipulating." A tall, lanky, red-haired man stepped into the living room with his proclamation, interrupting my ramble with one of my trigger words. *Manipulating*, I thought. *How many times had I heard that before!?*

Despite his marksman-like precision and my suspicion that he was correct, I became defensive without thinking. "I never said I was manipulating anyone." I shook my hair in what I hoped conveyed a cavalier attitude.

"James meant 'you' in the rhetorical sense," answered a smaller, dark-haired man who followed close behind. He had a slight lisp and a gentle way about him. His eyes were a rich, dark chocolate and emanated power like a cannon.

James shrugged as if my response merited no further reply. He didn't believe me and didn't feel the need to save me, either. His hollow cheeks and mournful eyes could look straight into your soul.

"So, why did you assume that's what James meant?" Connie asked. Her voice was tender, offering a gentler path through this realm of new thoughts and perspectives.

Unbidden images of the fight I'd had earlier with my husband flashed before my mind's eye. That morning, I had done everything in my power to lash out at him to make him feel small and shattered because of the holiday fiasco. My razor-sharp tongue's payback alighted on my consciousness and filtered through my awareness as the trio waited for my revelation.

I dropped my head. "I am trying to force my husband into being the man I want him to be." I looked up and held Connie's gaze. "But I can't imagine how to stop wanting a partner who is *actually willing* to grow and evolve with me."

The shorter man took Connie's hand and said, "Jamie, my dear, we all want that."

Connie squeezed his hand, "This is Michael and James." She nodded to James, who had crossed the room to sit on Connie's couch. He nodded back. "I have been looking forward to introducing you to each other," Connie said.

Michael leaned down to where I was sitting, and I reached up for a hug. As we pulled away, he held my chin. "You are so precious." He smiled with full, red lips as my tears started up again. He stood, held my gaze a moment, then went to sit next to James on the couch. He nested into the soft cushions of the pillowed divan like Merlin the Highlander Cat. Once settled, he took James's hand. They kissed quickly but tenderly.

My tears welled up at their love. "Why can't I have chosen a partner who understands me or believes in Magick?"

"It can take a while for a Witch to find the right partner," James said.

"Sometimes people need a restful life when they are not slaying dragons for others but tending to their own needs," Connie said. Noticing my dubious expression, she added. "And yes, even drowning in their own sorrows."

"We bonded over our wounds and I don't want to be the victim any more. All this baggage with men has to do with my dad taking off when I was a kid." My voice started to shake. "I want a real *partner* now." I felt an anxiety that felt closer than my skin. It was as if this panic was the only facet of me that I listened to, forgetting and abandoning all my other selves.

"You are whole as you are," Connie offered.

"Marry yourself," Michael suggested brightly.

"You need to do the work, love," James said.

Connie placed a hand on my cheek. "You are the yin and the yang, the God and the Goddess. Learn to love yourself for all that you are and bring to this world." She handed me a white seven-day advent candle ensconced in a glass container. "I wanted you to come over today so I could give this to you. The timing couldn't be more perfect." She held up a lighter and flicked the candle to life.

"This flame from this lighter was held to Brigid's sacred flame in Ireland. Her Magick is in this fire." She held the flame to the wick of the white candle. "Brigid is the Bright One, the bride who will give you the vision of your heart's desire, comfort you when you need it most, protecting the flames of your internal fire. She will be your sword and the spark of creativity that weaves through your words." Normally one prone to fits of giggles, aflutter with pink light and white bubbles, Connie was now solemn, having summoned her extensive power, which emanated from her in waves. "Brigid's Magick is with you now."

I held this connection to Brigid in my hand, deeply grateful. I drove home with the lit candle tucked into a box at the wheel well of the passenger seat. When I got home, I held an incense stick to the candle's flame, and when it sparked to life, I touched the fire to my pilot light so Brigid's protection would fuel the heat of my family's home, warm our bodies, cook our food, and spread her protection, creativity, and light.

MARRY YOURSELF

The Goddess is alive in every human being. All of us have both god and goddess energies working together within us to make us whole and balanced. Marrying the God and Goddess within is a Witchcraft *practice* for a reason.

Witches endeavor to actualize our entire divinity and rid ourselves of societal programming so we can honor the fact that we are an ever-evolving, unique, and harmonized amalgam of the Divine Feminine and Divine Masculine. A balanced life is one that flows between these dualities of the god and goddess energies so they blend and morph together in a way unique to each one of us. We are each a divine masterpiece.

The surge to discover the shadow or uplift the Goddess helps us integrate the largely ignored and often maligned dark: our mystery, yin, rest, self-care, the Divine Feminine. We have been conditioned to hide away parts of ourselves. The time is now for us to learn to accept all of ourselves and shower ourselves with kindness and divine reverence. Our Magick depends upon us doing just this.

We can marry the God and Goddess within when we learn to love all that we are and become our best cheerleader, confidant, caregiver, and counselor. Think about it—who could take you on a better date than yourself? Who gets *all* of your jokes? You know all your favorite tastes in food, music, and art. You know when you are tired and need a quiet night or when you feel like celebrating in a rowdy room. You know whether rest or action is needed. Stay true to you.

If you have forgotten some of your favorite things, ask yourself this question: *How did I express my creativity as a child?* Remembering your creative roots opens a portal to the Divine Creator within. Did you make mud pies or pretend to be a teacher, scientist, ball player, or artist? I used to climb trees with my friends and pretend to be Charlie's Angels; our separate apartments were the long branches of a pepper tree. I would pick out shapes in clouds and create new colors, such as "elephant blue," to represent the summer sky. Remember what sparked your creativity. Feel into what makes you tick, what fuels your fire, and what delights you about the person you are deep inside. This is how you marry yourself.

Handfasting is a Pagan wedding ritual between two people, but you can do as Michael suggested and marry yourself with modifications that suit your needs and preferences. You can perform a ritual like this, in which you promise to be loyal to the God and Goddess within, when you are rebirthing after divorce, debt, disease, death, or some other major ending in your life. You can also infuse the intention of bonding for a life with your beloved mate with this handfasting ritual. Beginnings or endings, alpha or omega, you decide. I found this ritual among Connie's papers, handwritten on a yellow legal pad. I hope you love it and remember to make it your own.

🔥 Handfasting Ritual

Gather the following supplies:

- Altar table for elemental tools

- Wand

- Sword

- Chalice

- Pentacle

- Thick red ribbon

- Rose petals

- Cornmeal

- Rings

- Broom

A beloved friend or officiant asks the couple one at a time, "Who comes to be joined together in the presence of the Goddess and God? What is thy name?"

The couple each responds in turn by saying, "I am (your name), ready to be joined in holy communion with (your partner's name)."

The officiant says, "Unity is balance, and balance is unity." Then, they pick up a wand and say, "The wand that I hold is the symbol of air. Know and remember that this is the Element of life, of intelligence, of the inspiration which moves us onward. By this wand of air, we bring to your handfasting the power of mind."

The officiant puts down the wand, picks up the sword, and says, "The sword that I hold is the symbol of fire. Know and remember that this is the Element of light, of energy, of the vigor which runs through our veins. By the sword of fire, we bring to your handfasting the power of will."

The officiant puts down the sword, picks up the chalice, and says, "The chalice that I hold is the symbol of water. Know and remember that this is the Element of love, of growth, of the fruitfulness of the Great Mother. By this chalice of water, we bring to your handfasting the power of desire."

The officiant puts down the chalice, picks up the pentacle, and says, "The pentacle that I hold is the symbol of the earth. Know and remember that this is the Element of the law, of endurance, of the understanding that cannot be shaken. By this pentacle of earth, we bring to your handfasting the power of steadfastness."

The couple then exchanges their personal vows and places their hands one on top of the other. The officiant binds their hands with red ribbon, sprinkles rose petals on the couple's bound hands, then says to the couple, "Repeat after me: By seed and root, by bud and stem, by leaf and flower and fruit, by life and love in the name of the Goddess, I ____ take thee ____ to my hand, my heart, and my spirit at the setting of the sun and the rising of the stars. Nor shall death part us; for in the fullness of time, we shall be born again at the same time and in the same place as each other; and we shall meet and know and remember and love again."

The officiant sprinkles cornmeal over the bound hands, then says, "Repeat after me: By seed and root, by bud and stem, by leaf and flower and fruit, by life and love in the name of the God, I ____ take thee ____ to my hand, my heart, and my spirit at the setting of the sun and the rising of the stars. Nor shall death part us; for in the fullness of time, we shall be born again at the same time and in the same place as each other; and we shall meet and know and remember and love again."

The officiant then unbinds their hands and begins to exchange rings.

The officiant says, "Let the sun and the moon and the stars, and these our brothers and sisters, bear witness that _____ and _____ have been joined together in the sight of the God and the Goddess. And may the God and Goddess bless them as we do ourselves. So mote it be!"

The officiant lays a broom down for the couple, and hand in hand, they jump over it. The broom is then picked up, and the circle is ritually swept.

DEITIES

The world's pantheons are a collection of personified deities, archetypes that represent an aspect of the Divine Source. For example, the goddess Athena represents strategy, and the god Mercury symbolizes communication. Each deity has their own realm of knowledge and magickal connections with nature. Oshun from the Orisha tradition reigns over the sweet waters. Nut is the Egyptian goddess of the sky, stars, and cosmos, and Demeter, Greek goddess of grain, influences the fertility of the earth through the seasons.

In addition, each planet is assigned to a deity and has its own reign of influence. Mars is the god of war and agriculture; Mercury is the god of communication; Earth is the goddess of Mother Nature, also known as Gaia or Maya; Venus is the goddess of love; Saturn is the god of time and discipline; Jupiter is the god of expansion; Uranus is the god of the sky; Neptune is the god of the ocean; and Pluto is the god of death and the Underworld. The deities are multidimensional and have a broad scope of influence and power.

In Connie's treasure trove, I discovered five soliloquies from a ritual play that was typed in dot matrix with the pages still attached to each other, like an accordion. Magickal rituals can serve as plays in which you live in the "skin" of the deity to be invoked. In this play, you will meet the god Hermes (known in Roman mythology as Mercury), who is gender-fluid and has the ability to see from both god and goddess perspectives; Mother Maya, Hermes's mother, goddess of the Earth, and the essence of the Great Mother; and the beautiful and wise Hecate, the goddess of the Witches. These invocations read Shakespearean and lyrical to help you envision these deities and relate to the personas and powers they represent. You can read this silently or aloud, depending on whatever feels right for you, but perhaps, since a large part of Magick is playful creativity, you and others can perform the following invocations as part of a ritual.

MERCURY/HERMES AT THE TIME OF BECOMING

Oh, world of human,
Rejoice and lament.
For the son of Maya is among you!

I am the truth, lost in plain sight.
As pervasive as a nighttime mist,
As intriguing as the open road.
As fleeting as a wink,
As endless as the Horizon.

I am the words in cleverness used.
Oh, world of human,
Smile past your tears.
For the son of Maya is among you.

I am the humor that softens great pain.
As open as a child's face,
As closed as a miser's chest.
As shallow as a gripped hand,
As deep as an ocean floor.

I am the mirror never seen clearly.
Oh, world of human,
Acknowledge your desires.
For the son of Maya is among you.

I am the wishes felt yet unspoken.
As shy as the fox,
As wise as the owl,
As staid as the ox,
As busy as the hummingbird.

I am the skills used to survive.
Oh, world of human,
I follow and lead.
Maya's son, Hermes, is among you!

I am the guide to awakening!

HERMES'S CALL FOR A COUNTERPART/CONSORT

Oh, my Mother Maya,
Known as the Grandmother of Time,
You hold within you the knowing of when
And of what that was, that is, and that is yet to become.
I am of
Your love at one time.
You hold within you the answers of who
And how I was, I am, and that I have yet to become.
Oh, Mother Maya,
Please solve my vain search.
You hold within you the solution of one
Like me that was, that is, that has yet to become.
One that may
Share with me time
And beside me complete the riddle of what,
And when, and where, and why I lead.
I call for a counterpart, a consort.
As deceptive
As strong
As perceptive
As completing of existence
As I am myself.
Oh, Mother Maya

By your power,
LET HER BE!

INTERMISSION

Without hesitation, we meet the Goddess Hecate, guardian of the crossroads and thresholds, keeper of the keys, and guide between life and death and all transitions. She walks with us as we cross the veil between the living and dead. Hecate's companions are great dogs that give warning when their mistress is near. She holds the key to your heart's desire. She is the Inner Light at the moment of decision, at the crossroads of your life. Hecate arises as the consort for Hermes.

APPEARANCE OF HECATE

Your call, it is heard
And I alone know your need.
I hear all things in my place,
Behind the darkest veil
All shall come to visit me,
And they shall be received,
Only at their proper time.
My strong and gentle arms
Shall warm and comfort them
From the journey through the veil.
But know ye well, my gifts of peace and surcease
Are not without their price.
For me to give my all to you,
You must give freely your very self,
For no less would either satisfy.
To the unprepared, I inspire fright
For all that can see
Is my shadow cast upon the veil.
My beauty is that of dreamless sleep
And the calling songs of owl and wild canine
Cast out upon a moonless night.
I am your maiden, older than mother,
The final lover, more than just crone.
Hermes, my partner,
I am your true consort, Hecate.

HERMES'S WELCOME TO HECATE

Oh! Great Lady,
Welcome, thrice welcome,
Into the existence of my being.
It was for you,
And truly you alone,
That I did search for and wait upon.
To the ends of the earth and past
Have I gone, looking, hoping,
Until now, all in vain.
The time passed until now,
So heavy did it weigh upon me.
To be patient is hard, upon such as I,
The embodiment of existence on earth
To my motion, you are stillness.
To my noise, you are silence.
To my wit, you are wisdom.
To my exuberance, you are restraint.
To my boldness, you are discretion.
To my wandering, you are homeland.
To my needs, you are completion.
To the truth of myself
Has your wisdom pierced my web of words?
I am Lord of Travel, Trails, and Pathways.
That I might pierce your veil
To the truth of yourself
In return for yourself,
I offer myself without reservation.
With your acceptance,
LET US BE TOGETHER!

THE PARTING OF HERMES

I must now leave
Humankind's direct sights,
Yet only look,
And you shall see me everywhere.
No longer do you hear
My words to you directly,
Yet only listen,
And you shall hear me in wind and silence.
I must now leave
Humankind's direct perception.
Yet ever know,
I am within yourself, always.
No longer do you feel
My leading influence,
Yet going ahead,
I shall be with and before you.
I could not leave
Humankind's inner self,
Yet so far,
Within the deepest part of all of you.
True blessings upon you all!

INTERMISSION

As quick as a whip, Hermes is on the move again, and we are left to wonder about Hecate. Who is the mysterious one who guides you to that inner light? Who is so strong that no threshold is too high?

Does she care that her lover has come and gone so quickly? No, she knows her consort is "as fleeting as a wink," and she has her own territory and authority to command.

Hecate is a goddess of complexity and great power. She is known as triple formed or faced because she can look from all directions. You need to be honest and willing to accept the implication of working with such an immense force. She is known as the Goddess of Witches and is called by many names or epithets. Some of them include:

- Abronoê: Gracious

- Adamanthea: Unconquerable

- Aidonaia: Of the Underworld

- Angelos: Messenger

- Ambrotos: Immortal

- Ameibousa: One Who Transforms

- Astrodia: Star-walker

- Brimo: Angry, Terrible One

- Dadophoros: Torchbearer

- Daeira: The Knowing One

- Enodia: Of the Ways or Crossroads

- Ephoros: Guardian

- Kleidouchos: Keybearer

- Makairapos: Blessed One

- Nychia: Goddess of Night

- Paiônios: Healer

- Pantrephô: All-nurturing

- Phosphoros: Light Bringer

- Polymorphos: Many-formed

- Propylaia: Guardian of the Threshold

- Psychopompe: Soul Guide

- Skylakagetis: Leader of the Dogs

- Trimorphis: Triple-formed

- Trioditis: Of the Crossroads

Honoring Hecate

Gather the following supplies:

- Pinch of salt

- One charcoal disc

- Eggshells

- Herbs associated with Hecate that speak most to you: garlic, cypress, mugwort, rue, hyssop, marjoram, fennel, thyme, rosemary, saffron, sage, lavender, wormwood, and/or dill

- Fire-safe mortar and pestle or cauldron

Remove the thin, white, membranous layer inside the shell so all you are left with is a dried, clean eggshell. Rinse the shells with soapy water and let them fully dry. You can also bake the shells at 400 degrees for ten minutes. Crush the shells with a mortar and pestle until you have a very fine powder, also known as *cascarilla*.

Light the charcoal in a fire-safe mortar and pestle or cauldron. When the charcoal turns white, add the herbs one at a time, imagining where each was harvested and the special spirit and medicine the herb brings to this ritual. Choose the number of herbs based on numerology. You can reference the meanings of numbers on page 72. For example, if you need the guidance of Hecate's torch for a murky path, you might just choose one herb to represent singularity of purpose, or nine herbs to symbolize the Hermit. If you need to invoke the power of three for creativity or ingenuity, then you might use three herbs to invoke Hecate's triple form. After the charcoal has burned out and cooled off, mix in the eggshell powder. Add the salt and mix well in a counterclockwise direction to call in Hecate while chanting:

God and Goddess Energy

"Hecate, Hecate, come to me I call you in as
[choose one of Hecate's epithets that most fits your needs]
to bless me."

You can choose to sprinkle the mixture on your altar, at an actual crossroads, on the grave of a beloved, or anywhere that you feel most inspired to evoke and invoke the aspect of Hecate that you most need for guidance and support.

7

Wheel of the Year

There was a time when no one needed to tell us it was high summer or nearing Halloween, or that the days were shorter and nights longer. When we were young, many of us lived attuned to the seasons, not to clocks or schedules. Riding the rhythms of nature, we were little Pagans, which is why Wicca and other earth-based spiritualities make sense to children. They can often feel the changes and lessons that come with each season.

Wiccan and Pagan holidays, known as sabbats, are spaced six weeks apart and embrace special, sacred points on the Great Solar Wheel of the Year, also known as the Mandala of Nature. The major sabbats are the holy days dedicated to planting and harvesting and mark the peaks of each season. The minor sabbats are the holy days that honor and track the sun's movement (solstices and equinoxes) and mark the beginning of each seasonal peak.

A mandala is an object of meditation to aid in one's spiritual development. The sabbats are more than holiday markers on the calendar year. These holy days become signposts for the spiritual energy that is rising and falling, expanding and contracting, in nature. Each of the Pagan sabbats offers a lesson: for every season, there is a reason. In addition, a mandala often includes a geometric configuration of symbols. Consider the illustration at the beginning of this chapter to see evidence of eight isosceles triangles within a circle that mark the Mandala of Nature.

The more we embrace nature's guidance, whether by decorating an altar or singing a song to the changes of weather, the deeper we will sink into the cadence of all life on earth. Our energy and Magick increase when we are in sync with nature's rhythms and flow. A stick, leaf, or boat will naturally follow the river's current. We strengthen our bond with nature through seasonal altars, gardens, and even seasonal desires. Once we meld with the flow, we are imbued with the feeling of added support and the calm strength of belonging to something bigger than oneself. The dates offered below are for the Northern Hemisphere. These holidays are opposite in the Southern Hemisphere; for example, when we celebrate Beltane in California, Witches in Chile are celebrating Halloween.

"Participation in the turning of the Wheel connects the Witch with the divine emanations behind the cycles of Nature."

Raven Grimassi, *Spirit of the Witch*

CANDLEMAS

Candlemas, also known as Brigid's Day and Imbolc, begins on sunset of February 1 and lasts until sunset of February 2. This holiday honors Brigid, the goddess of fire, inspiration, and wells, when, from the dark of a winter's night, the first seeds of light and inspiration are planted. This is the quickening when you crystallize your desires into a single flame. At the beginning of the year, we can connect to the powerful new life that is stirring in our spirit, awakening in the depths of the earth, and channel this light energy into an upsurge of personal power. Altar suggestions include candles, incense, seeds, nuts, vessels of water, saffron, basil, or rosemary.

As Candlemas is the first planting holiday of the calendar year, try planting your favorite plant ally from seeds. Place the seeds in your mouth for nine minutes while focusing your thoughts on your connection with the plant. The concept that your saliva will activate the seed's growth was popularized by the book *Anastasia (The Ringing Cedars Series)* by V. Megre. Bury the seed in soil and ask for Brigid's guidance for its protection, growth, and medicine.

SPRING EQUINOX

On the Spring Equinox, or Ostara, which falls between March 20 and 22, depending on the year, night and day last equally as long. *Equinox* means "equal night." This celebration of rebirth and growth is preceded by brushing off the winter with spring cleaning that revives enthusiasm and hope in the new life that is blooming everywhere. Ostara is the time of year to give birth to new ideas, turn over a new leaf, believe in your abundance, and allow for emotions to come and go like spring rain. Ostara rejoices in the beauty of our unique selves blooming and playing with impish delight.

Altar suggestions include representations of spring and new life (such as rabbits, birds, baby animals, or flowers), images of fertility (such as eggs, nuts, or seeds), or flowers of jasmine, lily, and rose.

In this season, create an altar and chant this song in honor of Ostara, the German goddess of rebirth, dawn, growth of all things green, fertility, and abundance.

"Ring bell, sing bell, Spring bell chime!
Ring out the joy of happy time.
Winter is over; the darkness is through!
Ring out, sing out, the earth is born anew!"

BELTANE

Celebrated April 30 through May 1, Beltane, also known as May Day, celebrates the joy of being alive with wild abandon. It is the great spring festival of the marriage between Goddess and God. The love between these energies of rest and action, light and dark, has created life in its passionate fecundity. We plant our gardens, hibernating animals awaken, and all forms of creativity are celebrated. Beltane is also a fire holiday of fertility, passion, and the power of creation. We must have respect for fertility's strength and the results it brings, and wait for the time when we are mature enough to handle the outcome.

Altar suggestions include flowers (either in a basket or alone), images of faeries, creamy treats for faeries, joyful pictures of yourself, maypoles, ribbons, and oak leaves and branches.

On April 30, light an outdoor bonfire and celebrate with red wine, the symbol of Bacchus, the revelry god. The next morning, erect a maypole (symbolic of God) and wind ribbons (representative of Goddess) around the pole; this symbolizes the abundant harvest (representing the child) and the many blessings we hope to have throughout the year. Or braid multicolored ribbons around a stick for your altar.

SUMMER SOLSTICE

The summer solstice, also known as Midsummer or Litha, is celebrated June 20 through 22, when the sun is at its strongest in the Northern Hemisphere. In alignment with this solar power, this is the time to cast spells to direct your Magick for self-empowerment and gather herbal allies that are important for your well-being. This is the holiday for luxuriant self-care. Midsummer is also the time to celebrate the joys life has brought you and practice letting go of things that no longer serve your highest good. Make peace with the impermanence of life and release painful relationships, old possessions, or a negative, destructive attitude. Bloom where you are planted. Hug yourself. You are one with the infinite sun.

Altar suggestions include flowers (especially roses), healing herbs, and pictures or other representations of the sun, such as an orange, lemon, or sunflower.

As a ritual, use a magnifying glass to direct sunlight onto a piece of wood and burn four interconnected Vs to make a star. With each V that you score, imagine a word that begins with the letter V, such as victorious, vivacious, valiant, or voluptuous. As this eight-pointed star forms, recognize that you are calling in these traits for yourself.

LAMMAS

Lammas or Lughnasadh, also known as the Festival of Breads, is celebrated on August 1 through 2. During this first harvest, we reap the rewards of our hard work as we gather corn and wheat and bake bread that we will later break with friends and family in a gesture of community to carry us through the coming winter. Bless the tools of your trade in order to honor the gifts that allow you to provide sustenance for your body and purpose to your life. Make a commitment to honor your strength and skills. Find the beauty in the mundane. Although the days are probably still warm, winter—also known as the "dark season"—is approaching, and so much can happen. Share your harvest and your light energy with others.

Altar suggestions include breads, corn, berries, grains, harvested fruits and vegetables, or pictures and symbols of all your hopes and fears for the coming year.

Ritual suggestion: Create a figure of a corn dolly from corn husks (step-by-step instructions are on page 56) or prepare your favorite bread while repeating the following chant:

"Cut the grain, bind the sheaf
Harvest time of joy and grief.
Our Lord goes to be reborn
Cut the grain, cut the corn."

You may choose to burn or bury the corn dolly to represent the god energy inherent in the vegetation, which slumbers in goddess energy of earth to be reborn in spring. Or you can put the corn dolly on your altar or write wishes on corn husks with a Sharpie.

AUTUMNAL EQUINOX

Celebrated from September 20 through 22, the autumnal or fall equinox, also known as Mabon, is the other day of the year (along with the spring equinox) when night and day are in balance. This holiday calls for harmony and for us to honor the cycle of birth, death, and rebirth as we begin the dark season of the Goddess, when the warmth of the sun is fading and the nights are getting longer, offering a time for reflection. The autumnal equinox is the Wiccan Thanksgiving, the second harvest of the year when we gather the abundance of ripe vegetables, fruits, and nuts. This is the time to give thanks for our many blessings and release what drains our energy as we bring our focus to our inner core.

Altar suggestions include garlands of greenery and apples, harvested dried corn, winter squash, pomegranates, grapes, wine, pumpkins, autumn leaves, nuts, seeds, and myrrh.

Ritual suggestion: This holiday, celebrate Dionysus, god of wine, and Demeter, goddess of the harvest, with a Thanksgiving feast made from local products only. Circle the table, asking guests to claim their natural gifts or talents aloud. On the next round, ask them to share aloud the skills they have learned. On the final round, ask them to share their blessings.

SAMHAIN

The next sabbat is Samhain, also known as Halloween. It is celebrated on October 31 and is the third and final harvest and the Witches' New Year. *Samhain* means "summer's end" and is the twilight of the year, when nature recesses into the quiet barrenness of winter. We reflect and let go of what no longer serves us, just as the leaves have let go for the survival of the trees. It is the time of year to engage our shadow selves, the hidden parts of ourselves that house our damaging tendencies and negative self-talk and habits. Through the portal of Samhain, we recognize death as part of the natural cycle of birth and rebirth. We sit in this cauldron of what to release before we can make way for new beginnings, hope, and manifestations in the new year. During this holiday, we gather the information needed for our manifestations by traveling through the thin veil that separates the world of the living and dead, human and faerie, and other parallel universes or realms of knowledge.

Altar suggestions include pomegranates, apples, pumpkins, gourds, pictures of deceased loved ones, autumn leaves, and marigold plants.

Ritual suggestion: Create an altar for your beloved dead with marigolds, candles, and their pictures and favorite foods. Talk with your beloved ancestors about the shadow self and journal any response you receive. If we can pass down ancestral trauma, we can also receive ancestral healing.

WINTER SOLSTICE

Winter solstice or Yule falls between December 20 and 22, signaling the longest night of the year in the Northern Hemisphere. *Solstice* means "sun stand still" while *Yule* translates as "wheel." The wheel is symbolic of the Wheel of the Year, which teaches us that life exists on a continuum of an ever-changing, never-ending cycle of birth, death, and rebirth. The longest night of the year represents the darkness, the womb, where all creation originates. It is a time of quiet reflection, rest, and peace before we are born again. This holiday guides us to breathe deeply into the present moment.

Altar suggestions include evergreens, pinecones, wreaths, mistletoe, holly, candles of red or green, juniper, berries, and images of the sun.

Ritual suggestion: Light a white candle and meditate on our collective role as midwife to Mother Earth as She births the sun. Gaze at the flame in the dark of winter solstice night. Chant, "Mother, birth thy sun and grant us light. From your womb we are reborn this night." Focus your attention on your ability to give birth to any creation you can imagine and boldly shine your unique light.

A single candle flame can provide the inspiration needed in midwinter, and the blessings of fresh flowers for spring can feel like a miracle of hope and renewal. Pay close attention to what it feels like inside your body to build your gratitude as you near the fall equinox, gather pictures of beloved dead for Samhain, or bring in the tree for winter solstice. For the Witch, following the Wheel of the Year is not simply a duty; it is also an honor to learn from nature.

✳

I donned my green cloak into which I had sewn quartz crystals and red clover herbs along the hem, kissed my sons goodnight, and drove off to the Imbolc ritual at Connie's. It wasn't easy to drive in the cloak, with its plush velvet on one side and a twin-sized tapestry of Celtic knots on the other, especially when the silver clasp rode too high on my neck. But I was feeling the influence of the season upon me, and I saw the drive as the long passageway between my mundane world of stay-at-home mom to the magickal space of ritual. Connie had asked me to come early to help set up for the ritual. I think she knew I was nervous about meeting her other magickal students and coven members.

I opened the front door to a blaze of candles on every surface in Connie's living room. Connie stood next to the dining room table, which had been cleared of its usual chaos of opened and unopened mail and meals prepared by her students. I set my things on the kitchen counter and helped Connie spread out a red tablecloth.

"Did you bring your chalice?" Connie asked.

"Yes ma'am," I replied, holding up the delicate silver chalice with the Triple Moon symbol engraved on it.

"Good," she replied. "Ah, you brought the spanking spoon." Connie laughed as I set out hummus and a wooden spoon engraved with "The Wicca Cookbook." At Renaissance festivals my uber-savvy marketing tool backfired when the spoons were co-opted by more than a few Pagan derelicts for the purpose of spanking each other. I was definitely taking a risk with this crowd.

Nick sniggered from his position on the couch.

I shrugged. "You know what they say, us Capricorns age backward. I'm trying to lighten up."

Connie laughed until tears glistened in the corners of her eyes. "It's good to see you," she said, giving me a hug. I had recently returned from leading a goddess retreat on Kadavu Island, Fiji. My friend Nila and I had taken ten women halfway across the world so they could experience themselves as four faces of the Goddess: maiden, mother, enchantress, and crone. I saw the Southern Cross for the first time and had begun to pay more attention to the night sky.

"What does the ring around the moon mean?" I asked as we went about creating an altar centerpiece for the ritual with paper chain snowflakes, candles, and a handmade Brigid's cross. The night before, the sky had been crystal clear with a distinct iridescent circle around the full moon.

"Rain." Connie gestured to the open window. The metallic scent of rain on the sidewalk and asphalt mixed with the wet, earthy scent of rain-soaked grass. "A ring around the moon means moisture in the air and determines when certain crops should be planted or even protected from frost. Wicca is an agricultural religion, first and foremost, a life-affirming spirituality based on seasonality and cycles. Pagan or not, farmers have long gardened by the moon."

"I love the practicality of Witchcraft," I responded.

"We are each a garden that can never be rushed." Connie smiled ruefully. "You must live these holy days for several years before their wisdom truly sinks in. With each passing year, the sabbats have been my best teachers." She lit a white taper candle.

"I feel like returning to seasonal lessons year after year is symbolized by the Glastonbury Tor or the last scene in C. S. Lewis's book *The Last Battle*," I said. "They all spiral up toward some unique knowledge or lesson that's stored in the same vertical column of awareness. Further up and further in, we return again and again to these lessons with this circumnavigation."

"Oh, I love that vision." Connie closed her eyes as if she was watching what I had described. "You have such a way with words." Connie opened her eyes and looked at me directly, expanding on my idea. "Flatten out that conical shape to a circle, and you would have the Mandala of Nature." She paused to allow the symbol of the Mandala of Nature, or the Wheel of the Year, to surface.

"The first Pagan sabbat I ever attended was run by an eclectic fae Witch named Jeanette. She had the coolest faery garden in front of her house, protected by fifty-foot eucalyptus and pine trees. There was a pond and a huge, cracked, cast-iron stove that we used for the bonfire. I loved the hand-painted sign over her front yard that said 'REMEMBER' in all caps. It made me feel like I was *remembering* what it meant to be Pagan and a Witch. As in re-membering, putting myself back together. But the funny thing is, years later, Jeanette told me there had never been such a sign. I saw what I was supposed to see."

"Of course you did," Connie said with a smile. "The Wheel of the Year teaches us that we all belong to this evolving circle of life."

The squeals of coven members dashing through the rain woke Nick, who bounded off the couch like he didn't want to be caught sleeping. The door flung open and five people rushed into the small home. We loaded up the table for our feast as the full coven arrived. Everyone treated me like a family member who had just moved back home, especially a small, powerfully built woman named Sariel.

My cheeks flushed with joy as Connie instructed us all to bring our chalices into the magickal circle with us. Thirteen of us stood up, crammed in Connie's living room, and formed a circle. Michael traced a pentagram in oil on our foreheads, and James blessed us with the smoke from a smoldering mugwort bundle. Together we drew a cabalistic cross and raised a cone of protection. Connie welcomed in the four Elements and seven directions.

"Witchcraft is the Craft of the Wise as long as you are living it," Connie began. "The Mandala of Nature is more than just a collection of celebrations and rituals; the sabbats are when we access the wisdom of natural cycles outside and within. This is why it is also called the Mandala of Nature." She handed us each three pink and red ribbons tied together with a loop at the top. "Loop these ribbons onto your chalice like this," she said as she demonstrated passing the end of the ribbons through the loop.

"Now think of three blessings of this year that you would like to continue to receive next year," Connie instructed. "Braid the ribbons together, focusing on one blessing at a time. Tie a knot in the ribbon at about one-third of its length and say to yourself, "So mote it be." Consider the same or another blessing and repeat the process for a second and third knot."

Connie played a brass singing bowl while her coven members crafted their knot-work Magick. She crooned, "You can do your Magick even on a desert island. Remember that Elements live in you. The sabbats are your teachers and playmates. Listen to the Wheel of the Year."

(◔)) Cabalistic Cross

The Craft speaks of energies often, and it should be understood that these energies are indeed real and may be directly perceived. The energies used in Magick are akin to, but not as "physical" as, the electricity, fire, or magnetism we use in daily life. The mind and body are capable of drawing, channeling, and projecting energies that can be felt as physical sensations. With practice, these energies can be filtered, colored, and generally manipulated for the specific task at hand.

In Magick, it is desirable to provide a solid link to an energy source for both drawing and returning excess energies. In the Craft, this is commonly known as grounding and centering, establishing a link to the earth. Centering your energy through the ground link allows any excess energy to immediately bleed off into the earth, while any energy drawn is directly supplied by the earth as well. This is accomplished by a short ritual known as the cabalistic cross, which originated in the mysticism of the Hebrews. A cabalistic cross ritual can be performed silently and anywhere or anytime you may feel the need to ground and center yourself. It will bring your chakras and aura layers into alignment.

The words *Ateh Malkuth, ve Geburah, ve Gedulah, le Olam Amen* translates as, "Thou art the Kingdom, and the Power, and the Glory, forever, amen," which is a prayer uttered in many places of worship. In the cabalistic cross ritual, *Ateh Malkuth* creates a link through yourself from the above to the below. Then *ve Geburah, ve Gedulah* centers your energies on this link from right to left, and *le Olam Amen* establishes and seals the connection.

Begin with three deep breaths from the diaphragm. On the third exhale, raise your hand over your head (position one), and while visualizing a ball of white energy forming there, chant the first word for the length of an exhale: "Ah-TEH." Then, as you inhale, draw a strand of white light down to a point just below your feet (position two), visualizing another ball of white energy, exhale, and chant the word "Mal-KOOTH." Allow the resonance of the chant to reverberate through your chest. Then take your hand while inhaling and move it up just past your right shoulder (position three). As you exhale, chant "Vay-Ge-Boo-RAH." Remember to visualize a ball of white energy as you chant. Now draw a strand of white light energy across your chest to just past your left shoulder (position four) and chant "Vay-Ga-Doo-LAH" while exhaling and visualizing a ball of energy. Then place your hands over your solar plexus (position five). This time, visualize a lotus flower opening up, and as you exhale, chant the words "Lay-OH-Lahm." The last step is drop your hands to your sides with palm facing out as you chant "Ah-MEN."

Words shown in parentheses are phonetic pronunciations, and the capitalized syllable denotes emphasis.

1. ATEH (Ah-TEH): "Thou Art"

2. MALKUTH (Mal-KOOTH): "the Kingdom"

3. VE-GEBURAH (Vay-Ge-Boo-RAH): "and the Power"

4. VE-GEDULAH (Vay-Ga-Doo-LAH): "and the Glory"

5. LE-OLAM (Lay-OH-Lahm): "forever"

6. AMEN (Ah-MEN)

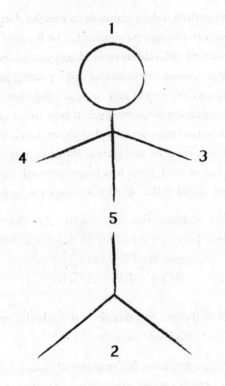

Return to Me

Gather the following supplies:

- Long-handled mirror

- Water, about a cup

- Pinch of sea salt

- Chalice, cauldron, or bowl

- Incense or bundle of herbs (mugwort is a great choice for this ritual)

As with every ritual, take a moment to breathe deeply and bring your awareness into the present moment. The focus of this ritual is to begin to see yourself as Goddess or God sees you—a perfect reflection of Divine Source. Gazing into a mirror and repeating positive thoughts softens the edges of self-doubt and suspends disbelief. This dynamic form of communication helps strengthen your inner guidance system. Consecrating a mirror turns an everyday object into a magickal tool by cleansing it of past energies and setting the intention to look at your reflection with eyes of the Divine. Mix pure water with sea salt in a chalice or cauldron and sprinkle the salted water over your mirror and say:

"I cleanse and bless this mirror with water and earth,
So that I may see the purity I was given at birth
To express the Divine uniquely as me
By my will so mote it be."

Light a stick of incense or a bundle of dried herbs, wave the perfumed smoke over your tool, and say:

"I cleanse and bless this mirror with fire and air,
So I might protect my wild nature with care
I now see my free soul looking back at me
Return to me, return to me.
By my will so mote it be."

You can also choose to decorate the outside of your mirror or the handle to further designate this magickal object as sacred. When your mirror is ready, look directly into your eyes and speak to yourself in the second person. "You are loved" settles differently in the brain than "I am loved." It resonates more like a command than a suggestion or statement. Think about a time when you had to give yourself a pep talk for an interview, competition, or some other life challenge. When you say, "You can do this," the encouragement comes from an inner confidence that speaks directly to your anxiety or uncertainty. It is a directive and a boost for you to step into your power.

CEREMONY INFUSES PURPOSE

Ceremony infuses our life with purpose. Magickal rituals that incorporate movement deepen the lessons of the season. Gesturing with delicate finger movements as the Maiden of Spring while wearing flowing, pastel garments allows the message of youth and beauty to well up deep within. By moving with the jovial step of Jupiter, we can begin to feel his expansiveness.

Pagans have long rejoiced and learned from the power of ceremony to more deeply integrate the lessons of each sabbat. Ceremony teaches us practical ways to infuse Magick into our daily lives so that with each turning of the Wheel of the Year, we can feel more deeply into the mystery and listen more carefully to the wonderful conversations happening in nature every day.

8

Shadow Work

Accepting your power is the first threshold for embodying your Divine Essence. The second threshold on this hero or heroine's journey is to face our shadow, the hidden or imbalanced aspects of ourselves or our immediate reactions to triggering events. Carl Jung is often credited for introducing the "shadow" concept in analytical psychology; however, the underpinnings of Magick have always included the shadow in a practical study of spirit and soul, exactly as the word *psychology* connotes: "pyscho-" relating to spirit or soul and "-logy" meaning study.

For centuries, Witches have answered the calling to be healers of the mind, body, and spirit; protectors of the wild within our souls and in nature; guardians of the mysteries; and weavers of the magickal arts. The irresistible yearning to create, cure, and connect will not be denied. To walk the magickal path is to heal oneself through recognizing our wholeness, then heal others so we can heal our world together.

Shadow work is a relevant topic because the time has come for each of us to face every expression of ourselves so that we can evolve as a whole—as people, communities, and a collective consciousness. We can no longer pretend or merely hope for change in the world; we must strive to be the change we want to see, to paraphrase the Buddha.

Our shadow selves can be our best teachers because they express our raw, vital energy that will not be tamed by society. There is a feral tenacity for life and growth that encourages us to take risks. In each of us, there is some version of a dream chaser, inventor, artist, and/or Magick maker who holds our hand as we pursue the most fervent desires of our inner heart. Every shadow has this gem of pure, natural energy.

In today's polarized social landscape, it can be courageously unconventional to assert there is nothing inherently good or evil about the shadow. We have been taught to fear our shadow, hiding our less socially acceptable selves from the public eye, feeling shame for bad decisions, and sometimes feeling guilty for not trusting our gut or being able to release a painful, traumatic experience. We have forgotten or altered key events in our lives to make us look better or feel safe, loved, and accepted.

What you resist persists for a very good reason.

"The shadow is the greatest teacher for how to come to the light."

Ram Dass

There is gold concealed in our shadow. It is a treasure we must mine from the recesses of our most unseen selves. The shadow can reveal how our greatest weaknesses, the places where we are "broken," can actually be the gateway to our greatest strength. We must coax our fragmented selves back into wholeness while patiently heeding divine timing and balance. As we do, we discover that changing the story can heal the wounds of the past.

Shadow work points the way to our greatest joy by urging us to accept all parts of ourselves, even, and most especially, when we "make mistakes" or react from a vulnerable or fearful place. These involuntary impulses can be our best teachers because they direct us toward our personal development through the Spirit Hole—a portal for emotional growth. We each have a shadow that can affect and manipulate our actions and beliefs, whether we realize it or not. Let's take a deeper look at some examples of how our shadows can present themselves.

1. Unacknowledged aspects of our personality

We all have qualities that we have difficulty acknowledging, such as self-centeredness, rigidity, or pride. With effort and work, we can shift the focus of these shadowed qualities and channel them toward something positive. For example, our self-focused desire for alone time could be the impetus to lobby for free childcare in the community, our fussbudget streak could help us grow a healthy savings, and our pride could push us to meet deadlines.

2. Qualities that are out of balance

There are parts of our personality that are very familiar and safe to express, such as the nurturer, peacemaker, or provider. But any qualities we possess, even the positive ones, can become imbalanced. We can neglect our bodies as we care for others to the point of illness, silence our voice in favor of peace, work ourselves to distraction or death in an effort to provide for ourselves and our families.

3. Stories that prevent us from moving forward

The meanings we give events, experiences, and relationships can impact us for our entire lives. We may replay or repress sad, frightening stories until we "forget" them as they originally occurred. Stories can take on a life of their own, becoming entrenched in our unconscious and calcifying on a merry-go-round, resulting in a pattern or groove that elicits the same reaction whenever we are triggered, like emotional scar tissue.

We can learn to see these stories from a different perspective and grow from the experience or find peace. For example, my Nana Della, who enjoyed drinking alcohol, died of cirrhosis of the liver. Based on how her death negatively impacted my mother and my childhood, I attributed my nana's death to alcoholism, which allowed me to blame her for leaving us. Years later, my cousin showed me studies that proved how the chemicals sprayed on the citrus fields where nana had worked for years had caused liver damage in some workers. The new information completely changed my perception of my nana, softened my heart, and gave me solace.

When the shadow takes over, we tend to refuse accountability or responsibility. Sometimes the reasons for our impulses are so tender, buried, or frightening that we lash out, deny, or withdraw when they are pointed out. Other times we may project an unacknowledged story or personality trait onto another person. For example, one could accuse a current spouse of cheating because their ex-partner was disloyal or maybe they're actually the one who is not living with integrity. It is usually true that when we point one finger forward, there are three fingers pointing back at ourselves. Only we can change our perspective, unstick ourselves from the past, and free ourselves from patterns we have outgrown.

Knee-jerk reactions to uncomfortable or unfamiliar situations reveal our shadow, perhaps in an unrefined or uncouth way, yet vibrantly alive.

We don't hold back; rather, we let all our big emotions fly. The truth rings out, but a discordant twang comes from the fact that we are reacting versus responding. Reacting to a situation from the shadow can stem from years of patterned response, where we live in a groove of unconscious behaviors. We may yell at our children or view ourselves as a victim because our childhood was rife with emotional abuse. We may treat others with mistrust because we were robbed, resist sharing because we experienced poverty, or feel we don't need to work hard because we didn't have to do chores as a child. On the other hand, when we respond rather than react, we take responsibility for our actions and choose to do better next time.

The stories we tell ourselves shape how others see us and reveal our outlook on life. We teach others how to treat us by the way we treat ourselves. Still, we do not always have all the information. We cannot assume, predict, or prophecy the outcome of our unchecked reactions that lead to us repeating the same story or following the same path year after year. We can only hope that with the passing of each season, we allow the wisdom of this physical experience to teach our mind and spirit some good that will evolve the soul.

Our brains purposefully shelter our consciousness from painful experiences. When you are ready to face the shadow, it is considered wise to set up some protection and a safe space where you will not be interrupted. You may want to cast a magickal circle (see page 178) or reference the protection spell (page 90). You may also choose to augment your healing with the aid of professional therapy. The following ritual was designed to help you accept hidden aspects of yourself, redirect imbalanced qualities, or release stories that have worn out their welcome and are causing more harm than good.

Working with the Shadow

Gather the following supplies:

- Salt from the Hecate ritual in chapter 6 (page 114)

- A Y-shaped stick to represent the crossroads epithet of Hecate

- Black candle

- Bowl of water

- Copal incense

- Magazines, scissors, glue, and paper

- Journal

- Pen or pencil

Take a moment to ground and center yourself with calming breaths. Prepare the salt with the intention of delving into the deepest, most mysterious recesses of your consciousness. Place the Y-shaped stick next to the black candle and water bowl. For protection, sprinkle the salt around where you will sit for this ritual. Light the candle. Ask Hecate to guide you on this mysterious journey to your hidden self. You may choose to place a picture of yourself and/or Hecate on your altar.

It takes courage to address your most furtively held secrets and let the light shine on them. We grow through these long, dark tunnels. Write a short list, no more than three, of any unhelpful personality traits or sad stories you haven't yet released. It doesn't matter if this quality is something someone else would admire. All that matters here is how you feel about this trait or story. Next, write down three unfavorable qualities that others have repeated about you. Everyone has both strengths and weaknesses, so try not to be intimidated; after all, this information is only for you to explore. Choose one quality from either list that jumps out at you or perhaps appears in both lists. You may always choose a trait or story that is less traumatic if you need an easier introduction to dealing with the shadow. This is heart-centered work, so follow your own pace.

Make a small collage using only images to represent the shadow you are willing to face. Avoid using words so the logical part of your brain can take a break. The images will speak in a symbolic language that is easier to feel and integrate than words. Remember that our brains are image processors, and when we work with visuals, we can tap into even deeper parts of ourselves.

After you have completed your collage, ask yourself some questions: *What is my shadow most afraid of? What is my shadow trying to make happen? What does my shadow need?* Your shadow might ask you questions: What is the trick to keep money flowing in? How will I ever learn to stop blocking love? When will I stop needing their approval? How come others have more than me? Place your hand on your heart and focus on the raw, honest questions to release what is underneath. Breathe into your heart center, and then journal your answers. Try to avoid spiraling too deep into labels, such as "I am trash, dirty, incapable." Remember, the voice of Spirit is loving, slow, and calm and never screams at you. You can use a timer to create a boundary for the journaling if you are concerned about managing these big emotions.

Recognize your shadow as an ally and give it a new assignment. For example, if you tend to be hyper-protective, invite your protector to take a break from its constant vigilance and only send you a sign, such as tingles on the back of your arms, when you need to add an extra layer of protection in a hostile environment or situation that elicits an imbalanced or habitual reaction. If your perfectionism functions well at work but wreaks havoc with your family, then you will need to set boundaries with yourself to not allow your penchant for precision to negatively impact your relationships.

Go slow and be polite as you get to know your shadow. It has been hidden in the dark for a very long time, in the mysterious goddess realm. Ask that the tenderness of the Divine Feminine be with you during this process. We can achieve deep self-love and find true peace within as we learn to calmly, slowly, and respectfully talk with our shadow.

*

I arrived at Connie's house with an intense desire to confess and take a deep dive into shadow work. I assumed most people knew when they'd behaved badly, but I wondered what *they* did with their feelings when they knew that, given a second chance, they wouldn't act any other way. I loosened the clench in my jaw as I rapped on the screen door, pulled it open, and walked into Connie's home. I handed her a hardcover of *Harry Potter and the Goblet of Fire* and plopped down on the beanbag in front of her chair.

"Oh. Thank you." Connie beamed at me. "How was the midnight release party?" she asked as she flipped the pages, releasing the scent of a brand-new book to mingle with her nag champa incense.

I thought back to last night. I had draped my stepdaughter, Ali, who was twelve years old, in a black gossamer Witch's cape with webs and spiders sewn in silver glittery thread. I donned my heavy green velvet cloak that swished as I walked and emanated my unique Magick, making me feel as powerful and invincible as a queen.

"Ali is the reason I ever read a Harry Potter book. A couple of years ago, she convinced me that J. K. had gotten some things right about our witchy world. At the same time, radio and newspaper journalists were poking fun at me, asking if Witches rode brooms like in Harry Potter. I wanted to get on a soapbox and explain that Witches heal with herbal medicines and holding onto the old ways of seasonal living, but instead I joked that we've upgraded to dustbusters for short trips and vacuums for longer journeys."

"That's a good comeback," Connie mused.

"My friend Victoria gave me that one. I don't like being teased. I take it personally and feel like someone just stole my energy. I work so hard to help the mainstream see Wicca and Witchcraft for its goodness, yet far too often people treat me as a joke—or their worst nightmare."

"Treating someone as a non-person is the path to marginalizing them," Connie said.

"Exactly!" I nearly shouted. "The more the world treats Witches as not real, the easier it is for them to ostracize and dismiss us." I bit off the nail of my forefinger. "So, last night . . . I loved celebrating the Magick of Harry Potter with Ali, but I was conflicted by the possible damage created by perpetuating Witchcraft as a pretend lifestyle, even though I do love the books now."

"What did you do?" Connie asked, intrigued and horrified.

I paused. "We were in line to buy the books. The Harry Potter theme song filtered throughout the bookstore, which was ablaze with lights, and workers ran around dressed as characters from the book. Wearing that green cloak put me in the patronizing attitude of Narcissa Malfoy from the Slytherin house. My frustration was growing when this frumpy woman standing in front of us in line turned around and said to me, 'Oh, I just love your costume.' It was too much. I looked at her with utter disdain and snarled, 'This. Is. Not. A. Costume.' The lady turned around so quickly." I sniggered in spite of my attempt at being remorseful in the presence of my mentor. I sobered up for my true confession. "I looked smugly at Ali, whose pale blue eyes clearly asked why I had to scare the muggles. My daughter was not impressed with me."

"An eye for an eye?" Connie asked, raising her eyebrow as she inspected me. "Makes the whole world blind," she finished Gandhi's quote. "You'll never help the collective consciousness rise in vibration if you unkindly take justice into your own hands," Connie remarked.

"I don't like feeling invisible or marginalized when it's so undeserved. I tend to react with a condescending attitude that I think I got from my Nana Della, who carried herself with haughty confidence because it was the only way to rise above the propaganda against Mexicans and Latinos. Her motto was, 'If you walk fast enough, they won't notice you're brown.'"

"Is that the legacy you will teach your daughter? Della deserves more respect than carrying her burdens as an excuse to be condescending." Connie paused and then brought down the hammer. "Stuck in a separate reality of us versus them, you will eventually lose your faith in the connection to all life. Your Magick will cease to work when you focus on yourself as separate, above, or better than others. You manifest everything through this interdependent network."

"'We all live downstream,'" I repeated a favorite saying about how our actions eventually catch up with us. "It's embarrassing how many times I have manipulated others to fill my cup when I'm feeling drained."

"You are not in charge of the divine timing to face, integrate, or cut your hidden shadow," Connie said. "That's the universe's job. You just need to be ready."

TIMING THE CUT

Shadow work is like gardening. There will always be more to do. You will need to pull weeds and pluck damaging thoughts often, and that is okay. You will tend to the blooms and reap the rewards of redirecting your energy. You can enjoy more of the fruits of your labor by finding the right balance of sunlight, water, and nutrients for optimum growth.

Shadow Work

It is a matter of seizing the opportunity to learn about your unique spirit at play in the world versus condemning yourself for not recognizing a better choice or reacting thoughtlessly in the moment. We fracture our spirits when we judge ourselves for the mere existence of our shadow side. It's a double whammy to get upset with the ubiquitous work of the shadow. We could unintentionally become the abusers by constantly reliving the stories that caused us pain and need professional help. Reading books like Sandra Ingerman's *Soul Retrieval* really helped me move through my unresolved stories.

Early abandonment from my father gave me a wealth of stories, from blaming myself for someone else's limitations to allowing a fear of rejection to create anxiety and letting hate corrode the vessel that contains it. The brain doesn't know the difference between something that is happening in real time and a memory. Yet we may not be able to change until we can face the obstacles that test our will to grow. By facing our shadowed stories, we can free ourselves, finally accept without judgment, and commit to vitality. Invite the shadow, your fears and secrets, over for tea or a cuppa, and really listen.

If you experience a block in moving forward, it is always a good idea to thank your shadow, which may have helped you survive by protecting you when you needed it most. Yet what served to protect our fragile spirits when we were young does not always serve us as adults. There comes a time to let what was once good, and now soured, go. It's like keeping milk in the refrigerator past its expiration date. Eventually, the more we accept ourselves, warts and all, the more our shadow settles into useful work on our behalf.

As with all Magick, shadow work depends highly upon authentic effort and divine timing. There is no Magick trick or spells to help you accept your shadow. You may need both time and tears to prepare your mind to accept a difficult situation or "character flaw." You may need professional help. I consider therapy like getting an oil change; it's what you do to keep the engine running smoothly. But I also get a plethora of therapy from bodywork, collaging, writing, and talking. With time and distance, we can gain a clearer picture or come to understand the motives of others or even a younger version of ourselves. Feeling all the emotions by letting them rise up and out is courageous, healing work.

You cannot rush acceptance because each step deserves to be processed with dedication and attention. You cannot hurry the ripening of the garden any more than you can force your way into enlightenment. Personal changes evoke cultural changes, and both take a long time. Yet it is important to realize that you will remain under the power of your shadow, which moves like a subterranean river, until you are ready to face it. Author and Jungian psychoanalyst Clarissa Pinkola Estés, PhD, calls this clandestine influence "Rio Abajo Rio," the River beneath the River. She addresses the many cultural shadows that attack and suppress women in her iconic book *Women Who Run With the Wolves*.

As the shadow can be one of our greatest guides, it often remains hidden from our awareness until we are called upon for transparent accountability. In this cyclical world of Magick, the seed of awareness and acceptance does not sprout until the timing is ripe. Dr. Estés's book barely made sense to me when I first read it in my early twenties. I wasn't ready for the material. Twenty years later, I understood every line. Have you ever read a book, parable, fable, or myth that only made sense once you gained clarity from your experience?

Some of us have come into this life to heal ancestral trauma that we carry as a shadow, an additional burden, or as unseen blocks or beliefs about our inherent goodness. These may take the form of self-sabotage, self-centeredness, or victimization. As if you're a helpless ant at the bottom of the Grand Canyon, the shadow says that these walls are too high for you to vault over. Perhaps our ancestors couldn't push back against society, but now the time is ripe for us to do so.

Shadow work is the "reward" step in the hero(ine)'s journey, a time for us to accept and integrate our unexamined nature in order to experience wholeness. As our wholeness strengthens from within, it emanates outward and gives people permission and also guidance to love themselves unconditionally. When we fully accept our shadow, we can begin to direct the energy where we most want it to go.

The magickal tool for directing energy is the athame, or the Witch's black-hilted knife. It's an instrument used to draw magickal circles and other diagrams in the midst of which spells are cast. There were two versions from Connie's notes on blessing athames. A basic one is discussed in chapter two; I have saved the more complicated ritual presented here for cutting away at the shadow and redirecting its energy. The approach to our Magick changes within a tradition and evolves within a person. Witchcraft follows nature's constant change and morphing, which is why no two versions of the Craft can ever be the same.

⟨⟩ Grand Blessing of the Athame

Gather the following supplies:

- Steel knife with a black handle. The blade should be about five or six inches long. You can choose to buy a special knife or you can bless and consecrate a knife you already have.

- Herbs connected to Mars, such as aloe, basil, bearberry, benzoin, coriander, hops, and wormwood

- Bowl

- Water

- Thurible (incense holder)

- Charcoal

When the moon is waning, infuse distilled water with any of the herbs associated with Mars, the god of action. Light a charcoal round. Cleanse the knife with water from your cup. Once the charcoal turns white, sprinkle some herbs on top of it. Move your knife through the smoke of the aforementioned herbs burning in your thurible. Then, proceed to heat the blade of the knife on the coals until it gets as hot as possible. You will have to stoke a good heat by pressing the knife into the coal. When the blade is good and hot, plunge it into your waiting brew, chanting these words and visualizing the knife glowing with power after each immersion:

"Blade of steel, I conjure thee
To ban such things as named by me
As my word so mote it be!"

This process of tempering, or forging as it is called, should be repeated three times.

Having accomplished this, you must now magnetize the blade by stroking it repeatedly with a lodestone or bar magnet. Hold the athame in your left hand, the magnet by one end in your right, and beginning at the handle end of the blade, draw the tip of the magnet down the whole length of the blade to the very point. Keep this up for a good five minutes, always stroking in the same direction and on both sides of the blade, and chanting these words with each stroke:

"Blade of steel, I conjure thee
Attract all things as named by me
As my word so mote it be!"

Finally, paint symbols that are important to you upon the handle in white paint with which you may again mix any of the herbs you have chosen to use. Chant the following words to charge each rune:

"Blessed be thou, knife of art!"

Then paint your Witch name on the reverse side of the handle. If you do not have a Witch name, you can use divination to receive one from Spirit [see page 224 for the full ritual]. Spell the letters out loud to charge them, then finish with your usual words, "So mote it be!"

Finally, bury the athame for three days and three nights in the earth, point down. At the end of this time, you may dig up your athame, wrap it in a piece of cloth, and tuck it safely away until you're ready to use it. You can combine Elemental Magick with the power of the athame by drawing specific pentacles as seen in the strokes of the following athame diagram.

Strokes of the Athame

Spirit
Air — Water
Earth — Fire

NORTH - GREEN

Earth Evoking   Earth Banishing

EAST - YELLOW

Air Evoking   Air Banishing

SOUTH - RED

Fire Evoking   Fire Banishing

WEST-BLUE

Water Evoking   Water Banishing

✳

I could barely contain myself as I drove to Long Beach. I was seething from an argument I'd had with my mother after I was late coming back from a date with my husband while she babysat. I was so upset with myself for reverting to old patterns, terrified of her screaming at me for keeping her waiting as if I was still a child.

The roiling clouds of spring rain fueled enough anger and courage for me to confess to my mentor and deal with the painful emotions once and for all. I took a deep breath at Connie's front door. In my mind's eye, I willed structure and order on the chaos of my mind, as if magickally reassembling a broken chandelier.

"You're feeling all that much?" Connie called from her chair directly inside the door.

I opened the screen door. "Oh yes," I said, handing Connie her beverage and plunking down on the pillow next to her chair. I glanced over at the couch to see that Nick was there again, asleep on the couch. He had the aura of an orphan who needed love, though he pretended he didn't. Of course, he had been at the last sabbat, where we once again did knot work to add another braided and knotted ribbon to our chalices.

She licked the whipped cream. "Delicious. So, what happened?"

I recounted the night's events. The shame at my childish, rote response enflamed my cheeks, and I shook my head. "When I entered my Saturn's Return six years ago, my number one goal was to release my anger at my mother. I refuse to make her the author of my every misfortune. She doesn't deserve it, and I need to play the lead role in my life. My friends and I found this woman, Katherine Morningstar, who practiced the healing technique called rebirthing. She guided us in meditation, and our memories went back as far as our consciousness would allow." I paused to take a breath.

"In one session, I remembered my birth. There was a dark tunnel, a prism of light in front of me, and the shadow of my nana's ghost to my right. I was suddenly so mad at my nana when I realized she was not on this side of the veil. She was no longer alive." I snickered to hide the pain. "I pulled myself out of the trance and said I had to pee. Katherine asked me what I was so pissed off about. 'The body always speaks to us,' she said."

A lump rose in my throat, and with years of practice, I swallowed it. "I felt rage from dealing with my mother crying regularly over my nana's death until I was at least ten years old. My mom said that at her mother's funeral, when she was nine months pregnant with me, she tried to throw herself onto the grave."

Fresh tears started to flow, and I wanted to stop, but a cool breeze billowing through the screen door emboldened me and I kept going. "I don't know why I am acting like an unloved child. My mother adores me." I wiped away tears and tasted them, as the Mexican tradition teaches, so I would not feel the same pain again. In many Mexican-American households, it's practically blasphemy to say anything ill about your mother.

"She was always yelling at me as a child," I almost whispered. "When I was young, I used to believe there was a finite number of people allowed on the planet at any given time. I assumed that for me to be born, someone had to be bumped off the planet and that I had killed my nana, and that's why my mother didn't love me." My voice was shaky and thin.

"That is far too heavy a load for a child to carry," Connie remarked with tenderness in her voice.

"Why couldn't she let go of her grief to raise me with love? I was also in pain and grieving the nana who would never hold me. I had heard her when I was in the womb."

"Your mother is the little mother. You are a Little Mother," Connie explained. "The Goddess is the Great Mother. We Little Mothers do our best to be like Her, like the Great Goddess, but we don't always get it right." She looked into the distance.

"Nana Mame says I stayed in the womb two weeks past my due date so I could be a tough-skinned Capricorn instead of a carefree Sagittarius. She said the stability of the Capricorn influence gave me a fighting chance."

"You came into this life with plenty of resources." Connie returned her gaze to me and smiled. "Many lives."

"Katherine helped me come up with an affirmation that I say while looking into a mirror." I rattled off the affirmation like it was the fine print at the end of a drug commercial: "I love you, Jamie. You are innocent. I forgive you for thinking that you are bad, wrong, evil, or guilty. You are good enough now and have always been."

"Why do you say it so fast?" Connie asked. "Can you say it slowly?"

I repeated the phrase as slowly as I could. It was so much easier to be quick about it.

"Why do you use those words: *bad, wrong, evil,* or *guilty*?"

"Bad for killing my grandmother. Wrong for temper tantrums. Evil for being a woman. Guilty for not healing the world immediately." I started chewing on my thumbnail.

"Why do you think being hard on yourself is such a good idea?"

"It's just how I have always done things. I'm hard on everyone."

"We teach people how to treat us by the way we treat ourselves." Connie lit a white taper candle. "It's up to you."

"Why can't people just know where my boundaries are?" I asked, hearing myself sound so childish. Yet, if I couldn't ask Connie, who could I ask?

"You want others to know where that invisible line is that protects you?" Connie asked, slightly amused.

"Well, now that you put it that way! But why do I have to be so influenced by others?"

Connie smiled tenderly and said, "Witches have a few extrasensory skills, and you are particularly gifted at picking up so much energy. You're like a satellite dish."

"Why do people always have to bitch-slap us as they wake?" I wailed.

"Waking a sleepwalker is always dangerous." The gravelly voice of Nick, who I'd thought was asleep, startled me. He rolled over and paid us no more attention.

Connie smiled at me. "You are a healer who can access the light, but you can only give as much as your resources will allow. You cannot pour from an empty cup." Connie raised her caramel macchiato and took a few satisfying gulps of the spiced, warm drink. She had added glitter stickers to the to-go cup.

"How can I say that I worship the Goddess and still have mommy issues?" I asked the candle's flame, not able to bring my eyes up to my mentor's at the mention of my darkest secret. I didn't want Nick to hear and I almost did. *Maybe my vulnerability could help him?* I thought.

Suddenly, a spring breeze blew in through the screen door, making the candlelight flicker. Warm, sensual air reminded me of my raw, vital energy, the part of me I usually suppressed lest it be too wild or untamable for Orange County, California, society.

"It doesn't always have to be this way. Now, breathe, just breathe, and listen," Connie crooned, and I closed my eyes. "Once, there was a family of women who made an extraordinary pot roast. The grandmother and mother had always cut off the roast at both ends, rubbed in herbs and spices, and placed the meat on the center rack. One day, the youngest daughter asked her grandmother why they cut off the ends of the roast, to which the old woman replied, 'Back in the day, we had to cut the hunk of roast to make it fit into the pot.'

"Sometimes we repeat patterns without knowing why we do them. We follow the methodology and tradition because that is how it has always been done. We repeat stories because they have become familiar. You have to get out of the rut of seeing your mother in the same light as you did when you were young. She will always be the little mother, trying her best to channel the love and wisdom of the Great Mother."

"But—" I interrupted.

"Sheltering in your shadow will turn cold and lonely, Jamie," Connie said. "You have prepared for this. Stare into the flame and repeat your matriarchal lineage as far back as you can go."

"I am Jamie, daughter of Cathi, daughter of Della, daughter of Eliza, daughter of Manuela, daughter of Maria . . ." I trailed off trying to remember the order of the next four grandmothers, whose names all began with Maria. As I fought to remember, I saw an image of my mother at nineteen years old, newly motherless yet holding me in her arms with love in her eyes.

As if Connie was watching the movie that played in my mind's eye, she said, "This family discord did not begin with your mother."

New images popped into view. I saw my mother leading a raucous standing ovation at a Whole Foods class in posh Napa Valley for *The Wicca Cookbook* even though I'd burned the meal trying to teach Wicca and cook at the same time. I remember the embarrassed but happy feeling of waiting in the parking lot of the Psychic Eye bookshop in Sherman Oaks while she asked the store manager for the event poster of my latest book signing.

"We don't have all the pieces to the puzzle," Connie said, eerily repeating a phrase I had heard many times before. "It's time you bury the hatchet."

A few days later, I approached my mom with the idea of letting go of our anger, and she wholeheartedly agreed. We created a ritual to address the obstacles between us that did not allow us to forgive the past, so we could build a new relationship. We buried the hatchet in her backyard, which was on the same land where eight generations of our ancestors had lived along the Santa Ana River. We like to think that our healing moment created a balm to mend the long line of the mothers and daughters in our lineage who may have benefited from this forgiveness ceremony. We can trigger each other at times, but we can always reflect upon this ritual with the knowledge that we love each other deeply enough to bury the hatchet.

Bury the Hatchet Ritual

Gather the following supplies:

- Paper for writing

- Pen or pencil

- Hatchet

- Small plot of land

- Shovel

- Sticks

- Candle

Create a peaceful environment in whatever way feels right for you and a loved one you are having a deep struggle with. Be sure this person is willing to explore their shadow with you. Light the candle, face each other, and while holding hands, look deeply into one another's eyes. Take turns telling each other why you love one another.

Release your hands, and take a few moments for you both to write down any past grievances between you and how the experience affected you. Be as honest as possible and focus on the feelings inside your body, mind, and spirit instead of projecting blame or shame. Take turns sharing your writings with the same love that emanated from your eyes and heart when you first began the ritual. When it is your turn to listen, make no excuses for how you have hurt the other. Refrain from debating about your loved one's feelings, which is the utmost sign of disrespect. When they're finished, simply say, "I hear what you say with an open heart. I love you."

When you're both done sharing, burn the petitions in a fire-safe container. As the flames consume your past, discuss your hopes for your future relationship, and write them down. Take your petitions for a more helpful and kind relationship outside with your hatchet, the container filled with ashes, a couple of sticks, and a shovel. Dig a hole with the shovel and place the ashes in the bottom of the hole. Place the hatchet on top. Read aloud your wishes for the future and place them on top of the hatchet; cover it all with dirt. Use the sticks to mark the spot in whatever way works best for you.

Even with heartfelt rituals such as this, it is important to accept that you may return to these lessons again and again, depending on the level of your vulnerability, the timing of the universe, and your soul's evolution. The joy in the journey comes from shedding whatever stands between you and your Divine Essence, even if that happens day by day, ritual by ritual.

"The holiest place on earth is where an ancient
hatred has become a present love."

A Course in Miracles

NURTURING THE SHADOW

The wisest Witches live with the clear awareness that Magick is at our fingertips every day, all through the year. To create Magick, we must consider all the possible or potential obstacles to manifestation, including those that lie within us. Embracing our shadow teaches us to let go of the notion that our less-than-desirable feelings or personality traits should be hidden because they are "bad." This thought process will keep us stuck in negative, unconscious patterns. Personal growth and metamorphosis begin when we courageously recognize and integrate the shadow.

We grow our self-love by accepting all that we are, which will give us a much better chance of positively directing our unique energy. Shadow work cleans each facet of your diamond so you can receive the power of universal influences in the form of your guardians and playmates. Yet there comes a time when focusing on the shadow is like chewing gum that has lost its flavor. We are not special because of our shadows or life challenges, so don't let your identity remain attached to your difficulties.

When you have faced your shadow and have accepted your allies and gifts, you will be rewarded with the Holy Grail, the everlasting cup of your Divine Essence for you to drink from whenever you need it. That's the whole point of the journey: to feed yourself by being the clearest, most truthful version of yourself that you can be and finding joy in seeing the best in others.

How do you really drink from the Goddess's chalice? Seek wonder, feed your curiosity, and live juicy. Listen for the message in birdsong or the warm breeze. Find the original innocence in yourself and even the world. Focus on the healing properties of plants, crystals, fresh air, burning bowl ceremonies, and the many other ways we heal ourselves. Find wonder in the small things. One day, you may realize those were the biggest moments of your life.

9

Universal Influences

I t is exciting to discover that the inherent Magick of the universe is at your disposal to transmute dreams or nightmares. As powerful as any spell that has ever been cast, a thrilling sense of "remembering" occurs when we listen to the whispers of trees and the sentience of nature. We feel empowered when we heal a small cut with herbal medicine, alleviate heartbreak with rose quartz, or feel our Divine strength rise up during a job interview. As we explore the power within and the allies and guidance offered, our awareness will expand to incorporate the power of universal influences into our magickal lives.

Universal influences include planetary movements, days of the week, our astrological and other natal charts, phases of the moon, the zeitgeist (the defining spirit, mood, and/or beliefs) of a particular time in history, seasonality and weather, cultural stories, societal feedback, terrapsychology (the soul of a place), family, and the lineage of our ancestors. Armed with knowledge, you can consciously create and play with the myriad energies in the world rather than be manipulated by them without your consent.

There is a universal influence that is associated with each day of the week. Each planet's area of influence relates to a different aspect of our lives and can infuse incantations with more power. There will come a time when you cannot cast a spell or ritual on the appropriate day, which is fine. If your focus is pure and strong, your Magick will reflect this. When possible, it is exciting to align your desire with the energy that the day and the planet may be exerting over you and others.

Sunday is ruled by the sun, which influences friendships, jobs, the healing power of the Divine, and intuition.

Monday is ruled by the moon, which influences emotions, love, home, family, clairvoyance, subtle changes, medicine, the ocean, and dreams.

Tuesday is ruled by Mars, which influences cardinal energy, battles, athleticism, hunting, surgery, physical strength, courage, contests, farming, agriculture, and competition.

Wednesday is ruled by Mercury, which influences communication, computers, learning, divination, teaching, self-improvement, writing, and intellect.

Thursday is ruled by Jupiter, which influences expansion, wealth, legal matters, money, materialism, abundance, generosity, and luck.

Friday is ruled by Venus, which influences play, lust, love, music, pleasure, joy, relationships, fun, and women.

Saturday is ruled by Saturn, which influences structure, the dead, endings, faith, solitude, self-discipline, self-respect, and banishment.

THE ORIGIN OF MOTHER EARTH'S ZODIAC CHILDREN

Since the mid-1970s, astrology has been taught through a parable in which God presents unique tasks for the different signs of the zodiac. This "origin of the zodiac story" was originally printed in *Karmic Astrology: The Moon's Nodes and Reincarnation* by Martin Schulman in 1975, and it has been reprinted thousands of times and appears in many places online. Several versions of the story appeared in the stack of Connie's magickal notes.

The problem with this material is that it perpetuates the misconception that the Creative Source expresses itself only as masculine thought, the Father God, with no acknowledgment or voice for the soft, feminine heart of the Mother Goddess. So, where the origin of the zodiac story speaks of "God's seed," I will use the term "My breath" to indicate the *inspiration* of co-creating with the Divine. Where the original version speaks of "My Idea," I will use "My Heart." I have not changed the gifts given to each sign of the zodiac but instead offer the Mother Goddess's perspective in bestowing gifts to each zodiac child to help make their tasks achievable and less arduous.

We will always have the masculine version of the original story, and now I present a similar conversation between the zodiac and the Creative Source, with the energy and tone of the Mother Goddess granting her gifts.

✳

"And it was a bright morning as Mother Earth stood before her twelve star-children and breathed a unique spirit of human life into each of them. One by one, each child stepped forward to receive their appointed gift.

'To you, Aries, I give the sacred fire as the first of my zodiac children so that you might have the honor of sharing it. For every spark of passion that you share, one million more will multiply in your hand, and your example will inspire others to ignite their co-creative abilities as children of the Divine. Your life is action, and the only action I ascribe to you is to demonstrate the power of passion and love so that others may admire and learn. For your good work, I give you the virtue of self-esteem.'

Quietly, Aries stepped back to their place.

'To you, Taurus, I give the power of tenacity, drive, and patience to bring ideas and dreams into substance. You will know and embody perseverance to stay the path until the work is done. You will know earthly pleasures. I grant you the fortitude to be true and loyal to yourself always so that you may teach others to trust themselves. You are the steady line, quietly stable and resolute, and I ask that you finish all that has been started. For this task, I give you the gift of strength.'

And Taurus stepped back into place.

'To you, Gemini, I grant an unquenchable curiosity and alert intelligence. I will fill you with delightful ideas and longing wonder at the illimitable possibilities. I give you the questions without the answers so that you may evoke an intelligent and playful conversation of what people see around them. You will engage heartily in the exchange of ideas, always seeking why people speak or listen, heal or stay stuck. In your quest for the answer of what is possible, you will find my gift of knowledge.'

And Gemini stepped back into place.

'To you, Cancer, I ascribe the fulfillment that comes from nurturing a deep inner life. Moonchild, you are the reflection and quiet of Goddess power. Above all, you are able to feel deep into the lunar Mother energy. You have the task of teaching people about the value and purpose of a rich emotional life. My hope is that you will evoke laughter and tears so often that others may develop fullness from inside by your example. For this, I give you the gift of family that your fullness may multiply.'

And Cancer stepped back into place.

'To you, Leo, I give the joy of leading others in the raucous celebration of life, in all its fullness and brilliance. Laughter is your medicine whether you wear the crown or jester's cape. Whenever you cavort and celebrate, showing others the importance of play, may you always remember that we create together, not alone. You are gifted with much vibrancy, valor, and color that grows when equally and freely shared. For this, I give you the gift of honor.'

And Leo stepped back into place.

'To you, Virgo, I ask for an honest and humble examination of your own humanity as well as humanity's work upon the earth. Through efficiency, you will attain a precise sense of an ideal sovereignty without falling victim to perfection. You are to serve others through perceptive analysis and astute clarity so that, through your observations, the collective consciousness may evolve their Divine Essence. For doing this, I give you the gift of purity of thought.'

And Virgo stepped back into place.

'To you, Libra, I give the mission of balance so others will be mindful of their duties to each other, learn cooperation, and foster the ability to reflect on the other side of their actions. You are blessed and challenged by the scales of justice. Your task is to apply the surprisingly healing balm of beauty upon the world. Because of your innate harmonious spirit, I will put you everywhere there is discord, and for your efforts, I will give you the gift of love.'

And Libra stepped back into place.

'To you, Scorpio, I ask that you dive deep into the mystery. In the shadowlands, you will be privy to secrets that may cause you pain because you feel so intensely. I will always be with you, dear one, through this very difficult task. Through your courage and example to face the unknown, all of humanity will better know the balance of light and dark. As yours is a journey of love and shadows, I give you the supreme gift of purpose.'

And Scorpio stepped back.

'To you, Sagittarius, I ask that you make people feel joy and remind them of childlike bliss. Through laughter, faith, and your free spirit, you will give people hope, and through hope, you will keep their attention on love. You are the adventurous arrow that goes forth from my bosom in search of new expression and fullest expansion. To you, Sagittarius, I give the gift of infinite abundance so you may spread wide enough to reach every corner of despair and bring it healing energy.'

And Sagittarius stepped back into place.

'To you, Capricorn, I offer you peace and satisfaction in the toil of your brow that you might teach others to view work as a tangible form of love. Your integrity stands as a monolith of what commitment to oneself and community can be in its highest form. You will feel humankind's labors on your shoulders; but the blessing of your burdens contains the abiding love for your human family and the power of the web that connects us all. For your efforts, I grant you the gift of sacred responsibility.'

And Capricorn stepped back into place.

'To you, Aquarius, I honor you with a glimmer of humanity's greatest potential. You will be blessed with a vision, a concept of the future that others do not see. You will be and appear revolutionary and sometimes feel lonely as you push humanity onward as a whole concert of light, rather than individual sparks. I give you the gift of freedom so that, in your liberty, you may inspire humankind wherever they need you.'

And Aquarius stepped back into place.

'To you, Pisces, I grant you the well of human emotions and ask you to collect all the world's sorrows and return them to Me, to Love itself. Your tears are ultimately My tears. You are the eyes of the world, the windows of the soul. The sorrows you absorb arise from people choosing fear over love, but you offer consistent faith so they may try again. Music is a salve for your soul. As you spread your sweet song upon humankind, I grant you the gift of compassion.'

And Pisces stepped back into place.

And then Mother Earth said, 'You each have part of my heart. You must not mistake that part for all of my heart, for each of you is perfect in your own expression. The circle of love is complete when each of you utilizes your gifts for yourself and all of life. Observe each other and how you relate to one another and you will see where I have hidden treasures of your soul for you to find.'

And each child was elated as they considered all the possibilities of this new mission."

COSMIC INFLUENCES

If you map the constellations onto a musical staff, the music of the stars can be heard. The stars tell us stories and sometimes offer insight regarding our place in the world or on the Wheel of the Year, such as the appearance of the summer triangle and the constellations of Aquila (eagle), Cygnus (swan), and Lyra (lyre). When the constellation Orion is fully visible, winter is coming soon. Polaris has helped travelers find north.

There are five constellations that circumnavigate Polaris, our North Star, which include Ursa Major, Ursa Minor, Draco, Cassiopeia, and Cepheus. This grouping of stars appears in the sky as images that represent five universally known archetypes of the Mother, Child, Dragon, Queen, and King, respectively. Cultures from all over the world have seen and recognized the energy of Ursa Major, the "mama bear" constellation, and have referred to Draco by some version of the word *dragon*. Yet even though we see the same outlines in the sky and associate the images of the constellations with the same characters, there are cultural differences in our interpretations. In the East, the Dragon archetype is a symbol of power, strength, and good luck. In the West, a dragon, like a snake, represents evil and must be slayed.

When you consider that the stories of the constellations have been told and retold for hundreds of years, it's easy to see their influence on human existence. For millennia, we have been watching the stars and creating myths about the constellations, observing how gardening and moods are affected by the moon's phases and the movement of planets. Would our world look any different if five other constellations circled our North Star? How much influence do the seasonal constellations (for example, the ones that only appear in spring) have? There is possibly more to learn than you could in a lifetime, so take it slowly—perhaps learn about the lore or individual stars of one constellation at a time. The universal energies will affect you without your knowledge; however, awareness of their influences and your perspective will determine their impact. As an example, let's take a look at the effect of Mercury retrogrades.

Mercury retrogrades have been occurring three times a year for 4.6 billion years. Ancient Greek astronomer Aristarchus of Samos (who lived around 310–230 BCE) proposed that we live in a heliocentric universe, meaning the planets revolve around the sun, but he gained few supporters. It took humanity another eighteen centuries until fifteenth-century Renaissance astronomer Nicolaus Copernicus produced a fully predictive mathematical model of a heliocentric system. The term "retrograde," in reference to when a planet is on the opposite side of the sun from our position on Earth, was first used in the 1960s. From our geocentric (or Earth-centric) perspective, when a planet is traveling with us around the sun, we appear to be going in the same direction. When any planet is on the other side of the sun, it appears to be traveling counterclockwise, or backward.

I find it helpful to envision the planet's retrograde movement through physical demonstration. Assign an object such as a saltshaker, an orange, or a cup to the sun, Mercury, and Earth. Move "Mercury" in a quick clockwise circle (left to right) around the "sun," while moving "Earth" in a slower, wider orbit. Notice how from the Earth's perspective, when Mercury is on the other side of the sun, Mercury could appear to move right to left, while Earth is still moving left to right. Since Mercury, the planet closest to the sun, completes its speedy orbit in eighty-eight days, there are three times during the year when the god of communication is on the other side of the sun from the Earth's perspective and appears to be moving backward, or opposite of our movement, for three weeks at a time.

From the 1960s through the 2010s, the lessons of Mercury retrogrades focused on seeing this three-week phase as an essential time of slowing down communication and activity, a cosmic naptime. Mercury retrograde not only gives us permission to pause and stop being so relentlessly productive, it also underscores an essential period of rest, reflection, reconnection, and reinvention (all the *re-* words). Magick often includes shadow work to help us see into the mystery, including parts of ourselves or relationships that aren't helpful.

Under the influence of a Mercury retrograde, we are thrust into the past to revisit, remember, and sift through our past actions and to decide what thoughts, emotions, or beliefs we should keep as we move forward. By stalling forward movement, Mercury retrograde can help us accept divine timing as we sit in the unknowing as chaos reigns. In this time of mysterious rest we can re-member ourselves to wholeness.

In some cases, you will experience what is called a paradigm shift when your mind lets go of its baggage and healing occurs. It's like taking a cinder block out of your backpack and noticing how much lighter you feel without it. This may happen or it may not; simply allow whatever you feel to be okay.

Today, fear has replaced the curiosity that once surrounded Mercury retrogrades. People are told their cars will break down, that they should expect fights with lovers and friends, and to beware of theft and scams. Our collective hyper-focus on the negative possibilities makes some people shudder when they hear that Mercury has gone retrograde.

Yet Mercury retrogrades need not be fearful occasions—how this and other universal influences affect you is entirely up to you.

Will you look at Mercury retrogrades as an opportunity to deepen experiences, or will you let negative stories sharpen the blade of fear? Will you welcome the disorder, knowing that when we release our rigidity, we are offered a new perspective that may allow us to grow more as light beings and children of Divine Love? Have you ever seen or been in a group in which each person held a single candle?

It is magnificent to behold the separate lights come together as one grand collection of individual flames. Each light is important and adds to the collective effect of all that brilliance. The same rings true when we collectively decide to see something in a particular way. Our combined thoughts carve a channel that can direct universal influence through one perspective. In other words, if people forget that Mercury retrograde is meant to be a welcome reprieve and, instead, only see pandemonium, then one day, that may be all we see.

It takes just one brave soul to trust their heart and see something new to make a difference in a field of single lights.

Mercury Retrograde Ritual

Try this ritual for a deep dive into what Mercury retrograde can teach you about personal transformation. At the beginning of retrograde season, take out your tarot deck and pull out the Hanged Man, Devil, Fool, and Tower cards. If you do not have a deck, you can Google and/ or print the images of these four Major Arcana cards. Or you can draw them on cards or create collages that represent these archetypes on scratched CDs.

If you are inclined to make an altar in honor of Mercury, you can include any of his magickal correspondences. Some of my favorites include citrine, feathers, bells, images of Mercury, butterflies or hawks, a caduceus (the double-snake-entwined staff with wings often used to represent Western medicine), and a pen, but I encourage you to incorporate any Mercury-related symbols or tools that resonate with you.

Shuffle the four cards and place them face down in a line, either horizontal or vertical. It is often easier to see the process from card to card if you go in a horizontal line, but if you want to place your cards another way, that is your choice.

Turn over one card and observe everything you can about what it is trying to tell you about your particular situation. If the tarot is new to you, then remember that the Major Arcana are archetypes (as discussed in chapter 5). These universal influences will help clarify what Mercury retrograde is teaching you in a particular season. You can review scores of books as well as dive into your own knowledge for what the Hanged Man, Devil, Fool, and Tower represent, but here is a start for what these archetypes could teach us during Mercury retrograde:

- **Hanged Man**: Release your hold on the situation. Look for a different point of view.

- **Devil**: Beware a potential ego imbalance. Something or someone must be released.

- **Fool**: Look for the humor. Remember to play. Don't plan anything; just go with the flow.

- **Tower**: Let it all crumble. Sift through the ashes for the gems left behind.

You might want to stick with one card per Mercury retrograde, or you can choose a card per week, with the final card being the overall message for the three-week season. The message from these four Major Arcana cards does not have to come through on a hugely grand scale. The archetypes could show you something minor that happens in a day, or the card could point out how a relationship has changed. You may want to document what you learned from Mercury retrograde in a journal, with a collage, or by talking it out with a friend.

MOON MAGICK

According to the tarot tradition, which dates back to the mid-1400s, the Moon archetype is an energy that represents reflection and the deeper, often hidden, messages. Since the moon rules emotions and reflects the sun's light, it is considered to be an excellent guide to mirror what we are feeling. The phases of the moon and the month we're in give us clues to go within and ascertain shadowed or hidden perspectives. Observing the moon's phases teaches us about timing and allows us to align our Magick with the universal influence of our closest planetary ally.

In the Wiccan tradition I follow, the moon is considered feminine and is a symbol of the Triple Goddess. In its growing crescent form, the moon reflects the Maiden and possibilities, the Mother when it is full and embodies fruition and the attainment of goals and dreams, and when it wanes, the Crone in all her wisdom. The new moon is the beat of stillness before growing again. The full and new moons are known as esbats, which are the occasions when major or profound magickal work is traditionally performed. And yet, every night that Moon Magick is available to you for whatever you need. Many people focus on four phases of the moon for their Moon Magick, some celebrate eight phases, and others explore sixteen phases as outlined by Lynda Emashowski in her book *Whispered Wisdoms of the Moon*. You can look up which phase the moon was in when you were born and observe how you feel now when the moon is in that phase.

New or dark moon is when the moon is hidden from our view. As such, it's the time to gain insight about yourself by making friends with your unseen or hidden aspects. We enter a period of stillness as we cast introspective spells or do magickal work for fresh starts and beginnings or just be still.

Crescent moon is when we see a sliver of the moon, a thin crescent in a backward-C shape. Representing the Goddess as the Maiden, this moon is the time to do Magick for hopes, wishes, and inspiration.

First quarter moon is the time to consider challenges, decisions, and the steps you must take to complete a needed task.

Waxing gibbous moon presents a time to adjust, refine, and edit your intentions so they are clear.

Full moon is when the moon is round and full. This is the time to perform positive works and manifest spells that release your most passionate desires.

Waning gibbous moon gives us time to show gratitude and enthusiasm for life and seek out new truths or perspectives.

Last quarter moon is the time for banishing or releasing spells, rituals for knowledge or forgiveness, and concentration on the Goddess as the Crone. The moon appears as a crescent in a C shape.

Balsamic moon presents an opportunity to surrender, accept, rest, recuperate, and decide where your magickal intentions should go next.

The moon affects the size of waves, the level of groundwater, menses, and everyone's emotions. There is an entire science devoted to gardening by the moon that focuses on how the moon's gravitational pull affects the water in soil. It is thought that the moon may also affect the water in the cells of plants just as subtly, encouraging them to grow more vigorously during certain moon phases. You can get very detailed by observing the exact phase of the moon, but for our purposes, we will look at the waxing and waning phases and the gardening tasks that are appropriate for each phase.

Waxing moon: when the light is increasing
from new moon to full moon

- Repot and groom houseplants

- Sow seeds of plants that grow above ground

- Fertilize

- Graft fruit trees

- Plant evergreen and deciduous trees

Waning moon: when the light is decreasing
from full moon to new moon

- Plant bulbs

- Plant crops that grow below the ground, such as potatoes and carrots

- Cultivate weeds

- Plant biennials and perennials because they need strong roots

- Eliminate slugs

- Prune shrubs

Communicating with the moon doesn't mean you have to cast a spell every month. You can simply observe how you feel as the moon morphs. You can utilize several magickal correspondences in your Witchcraft practice, but until you experience the interconnection between yourself and these moon phases, it's just rote memorization. The Magick is in the synergy, which deepens with experience, maturity, and time. This wisdom about yourself cannot be rushed, downloaded, injected, or indoctrinated.

MOON WATER

Moon water is simply water that has been placed under moonlight to collect its essence. To add more intention to your moon water, refer to each month's influence throughout the year in the appendix at the back of the book. You can choose to infuse water with the power of the moon during any of its phases. The most common practice is to prepare moon water under one of the esbats, either the full or new moon. You can also align your intention with the energy of the moon and its current astrological phase.

The full moon occurs when the sun and moon are opposing (or facing) each other, so their zodiac signs will be opposites; during a new moon, the sun and moon sit next to/on top of each other, so their signs will be the same. For example, the full moon in July occurs during the Cancer season and will be a Capricorn full moon (opposite sign of Cancer), and the new moon in July will be influenced by the sign of Cancer.

There are many things you can do with moon water, from blessing your home, cleansing your altar, adding it to a bath, drinking it, feeding it to your plants, using it in an essential oil diffuser, making tea, or offering it to your ancestors or moon goddesses like Diana or Artemis. You can also add herbs and crystals specific to your intention, but if you plan to drink the moon water, be very careful that anything you place in the water is food-safe and nontoxic. Also, do not place any crystal that ends in "-ite," such as selenite or malachite, in water that you plan to drink. Other toxic crystals include chrysocolla and garnet. Safe crystals include rose quartz, clear quartz, amethyst, citrine, and obsidian.

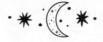

Buck Moon Magick (in July)

Gather the following supplies:

- Bowl

- Water (preferably spring or gathered from a living source, although tap water works too)

- Any black stones will work, such as black tourmaline, obsidian, or even a black rock

The full moon in July is called the Buck Moon because this is the time of year when bucks' antlers are growing. The name symbolizes a time for personal growth that corresponds with the persistent tenacity of the Capricorn sign, whose energy comes from Saturn, the disciplinarian, and the heart-centered, moon-influenced Cancer season. Place any black stones you may have in a bowl of water, then leave the bowl under the full moon. The black stones will absorb and dissolve obstacles that are impeding your goals. You may gain insight on some limiting beliefs, your relationship with rules, or a shadow or unseen emotion or feeling. Ask the moon water to reflect your responsibility so you can clearly see your path. Say:

> "I cast out negative energy under the moonlight.
> I am protected by this Lunar Goddess light,
> Surrounded and embraced by pure Love.
> As it is below, so it is above."

Write out your intentions and any actions you can take to fulfill them. The following morning, pour the water on the ground or underneath a tree so Mama Earth can regenerate the energy. This Buck Moon Magick will synergize the full moon with Capricorn's ambitious, hardworking nature; Cancer's loving, hearth-and-home energy; and the stamina and strength of buck animal medicine.

TERRAPSYCHOLOGY & SOUL FAMILIES

Have you ever noticed how some places resonate with a particular personality? Battlegrounds, cemeteries, gardens, forests, and beaches all carry their own kind of energy. What do you know about the terrapsychology, or the soul of place, where you live? Do topography and ecology affect the personality of the land? Next time you feel the spirit or soul of the land, welcome it and say hello. This soul essence is a conscious presence that can influence you as much as members of your soul family can.

Soul families are the souls with whom you experience an instant or powerful connection through shared lifetimes, wherein we tend to switch roles to experience the wholeness, oneness, and interconnectedness of all of life. Classic dualistic roles include parent/child, victim/villain, teacher/student, and boss/worker, but there are many more. This reincarnation lesson is based in nonjudgement, acceptance, and unconditional love.

Members of our soul family often teach us our life's greatest lessons. Sometimes they take a gentle approach, and other times, these teachings feel like a cosmic two-by-four to the third eye. We may meet our soul relations for "a reason, a season, or a lifetime," as the poem by Brian A. "Drew" Chalker goes. The length of the relationship does not determine the power of the lesson or its impact on our life. Human connections are essential, and everything that has happened has made you who you are.

This reciprocal relationship through eons of lifetimes is discussed in the children's book *The Little Soul and the Sun* by Neale Donald Walsch, author of the *Conversations with God* trilogy, and Caroline Myss's book *Sacred Contracts*, which discusses the karmic agreements we've made with other souls. Through soul family interactions, we experience our deepest relationships that offer us a mirror so we can clean up and shine more brightly.

There are times when members of our family get stuck in an interpretation or expression of how they see us. A classic example would be the parent who manipulates their adult child to remain dependent so the parent has a purpose, or the partner who refuses to acknowledge any change in their significant other over time. Because Witchcraft is a lifestyle that matches the cadence of our lives to the seasonal changes of nature, you are meant to evolve and be empowered to grow beyond outdated roles, stories, or people who stunt your growth.

This maxim is true for living family and friends as well as our ancestors. When you listen to the ancestral stories, particularly those that are infused with powerlessness, remember the power of the Witch to forge your own path. Your Magick comes alive with the universal influences that feed the soul. Discernment is required to help us sift through our experiences and relations and honestly determine who lifts us up and who brings us down. Even in service to the Divine, you must ensure that your cup is full.

"I am convinced that the deepest desire within each
of us is to be liberated from the controlling influences
of our own psychic madness or patterns of fear."

Caroline Myss

*

My anklet of deer hooves rattled as I walked up to Connie's door. A week before, Jimi Castillo, Elder of the Tongva people, had invited me to a naming ceremony and tobacco blessing, and I hadn't been able to take off this precious piece of my regalia.

"It's awkward to be at an Indigenous ceremony when I can only trace my family heritage to the colonizing Spanish of ten generations ago," I confessed as I entered. "Ever since I wrote a fact sheet for California's 150th anniversary six years ago, I've been obsessed with the feeling that I'm supposed to heal the pain my ancestors, the Catalan and Mexican soldiers and Californio ranchero colonists, caused the Indigenous people they enslaved to build their missions and pueblos."

"No small mission." Connie winked at me. She lit a white taper candle. I waited for the flame to grow stronger.

"It feels and sounds terribly presumptuous when I can only trace the Spanish and Mexican lines, and yet I feel so close to earth spirituality. I have ordered birth and death certificates, hoping to find a trace of Native blood in California. I haven't found anything."

"We are all native to somewhere. Perhaps your roots are deeper in Mexico," Connie offered.

"That's what the Native American curator from Bowers Museum said. This museum houses artifacts from Californio colonists and Indigenous people in rooms that are right next to each other. He also told me how exhausting it was for him to field questions from white women who want to be Native after watching Kevin Costner in *Dances with Wolves*." I sighed. "That's not me, and maybe I am trying to erase the blood from my hands, but I want to have my roots in California." I paused, waiting, hoping for Connie to interject something to assuage the tension in my belly.

When she said nothing, I continued. "I have been going on ancestral walks to sacred sites under the tutelage of Jimi Castillo. I was so honored when he invited me to the naming ceremony last weekend. My friend Melinda and I fasted for a day prior to the ceremony and brought herbs from our garden for a tobacco blessing ceremony. I was on my period, and it was unusually heavy, which somehow made me feel extra powerful and provoked me to tell Jimi. He surprised me when he said that I couldn't participate in the ceremony." I flashed back to the moment. Jimi had gone to find an Elder woman to explain to me the menses cycle from their perspective. I described the scene in my mind's eye for Connie.

"Jimi returned with a woman who had a soft, wrinkled face, braids, and a ceremonial shawl over her thin shoulders. The wise woman reached out and took my hands. 'My dear little one,' she said. 'You are already in the most sacred ceremony there is. It would be disrespectful to Life, to Great Spirit, to have a woman on her moon work doubly hard. You must honor the ceremony taking place. You need to rest and allow the others to take care of you.'"

I nodded in that moment as I had then.

"Then she said, 'While you are on your moon, you are in your most dominant, most powerful state of being. From this seat of power, you could inadvertently sway the public ritual to suit your needs.' She squeezed my free hand with surprising strength, and added, 'Being on your moon cycle means you are in ritual, like a snake who goes blind during the sacred transformation of molting. You are not being punished here. You are being protected and honored as a Carrier of Life.'"

I paused to watch the candle flame, then said, "It turned out twelve other women were also on their moon cycle. We sat in a separate circle and were catered to like in the book *The Red Tent*. It was such a seat of honor."

"You never would have known if you hadn't spoken up," Connie added.

"It was awe-inspiring to see thirteen menstruating women in our circle being honored for our moon cycle. It was hard to find a sponsor for the naming ceremony, someone who would stand beside Melinda and me since being on my moon cycle had changed the dynamic. But the challenge made the ceremony that much more meaningful. And now I'm never making dinner when I'm on my period." I laughed, then sobered up.

"Our sponsor told me to step into my power, and my test came a few days later when Skyler's public school kindergarten teacher sent home a note saying that the parents had to come up with 'Native' names for their kids, like Chattering Chipmunk or Mischievous Monkey. I was absolutely livid. I called the principal to give her a piece of my mind and pulled Skyler from school for the day."

Nick had rolled over onto his side and was watching me tell my story. Connie winked at us both.

"I was already pissed off at this school for the science table that had two labels, 'Live Things' and 'Not Alive Things.'" I started waving my hands around for emphasis, like a conductor of my own tale. "There was a freaking apple on the 'not alive' side of the table. How is that science? The apple grows, so it's alive!"

"Animism is the basis for all earth spiritualities," Connie said.

"Exactly. This belief in the spirit and consciousness of nature is what we need more of!" I sighed. "Anyway, the principal said they were progressive since they didn't force kids to say the Pledge of Allegiance. But in the end, she suggested that I homeschool." I took a long sip of my drink.

"Skyler and I started what we call our Bottlenose Dolphin School. We do jumping jacks and drumming for math, gardening and canning plum jam for science, and he's making his own flash cards for the alphabet. I let him use 'fart' for the F card, trying to make it fun, but I still made him draw the picture. We have the freedom now to make his education alive."

UNIVERSAL INFLUENCES AND YOU

The more you learn to trust your Divine Essence and give it a wide berth for its own expression, the better you can hold onto your core self, regardless of all the universal influences. Practice following your intuition to discern the difference between outside factors that can augment your magickal life and those that obstruct your forward movement. Listen for messages from the cosmos. Integrate the information slowly; take what you like and do not concern yourself with what doesn't resonate in this moment. We are all connected and will be affected by external forces to some degree, but your awareness of these forces can help you wield power in the direction that's most advantageous for you, your communities, and the planet.

10

Circle Magick

circle's Magick is that it raises more energy than one person can
alone, just as three candles are brighter than one. When we come
together for a single cause or purpose, we are driven by the truth
of the motto that there is "strength in numbers." When we are healthy, we
say we are "whole" and "complete," like a circle. When loss becomes gain or
fear morphs into love, we observe that our lives have come "full circle." In all
these cases, we experience the circle of life.

Linda Lenzke, writer of poetry, prose, comedy, and spoken-word mono-
logues, says, "The circle is both an image and metaphor of completeness
and equality. There is both protection and democracy within its confines
as people face each other without visual hierarchy. This facilitates intimacy."

The lessons offered from gathering in circles of friends and family and
the impact on our emotional, physical, and mental health are present in
every walk of life. The circle is a metaphor for a oneness and connection
that is vibrantly alive and impacts you based on your receptivity—not your
religion, melatonin, gut flora, sexual orientation, or height. In Perfect Love
and Perfect Trust, Circle Magick blossoms like concentric waves created by
a single pebble of truth.

Today, we are rewarded and encouraged by our culture to "go it alone"
and not rely on others. We try hard to stand out and be special, yet we yearn
to be in the circle of influence, power, or love. When we come to recognize
the power of our equality and need for connection, then the true Circle
Magick can begin.

The symbol of Witchcraft is the pentacle, a five-pointed star surrounded
by a circle. Four of the points have been designated as the four Elements,

and the fifth point, the one at the top of the star, has been reserved for the Great Spirit within us, nature, and the cosmos. The circle of life holds this star at its core. The four tenets that describe the inherent strength of the magickal circle are as follows:

1. Your word claims the space for healing and Magick to occur.

2. The circle protects the participants from outside influences.

3. It focuses intention by holding the space for dreams to manifest.

4. It establishes a sense of mutuality, meaning every participant carries reciprocal and equal weight.

YOUR WORD IS YOU

The first step in ceremony is to set the boundaries of where the ritual will take place. We strengthen the power of the circle and increase its Magick when we speak the words that establish a place as a ceremonial site and clearly hold this vision. Words have such power that when we collectively say a place is sacred and uphold those boundaries, the seal is set and the circle is real and can be sensed by everyone present.

In the best-selling book *The Four Agreements*, Don Miguel Ruiz says we must be "impeccable with our words" as we are the message and the messenger in a conversation with the Divine. We don't ever want to say something that goes against our highest good. Our word is our Magick because speaking and claiming something makes it real. We are all that powerful; it's just that a lot of us are asleep to the power inherent in our words. We toss them around when we should instead focus our words to be concise. Aligning our intention to create a magickal circle is the first Witchcraft we do together and presents the first opportunity to feel the power of a united, collective consciousness.

PROTECTED IN THE MAGICKAL REALM

The concentrated attention inside a magickal circle becomes a beam of light that blasts out of or rises above (depending on the tempo of the ritual) the mundane existence and opens a magickal portal. This portal is the long hallway between speaking your desire, perhaps by creating a spell or ritual, and experiencing its manifestation. In the altered dimension of a magickal circle, we create a doorway that expands out around us, establishing a protected space that exists between the worlds of earth and sky.

In this creative, numinous place, we express our wishes, spells, and intentions and release them to a receptive universe. Our ideas and feelings roam the cosmos, magnetically attracting experiences, people, and places and bringing them back to us in the form of manifestation. Our focus must be very clear and distilled to its core essence if we are to have any hope of getting what we want. The universe listens and answers back precisely, so be certain your intentions are just as precise.

A circle is a group exercise in which we commit to being vulnerable together as we transform in the cocoon of our magickal container. The boundaries protect us while we're in the trance of meditation. If everyone in the group wills it so, the circle will have impenetrable borders, and everyone involved will be safe to experience the intoxicating feeling that accompanies one who travels this mystical highway. This protection muffles the outer world with the undivided purpose to create Magick, transform, uplift, and safeguard. As long as the focus remains, the circle will repel distractions. Of course, things can arise that pull you away. You choose where you need to place your attention.

MIRACLES IN THE MYSTERY

A circle authorizes the moment for miracles. Being in a magickal circle can be similar to dreaming, when we don't question fanciful flights of flying or conversations with a deceased beloved. We can anticipate experiences, feelings, or thoughts in ways that defy explanation yet are real. We can be transported, transformed, and changed completely when we are immersed in the mystery, within the realm of the Divine Feminine.

Perceived as a protective womb, the circle is a symbol of the Divine Feminine's method of communication, which is focused on achieving mutuality in relationships. True awareness and meaningful growth stem from how much care we put into relating to each other and the world. Circle Magick is also evident in the Wheel of the Year, which shows how the seasons change, each one morphing into the next, giving way to each other with grace and completing a circle every year through a series of cycles and spirals.

The magickal circle prepares participants for magickal thinking and creating. The process of drawing a boundary separates this sacred space from the mundane and places the circle and the participants squarely in the realm of Magick. This ritual of establishing a circle is like preparing the soil for flowers or the soul for growth. It sets people in a mood to receive the miracles growing in its fertile ground.

MUTUALITY IN A CIRCLE

This notion of our combined strength is so ubiquitous in our society that we might be tempted to overlook its truth and power. We hear the words in a myriad of slogans, like "We are stronger together" in the fights against wildfires and pandemics. The story of the knights of the round table is one of the most famous examples that symbolize the equal merit of everyone present. In a circle, all are one; there are no leaders. The circle places emphasis on mutuality, the sharing of a feeling, action, or relationship between two or more parties. The most beautiful aspect of the power and Magick of a ceremonial circle is that by performing the ritual of casting a circle, we can embody its lessons.

· ✳ ⁚ ◯ ⁚ ✳ ·

Casting a Circle

There are many ways to cast a circle for Magick. What follows is an outline of the basic steps, which I have developed over a couple of decades of following the Witch's path, and through inspiration that has come from many sources, including in-person trainings, public rituals, DNA memories, and an indwelling of Magick from birth. For your inspiration, I have provided examples for each step from the first sabbats I attended as well as ceremonies I created. If you are called or drawn to try something different, Spirit or your inspiration is speaking to you in ways that only you can hear. Remember to always follow your unique Divine Essence.

1. Set up an altar in the center of where the magickal circle will be.

2. Bless, cleanse, and protect each participating member.

3. Draw the magickal circle with an athame, sword, or your extended forefinger and middle finger.

4. Invite the God and Goddess, Elements, and spirit guides.

5. Set up the cone of power, a visualized connection to the Divine.

6. The work: ask for your desire.

7. Share cakes and ale in a communal experience within the Magick circle.

8. Give thanks to the Elements, your guides, and the God and Goddess for being with you.

9. Close the circle.

ALTARS

There are typically five altars in a public magickal circle: one for each of the four Elements and one that serves as your central, aka "working" altar, which represents Spirit. The four elemental altars are consciously curated with a collection of symbols, colored candles, crystals, and other magickal tools that correspond to each Element: air, fire, water, and earth. On the central Spirit altar, there are two sentinel candles, representing the Divine Masculine and the Divine Feminine, which are placed to the right and left of a central candle. These three flames represent your spirit and soul in connection with the Divine that is beyond gender or exact name. Incense smoke sends your wishes upward to Spirit.

These altars can be elaborate or simple. What matters most is the connection you have to each item you place on your altar(s). If you are a solitary practitioner or simply do not have a lot of space, you can condense the five altars to one. In the DCWA tradition, a solitary altar for a magickal circle would be placed on an image of a pentacle—either drawn, engraved, or painted—to represent the magickal space implied by "As above, so below." Doing this expands the energetic space despite the limitations of physical space. Magickal tools such as a bowl of water, salt, an athame, and a thurible are often included in a basic ritual altar.

As you create your altar, consider the phase of the moon—dark, waxing, full, or waning—and what this energy brings up for you. Remember to be precise in your work as you prepare the words you will speak and the symbols you arrange. Your altar can be designed to manifest desires, profess gratitude for seasonal gifts, request guidance when your direction is unclear, or meet any need you have.

BESTOWING THE BLESSING

A welcome blessing is seen in places of worship all over the world. Whether with scented oil or holy water, ceremonies from every corner of the globe bless participants' third eye, even if they don't call it that, to awaken our inner sight to recognize the works of the Divine. In many Pagan ceremonies, the High Priest or Priestess dips their finger in a magickal oil and anoints each person by tracing a small pentagram on their third eye. Typically, these blessings happen on the lintel, or gateway, to the magickal world (a space denoted by the perimeter of the magickal circle) as a method of preparing the mind, body, and soul to enter the mystical realm. It's a ritualized act of casting off everyday problems to engage in the work of Magick. The blessing could also include herbal smoke from a variety of plant allies, like sage, mugwort, frankincense, myrrh, and lavender, based on what's in season, what you can sustainably harvest, or the reason for the ritual.

DEFINING A MAGICKAL CIRCLE

Using a combination of Mental Magick and physical action, the next step is to draw the perimeter of a magickal circle. You can walk the perimeter of your circle, tracing an outline on the ground or in the air with your athame, an extended pointer and middle finger, or even a sword.

Participants can be prompted to visualize the circle closing around them like a thick velvet curtain at an art house movie theater—or whatever visualization works for you.

At the eclectic fae sabbats, we sprinkled rose petals or juice around the circle to honor the Goddess and scattered corn meal or barley to celebrate the God. In Connie's rituals, the person who stood to the north would take their athame and walk the perimeter of the circle once with their blade down, starting in the northeast, to mark the boundary of the protected sacred space. In some traditions, circles are drawn through visualization, such as the Tree of Life meditation in chapter 2, where participants "ground to Mother Earth" and reinforce the power of the circle by aligning their energy with the life force of the fiery, molten core of earth.

WELCOMING SUPERNATURAL AID

There are endless ways of inviting in the Elements, Divine Masculine, Divine Feminine, spirit guides, and ancestors. As such, this seems to be the most personal of all the steps of casting a circle. DCWA rituals begin by bestowing the blessing with a cabalistic cross and then take a firm tone when we address each of the four directions, beginning in the east by stating, "All hail ye, Guardians of the Eastern Quadrant, Element of Air. I do stir, summon, and call you forth that you may bear witness to this ceremony. Bring us your gifts of inspiration, beginnings, levity, strategy, and new ideas. Hail and welcome."

If this feels right for you, then turn clockwise and repeat the invocation, adapting the Element and powers of each direction as you greet and welcome the four directions. South/fire has gifts of will, determination, power, passion, and play. West/water offers gifts of emotions, relationships, feelings, support, and dreams. And north/earth bestows gifts of security, belonging, ancestors, safety, and abundance.

The spirits of the four Elements, known as elementals, guard your circle and provide balance. At larger circles and gatherings, a candle of the appropriate color is placed on an altar decorated with items that symbolize the elemental energies. The candle is lit when evoking the Elements, also known as the Watchers. The DCWA color correspondences are yellow for east (air), red for south (fire), blue for west (water), and green for north (earth). As always, you can choose other colors that may represent the elemental energy to you.

In chapter 3, you will find more information on elemental correspondences for inspiration to welcome the supernatural aid of the Elements. You can choose flowery words that describe the power of each Element, you can enact the realm of each Element through song, dance, or poetry, or you can write a gratitude incantation about how each Element empowers you. You could name colors, archangels, animals, gods, goddesses, seasons, qualities, or powers for each of the Elements. The choice is yours.

CREATING THE CONE OF POWER

The cone of power is used to focus the energy of an individual or group for a purpose or goal and/or to provide an energetic connection with the Divine. If you do this alone, you can imagine the cone of power rising above your head like a Witch's hat. In a group ritual, the participants can imagine a current of energy spinning clockwise, or deosil ("sunwise"), around the circle. You could ask participants to squeeze the hand of the person on their left as you send the energy around. After the energy has traveled through participants' hands, you can then direct the energy through the hearts of each participant. Then, all together, you can visualize the energy rising up above everyone's head, above the treetops, higher and higher, until you anchor the energy on a star or perhaps the moon. I imagine this cone of power as a starry apex triangle, vibrating with possibilities and sealed with firm boundaries. It signals that it's time to commune with the Creative Source.

SPEAKING YOUR WORD, CASTING YOUR SPELL

Everything up until this point of casting a magickal circle has been like setting the table for a meal. Now is the moment many Witches call "the work." This is when you summon your will, breath, blood, and strength and ask for what you need. It's called the work because it takes effort to be so focused on the positive visualization of your manifestation. Spells work when you hold your vision with precision, repetition, and believability. The work, in essence, throws off distractions, self-doubt, and the shadow.

From Connie's treasure trove: "Wicca 101, January 1996. A spell is a work of Magick, which through ritual, the power of the mind is combined with the powers of the universe and used to manipulate and channel energy to create changes within the self and environment."

When you "do the work," you have asked yourself four discerning, spell-worthy questions (these are covered in chapter 11), you are clean from negative karma, and you are ready to accept the abundance that you are calling forth in the shape of your desired manifestation. Claim what you want. Speak your word, cast your spell.

SHARING CAKES AND ALE

"Cakes and ale" refers to the feast or joyous celebration after the focused intention of the magickal work. This feast can be large or small, but the food, drink, and spirit of the gathering will always match the season as we dine in the presence of our supernatural aid—the God, Goddess, Elements, and spirit guides. This moment celebrates that our desire exists in the spiritual world, and now we wait for its manifestation.

Cakes (or any grain) are symbols that represent the God or Divine Masculine, the seed of life. The ale, or any liquid substance (it doesn't have to be alcohol), represents the watery body in which we all lived while in our mother's womb and serves as an offering to the Goddess or Divine Feminine. When you align these two forces within your soul with love, your heart's desires materialize. Being at peace with yourself is how you live your best life.

This is the moment within the moment in the message of "As above, so below." When we love the Divine Feminine and Divine Masculine equally inside ourselves, it radiates outward, healing the planet and, in return, granting a deeper contentment than you could imagine. Magick begins in the microcosm (the material plane of the world, earth, and people) and expands to reach the macrocosm (the astral or spiritual plane of the heavens and deities). When we meditate in gratitude, we inhabit both worlds simultaneously, like a Venn diagram of Magick.

GIVING THANKS

Give thanks because the answer to your desire is already on its way to you. We give our gratitude before our dream has materialized. Gratitude that moves in a circle builds more energy for the things you want to manifest and breeds contentment.

CLOSING THE CIRCLE

Also known as the dismissal, we unravel the cone of power through visualization, then say farewell to spirit guides, the Divine Masculine and Feminine, and the Elements, beginning in the north and moving counterclockwise. We release anything that has been invoked from the higher realms. We draw back the curtain and return the magickal circle to the human, mundane world, often with this popular chant:

> "The Circle is open but unbroken
> May the Love of the Goddess
> Be Ever in Your Heart
> Merry Meet and Merry Part
> And Merry Meet Again."

Circle Magick

After the magickal circle is closed, we let go and release all expectations. Your Magick is now in the hands of the Divine, and it's best not to ponder or worry lest you muddy your desire with anything less than the pure Magick of your spellwork.

✳

Dandelions lined the walk to Connie's apartment. I needed her advice more than ever, but it would have to wait until after the circle and ceremony for high summer. As the coven joined us, Sariel gave me a fierce hug. She reminded me of an ancient warrior. Her position was to hold the northern quadrant in every ritual. She was the most grounded Witch I had ever met.

Connie gave us bright ribbons of orange, red, and gold for the summer solstice. I tried to step into the creative power of the high summer holiday, but I felt drained. None of the Crimson Dragon coven members had missed one holiday since our Elder High Priestess had begun including the knot work for each sabbat ceremony. By the energetic web that holds coveners together, we of Connie's covenstead instinctively knew this was an important year and that we needed to be present for every spoke of the wheel. Plus, the ribbons Connie gave—bestowed with Magick and empowerment—became more desirable than any rare collectible.

After the ceremony, Connie ushered everyone out the door gently but firmly. She turned to me as I gathered my things to go.

"Sit down," she said. "What's going on?"

We sat on the couch together. I felt a sense of relief that my mentor had seen through my charade. "I figured since Magick mended the pain between Mom and me, that I should tie the sabbat ribbon to heal my relationship with my dad." I took a deep breath and continued, "I found an address for my long-lost father in my mother's old address book and sent him a letter with my number and a picture of me and my boys. Yesterday I got a call from a raspy-sounding woman who wanted to know why I thought her husband was my father!"

Connie smiled sympathetically. "What did you hope would happen?"

"I had hoped to either cut the spiritual and karmic cords so that I can stop hoping to connect or start a relationship with my dad, but I got neither! I told the woman my father's age, and she realized her husband couldn't be my dad. Then she allowed him to talk with me, and he went on and on about the history of the surname Wolfgang. I didn't want to talk with him. I hoped if I cleared the karmic loop with my dad, I could be done with issues with men. Then I'd know how to find a way to make it work with my husband or have the peace of mind to leave. No such luck."

"Relationships and karmic lessons don't work like that." Connie shook her head. She lit the white taper candle. "We don't get to determine the perfect timing of our life's lessons coming full circle. Witchcraft operates on listening to the messages always coming from the cycles of nature and the cosmos."

"It's so perfect you would say that," I said, and I began to spin my story. "A while ago I took Skyler to a Waldorf kindergarten class, but he was so disruptive and upset; it wasn't working. Recently he started asking to go back to Waldorf and told me that he had been scared, but he wanted to play with the gnomes. Then last night, I got a call from Kimberly, the Waldorf kindergarten teacher. She had dreamed of Skyler so clearly that she decided to make room for him in her classroom this year. She said his spirit was adamant. I believe it! His spirit used to visit me when I was pregnant with him. Kobe is already accepted into the preschool program, too. I'm going to learn to knit. Waldorf kids learn to knit, so I want to help them."

"That's wonderful news." Connie smiled. She could not have looked prouder than if Skyler had been her own grandchild. "This was the Magick you wanted to create."

"But Magick doesn't fix everything," I mused. "It's just . . ." I trailed off.

"What are you so afraid of?" Connie asked tenderly. "Look for holes in the aura," Connie suggested. "Where are you leaking energy?"

I closed my eyes, and as I had been taught, I imagined the three layers of silver, gold, and blue light protecting me in an egg-shaped force field. I used every one of my six senses to divine a gap in the light. I felt an emptiness in my gut and my feet.

"I need to trust my gut and keep walking forward. Maybe I was just too weird to think meeting my dad could fix my marriage," I said.

Connie crossed her arms over her belly. "I only like the weird ones. We're all weird, only it was originally spelled w-y-r-d." Connie added a pinch of myrrh onto the fiery charcoal that she had lit for this moment. "In ancient times, the word *wyrd* meant that everything is connected by a weaving of intricate strands," Connie began. "Wyrd is knowing and responding with discernment because you can feel what is coming. Wyrd is the fate that connects our past choices to our present moment. Every day, we make choices that affect our destiny as well as the future of others. All lives are affected by the web of fate." Connie leaned over and gave me a hug. "You are being wyrd when you are paying attention and making the connections."

Her words were warm and comforting, but it hurt to close the book on my dream of reconciling with my father. "It's time for me to see my dad as a human being, not a vision of who I have always hoped he would be." I smiled at my mentor, hoping I had got it right. "And trust that what is meant to work out will, in its own time."

Connie rewarded me with a magnificent smile. I got a vision of her handing me a decorative urn, as if she had just passed down her family's secret recipe for award-winning olive oil, Magick of the Goddess Athena. A surge of warm love filled me for Connie as a soul family member traveling with me through this multidimensional universe.

"Patience is the key. Or, it may be the Divine plan that the answers you seek will never be revealed, or not for a long time to come. You have to find your own inner strength and be willing to close your own circle on the pain."

As Connie spoke these words, it was as if a fifty-pound load was lifted from my back. In my mind's eye, I saw a golden circle, a ring in the sky. It would have to be enough. Then, with a deep exhale of release, I remembered something other than my frustrations. "I haven't told you yet about PantheaCon!" I exclaimed.

"I haven't been in so long! How was it?" Connie asked in a tone that conveyed she was living through me, having missed out on one of the biggest annual Pagan conferences of our time.

"I went to the midnight ritual for Aphrodite and Dionysus." I sighed. "There were luscious altars, fountains of flowing red wine everywhere you looked, and *only* music by The Doors. I filled my chalice often." I held up my chalice, which had six months' worth of braided sabbat knot work tied to the stem. "I was so turned on, wearing a red corset, too. Well, I got a little carried away invoking the maenad." I laughed heartily, lustfully.

Connie curled her left hand under her chin and giggled. The sound was like happy waters spilling over rocks. "A flirt of the highest order and right down to the ground of this magickal earth."

"I danced myself dizzy at a whirling dervish ceremony." I laughed. "I went to my first sound healing ceremony and sat in on a conversation led by a sacred sex worker about sexual empowerment and healing. It still has me reeling. Grown men pay just to snuggle up and weep in her arms!"

"Male toxicity doesn't just hurt women," Connie said. "Everyone is affected."

"So true. Over the course of a couple of days, the classes started to really sink in. I was drawn to attend an Oshun ritual led by an Iyanifa. I sensed Oshun's multilayered power and had been waiting for an opportunity to be invited to attend an Orisha ceremony, especially after that incident with the Orisha warning me not to write the Santería book. 'Not yet,' they said. I hope for the possibility of learning more if I stay aware and ready."

"Tread lightly," Connie warned. "PantheaCon is a special event to learn about closed, initiatory, and heavily guarded practices from around the world, as its name suggests. One should never take the Orisha lightly. They are powerful entities from another culture than the one you were raised in, and they are not easily understood without direct guidance from an initiate of that practice."

I nodded. "I know Orisha ceremonies aren't something just anyone can attend at any time. I felt so blessed, so honored to be there. I was overcome by the time, care, and attention it took to adorn a ten-foot altar—it was covered in yellow and gold flowers, mirrors, bowls of water, dishes of honey. It shimmered! The ceremony was long and my hips started to cramp. I have always had very stiff hips, so I can't sit cross-legged for too long without pain. Instinctively, I stretched out my legs, and my feet ended up facing the altar."

Connie inhaled sharply. It was clear that she knew I had breached an unspoken code of conduct.

"My friend shot me a fierce look, then hissed at me, 'It's taboo to present your feet to Oshun's altar!'" I shivered. "I didn't realize how disrespectful squirming from a minor discomfort can be in a ceremony when the tradition arose from a lineage who has suffered so much. Connie, can you imagine if I had written about Santería, never having been to an actual ceremony? Blundering forward into a closed practice, I could have created a lot of trouble for myself."

"You listened to your inner guidance. Every tradition has their own boundaries and definitions of the sacred. It is important that we learn from each other and make course corrections when necessary."

"I say it was a very soft lesson come full circle. Thank you, Goddess Oshun! Asé!" I gave the honored greeting. Years later, my respect and integrity would be rewarded when Marcela Landres, the editor who invited me to write the book on Santería, recommended my work to a colleague, opening the door for me to publish my young adult novel, *Rogelia's House of Magic*, about three magickal Latina teens and their curandera mentor. Full circle healing.

"A healthy woman is much like a wolf: robust, chock-full, strong life force, life-giving, territorially aware, inventive, loyal, roving."

Clarissa Pinkola Estés

🔥 Elemental Magick Ritual

Gather the following supplies:

- Cakes and ale (any feast or meal, large or small, that matches the spirit of the season and current abundance of a local garden)

Anoint or bless yourself and others. Ground and center your attention. Draw the perimeter of your circle. Raise a cone of power, creating a sacred space that will protect you while you commune with the elementals. Welcome in the Divine Masculine and Divine Feminine in whatever way feels best for you. As you call out the welcome for each of the four elementals, imagine a flaming blue pentagram. Charge the pentagram by visually touching the center of the pentacle and anointing this magickal portal with your inner light. Take a moment to sit in silent salute with each of the elementals.

Invoking the east, say:

"Watchers of the East, Dwellers on mountains high,
Searchers of the earth, Hear my sigh, my plea to thee! Attend!
As you feed the flames, As you cool the earth,
As you dance with the waves, Hear my plea, attend!"

Invoking the south, say:

"Watchers of the South, Keepers of the lightning bolts,
Stokers for the volcano's fierce fire,
Hear my cry, my plea to thee! Attend!
As you are the furnace of the earth, As you are mate to the air,
As you float upon the sea in the sun's rays, Hear my plea. Attend!"

Invoking the west, say:

"Watchers of the West, Fleet shadows in the swift stream,
Riders of the waves, Hear my call, my plea to thee! Attend!
As you ground the flame, As cloud form you dance in the sky,
As you slake the earth's thirst, Hear my plea, Attend!"

Invoking the north, say:

"Watchers of the North, Guardians of the Mother of us all,
Dwellers in crystal caverns deep,
Hear my song, my plea to thee! Attend!"
As you are the cauldron for the earth's fire,
As you are chalice for ocean and stream,
As you wear the air as your robe, Hear my plea, Attend!"

The work of this ritual is to notice the elemental Magick at play in your life, etching the knowledge deeper into your psyche that your voice, the hurricane, and an inspired poem are all the air Element. Your passion and playfulness originate from the same elemental fire as the flames of a bonfire. The emotions that surge as waves within you all draw power from the water element. Your physical body and sense of belonging are of the earth Element.

Enjoy your cakes and ale in honor and respect for each of the Elements and how they support you in your life. Take your time and journal ideas on how you can become more aware of the elemental Magick that courses through your life. When you are ready, take down the cone of protection and close the circle.

Circle Magick

All magickal circles conclude with deep, abiding gratitude. It is important to close the loop of circle by returning metaphorically to the source of everything with gratitude. This is a moment of deep appreciation for the magickal journey of creating your desire and waiting for it to appear, over and over again.

11

Write Your Own Spells

You are casting spells with the words you speak every day. When the word *spell* originated in the 1400s, it meant "to write letters that formed words" (verb) and a "story or tale" (noun). A Witchcraft spell is a conversation between ourselves, nature, and other universal influences. Our words create ideas, beliefs, dreams, and health with or without our awareness or active participation.

Our body listens to every word we say. With words, we can heal bones and other illnesses by visualizing the body's wholeness, which is the root of all healing. When we speak ill of our bodies, we create dis-ease in the same way that speaking words of love or fear over a glass of water changes the molecular shape of the water crystals.

Our Magick can impact trauma seeded in ancestral stories of buried anger and fear. For this reason, rituals for ancestral healing may need our spellwork the most. Spells can be personal, geographic, global, or retroactive. Time and space do not exist in the hologram of the magickal realm in the same fixed way they exist in the third dimension of earth-bound life.

The universe is listening to the stories we stuff into our backpack every morning and carry around with us all day. They move like an underground river, impacting us daily without our conscious awareness. Creative Source mobilizes energy to manifest what you say you want in your inner dialogue as well as aloud. Just like with positive affirmations or mantras, we are always sending messages with our words and stories to an alive world that is listening. So, send love.

What you do reverberates because the world moves in rhythm. We are a Uni-verse, one song. It's time to join in the conversation. Fuel the desire to reconnect with your wild side. You know the truth of what it means to own your power and hear the voices of nature and the supernatural. Consider that an abundant harvest, the garden, is nature responding to your care and attention. Accept that the cool breeze on a hot day is a caress of love from the Element of air itself.

Speaking with intention, recognizing symbols, and utilizing magickal tools tells the universe and your subconscious where you want to direct your energy. Our altars are the visual representations of our spells, which I call prayers in 3D. (Of course, when you consider divine timing, you could argue that a spell is a prayer in 4D.) Anyone can write their own spells. You have just as much ability to connect with the Divine Creative Source as anyone else. There are no duds, just a lack of focus, right timing, confidence, or perhaps the outcome would not meet your highest good.

SPELLCRAFTING TOOLS

Let there be no doubt: magickal tools are reason enough to be a Witch. Glitter follows you wherever you go, and tendrils of vines reach out to touch you as you pass. You can find treasures in amethyst points, calendula salves, handcrafted silver chalices, antique brass thuribles (incense holders), and intentional candles sprinkled with crystals and flowers. It's just yummy. Your first lesson as a Witch is to remember that the most important and shiniest thing in your Witchy bag will be your self-esteem. Gather the tools of your Craft with intention and purpose. Take your time as you collect magickal items for your spellwork. Be certain they are sustainable and that your desire for a particular treasure doesn't harm others in its harvesting (see the appendix for more information about sustainable tools).

Rather than focusing on collecting or memorizing all the proper herbs or crystals, buy or gather only those tools that help you practice Magick for what you need in your life. In fact, it is best to begin with just a few tools so you can become familiar with the symbolism each represents within you. Witchcraft was preserved through symbols and everyday items. The cauldron was used to cook food, the knife or athame chopped food, candles were lit, and an everyday cup was the chalice. Make no mistake: these tools are alive within you. Below is a list of how different magickal tools affect our energy so you can better determine which tools you might want to incorporate into your spellwork.

Cauldron/chalice: holds energy

Athame/sword: cuts energy

Wand: directs energy

Mirror: reflects energy

Mortar and pestle: mixes energy

Crystals: project energy

Tarot and oracle cards: affirm energy

Censer/incense: purifies energy

Bells/drums: awaken energy

CREATING A MAGICKAL OIL

Some spells call for a magickal or intentional oil that corresponds with a specific astrological sign, planet, archetype, or feeling. For example, a spell supply list may call for Capricorn oil, Neptune oil, or peace oil. You can sometimes find these oils in esoteric or Witch shops, or you can make your own. All magickal oils begin with a carrier oil, such as jojoba, almond, avocado, coconut, or, my favorite, apricot kernel oil. Each carrier oil has a different consistency and aroma. Follow your intuition and preference. You can use a magickal oil to anoint a candle, your third eye, or your entire body. The choice is yours.

You might like to research and seek out herbs associated with specific powers of gods, goddesses, archetypes, or even emotions. Your intention and mood are important ingredients that act as binding agents when you create magickal oils. Spells will be more effective when you visualize the herb growing in its natural environment. Your recognition of and gratitude for the individual life force of plants increases your Magick because it strengthens your allyship with the plant realm.

BASIC INSTRUCTIONS FOR MAGICKAL OIL

Choose a carrier oil and a single plant ally or your own blend of allies in the form of essential oils, dried herbs, or flowers. You will also need a vessel for your oil, such as a small bottle with a dropper or a jar. You can add the essential oil to your vessel before or after adding the carrier oil and use it immediately. Herbal infusions—dried herbs soaked in a carrier oil—take up to six weeks for maximum potency, depending on the plant. Because living plants contain water, you'll want to work with dried herbs for oil infusions to prevent molding or spoiling. Typically, the ratio is one-fifth plant matter to four-fifths water, but this can vary depending on the plant and its purpose. Place the plant matter in a jar and cover it completely with oil, leaving no room for air in the jar. Seal the jar with a tight lid, label it, and store it in a dark place. I prefer to work with one plant at a time for my herbal infusions so I can really get to know how my body and spirit respond to working with the herb.

ASTROLOGICAL OIL

Place a bowl or clear bottle filled with carrier oil under a full or new moon to accumulate the essence of the zodiac sign that is influencing that moon cycle. You can find which astrological sign is affecting the full or new moon via an online search. As a reference point, unless it is a blue moon, the new or dark moon is always influenced by the astrological sign of that month (for instance, a March new moon will be in Pisces), and the full moon will be the opposite sign on the chart (a March full moon will be in Virgo). You can also choose to add flowers, essential oils, or crystals that are associated with the astrological sign (just be sure to use crystals that are nontoxic; see the moon water recipe on page 167 for guidance). If you are inspired, you can create a chant for the specific energy you are hoping to create with this astrological oil. Using water instead of oil, you can follow this same technique to collect moon water.

PLANETARY OIL

If you want to make a sun, moon, or planetary oil, pour oil into a bowl or bottle on the day of the week associated with a specific planet. Reference the power of the days of the week on page 156. Repeat your intention for the oil aloud. For example, Sunday is the day connected to the sun, so you could chant over your bowl: "I infuse you with the power of the sun. Warmth, joy, and friendship are won. By my will so mote it be."

🔥 Spell-Worthy Questions

In the Crimson Dragon coven, we are instructed to ask ourselves four questions before we begin any spellcasting. These questions are ingrained in DCWA Wiccan education as the pillars of integrity, humility, and responsibility. Honest, affirmative answers will strengthen the spell's energy, clarify your desire, and "keep your side of the street clean." The Witches' rede of "Harm none" means not to harm others or yourself by creating unnecessary karma.

1. IS IT NECESSARY?

Before you cast a spell, ask yourself whether or not you have put in the work and effort to make your dreams come true. If you want a career as an herbalist, have you sat with the plants, taken courses, and sampled the herbs? If you want to be a professional musician, are you playing your instrument daily?

2. IS IT WHAT YOU REALLY NEED?

Magick that is performed primarily for the sake of boosting your ego will not satisfy you in the long run. The universe has an expanded view of your highest good. Consider the phrase "This or something better" to ward off disappointment if your spell does not manifest exactly as you wished. Remain open to the infinite possibilities.

3. WILL IT HARM ANYONE, INCLUDING MYSELF?

Harm is different than hurt. Sometimes it is necessary to experience hurt before a need can be met. It hurts to realize that your limitations have held you back, but as you cast off unhelpful aspects of yourself, your Magick will grow and your spells will manifest more smoothly. Harmful acts, on the other hand, are those made in violence, anger, or cruelty.

4. AM I WILLING TO OWN THE RESPONSIBILITIES OF THE RESULTS?

Once you have asked the forces of the universe to move into action on your behalf, you must accept the form the universe has decided will best fit your need. It is like shaking a tree to get the fruit to fall. You cannot determine where the fruit lands, only the intent and energy you put behind your action.

✳

As I got out of the car, a strong gust of wind lifted my broom skirt and blew my long hair into my face. Unlike some, I love the electric Santa Ana winds that lifted leaves into the air like unseen hands. These wild, unpredictable, warm breezes made me feel unstoppable. Plus, Samhain was coming. It was the season of the Witch. Purple leaves of the Japanese maple tree lay scattered across the green parkway as I walked up to Connie's house.

"The Witch is in," Connie called to me as I opened the door.

"I hope so." I laughed as I sat down on the beanbag and handed her my tithe of a caramel macchiato and maple nut scone. I also handed her an ombre scarf of ocean colors.

"What's this?" Connie asked.

"A scarf I knitted for you," I replied, watching with pride as Connie wrapped the scarf around her neck. "You look beautiful."

"My hair is so oily I could cook with it," Connie said, touching her hair. She was making a joke, but it didn't sit well. *Why wasn't she taking showers? Was her hip bothering her again?* A sheen of glistening hair lay flat against her round face.

Then she smiled and batted a dismissive hand, and in that instant, her melancholy aura evaporated. She giggled and now radiated light and beauty, like the sun peeping out from behind dark rain clouds.

"What's new?" she asked. Connie took a sip of her drink and shivered with the unfettered delight of a burlesque dancer shimmying on a grand stage. She shook off whatever had been bothering her, and I followed her lead.

"Remember how I told you that my next book, *The Enchanted Diary*, is due to the publisher real soon?"

"Are you writing another teen spell book?" James asked, walking in from a back room. Somebody was always at Connie's lately. "I wouldn't do that." He shook his head. "All that karma they're going to reap with their adolescent petulance and bitter fears is going to come right back on your ass because you wrote the spell."

"I don't write anything that would boomerang like shit hitting the fan," I protested. I knew James was testing my mettle, but he still made me nervous. "At the Scottish Games last week, when I was signing books, a woman with a pinched look reached out to touch *The Teen Spell Book*, clearly afraid."

"The Celtic events always bring out as many Catholics as Pagans," Connie mused.

"I know," I replied. "She asked me if this book meant her daughter was going to cast spells on her. I leaned back in my chair and with a deadpan look asked, 'Do you deserve it?'"

"Jamie, you didn't!" Connie exclaimed.

"Well, I am so sick of having to defend myself from others' susceptibility to centuries of negative propaganda against Witches and spellcrafting."

"That's why I don't go out anymore," Connie replied.

"Is it?" I asked rather surly, then sucked in my breath, worried I may have gone too far.

Rumors had spread about a Witch war, or spiritual battle, between Eye of the Cat and Crimson Dragon covens, in which harmful spells were aimed at my mentor. I used Mental Magick to visualize harmony and walked between the two warring covens as if the fighting didn't exist. I refused to acknowledge the negative energy in the attackers' motives and actions; or, as Nick would say years later, "It was as if the sun shone out of your every orifice. Nothing could touch your light."

When, earlier, I'd watched Connie get up and go to the bathroom, her hip seemed to be really bothering her. For the first time, she seemed vulnerable. I worried that the negative energy directed at her had settled into her body. Or perhaps it was her tendency to try to save others and absorb all their fears. Regardless of what it was, my concern for her came out angrily. Connie stared at me with a hardened gaze, then softened.

"You are doing enough work out there for the both of us," Connie said as she waved her hand toward the open window. "My work is here."

"Okay." I held up my hands in surrender and circled back to my story, relieved to change the subject. "So, I told this woman that if her daughter lit a candle to her demise, with or without my book's help, she, the mother, still had the free will to accept or deny the negative energy. When someone hurls crap your way, it's like playing ball; you don't have to catch it."

"No hexing?" James crossed his arms and threw out his bony hip. "No love spells?"

"I only send out positive energy, so that way, I reap only goodness. The only love spells I write are to be cast over a room or yourself."

Michael entered, and the energy in the room shifted and became brighter with his jovial, elfin presence. He handed Connie a glass of water.

I smiled at his devotion to Connie. "There's nothing I write that goes against another's free will to evolve at the rate that is best for them," I said. "If there is one lesson I am learning, it's to let people learn their lessons in their time."

"Divine timing benefits everyone." Michael winked at me.

"What happens if one of your readers opens the door to the spirits and attracts a foul energy?" James kept on me.

I wavered in my faith and conviction, pondering this question. "I give them tools of protection and support to shine their light so bright that dense, negative energy cannot exist in the same space. I tell them that as humans, we have sovereignty over our physical existence, and as such we have the authority to exorcise any energy that hurts us. I give them protection with both a shield and a sword."

Connie looked at James and raised her eyebrows as if to say, "Are we through?"

James raised his hands. "You're right. She knows."

Connie lit the white taper candle and added dragon's blood incense to the thurible.

Michael smiled. "We'll watch over you like we watch over this one." He bent down and kissed the top of Connie's head. He took James's hand and smiled at me. It felt like the night watchers of ancient England had given me their vow of protection.

"I wrote *The Teen Spell Book* to heal myself of the anger and sadness I felt as I came of age, which I had been carrying with me for too long," I said. "I read the diaries I kept as a teenager and wrote spells, visualizations, and affirmations for all the times I felt lonely, unlovable, or lost. I collected my fragmented selves."

"Soul retrieval," Connie confirmed.

"It felt like going into a thick forest or underground maze to find parts of me I had left behind." I laughed. "I got into a car accident on the way to the book's first signing event. I felt so vulnerable, like I had published my diaries, which I had. But I wasn't going into my thirties with my mommy or daddy issues following me through my whole damn life," I said. "Each spell was created with the intention of strengthening our awareness of our Divine Essence. So that can boomerang all day long."

"In turn that gives others permission and a role model to shine their unique light," Connie said.

"How do you write your spells?" Michael asked.

"In the cave of inner silence, you shall find the wellspring of wisdom."

Paramahansa Yogananda

SPELLCRAFTING STEPS

These are the basic steps I take when I am writing spells for my books and witchy life:

1. Grounding

2. Centering

3. Finding stillness

4. Focusing intention

5. Creating the altar

6. Making the rhyme

7. Preparing an offering

8. Saying thanks

Spellcrafting begins with grounding and centering, by slowing down your breathing and bringing your awareness to the present moment. This means that your senses are heightened and engaged in your immediate surroundings, bodily sensations, and current desires. In this quiet, meditative space, your higher self can speak through the stillness. As your intention becomes more focused, ask yourself the reasons behind the desire you seek. The universe is alive and responds to our deepest truths, so it is important to know where your motivation is coming from. The spiritual manifestation of your spellwork is how this desire will make you *feel* once it has formed. Focus your intention on the positive aspect of what you want to experience.

Concentrating your attention on positivity may seem more obvious if you want to attract a mate, job, or prosperity, but if, for example, you want to be relieved of stress, anger, or anxiety, then ask yourself what is the opposite feeling of the emotion that is weighing you down. It may be that tranquility, trust, or security becomes your intention for the spell.

After you clarify your truest motivation and have tapped into the desired feeling, collect symbols, words, or items that match the vibration or correspond in some way with the feeling you want to manifest. For example, if you want to create a prosperity spell, you might put money on your altar. If you needed to forgive someone, including yourself, you might lay images of hearts on your altar. You give the symbol its power with your intention.

Next, create a rhyming chant that states the intention of your spell. The rhyme speaks to the right side of your brain, which is the creative side that does not need logic to understand how the spell will manifest. Your creativity is illimitable, numinous, and dreamy. Your incantation is a wish in a song that is created for you and the universe to experience something new that you dreamed up. It can be two lines that you repeat over and over, like, "I release to the fire what I no longer desire," or it can be several lines or stanzas. You want to chant until you feel the vibration of your song resonating in your heart center.

Traditionally spells end with phrases such as, "By my will so mote it be," which is a declaration of yourself as the Divine co-creating with the universe. Then, prepare an offering, such as a bowl of water, cakes and ale, cornmeal, herbs, or flowers. End with a written or spoken statement of gratitude, acknowledging that the spell is already on its way to manifestation.

Now that the spell has been written, you decide if you want to cast a full circle or simply apply Mental Magick to set the stage for your spellwork.

PAYING THE FERRYMAN

I suggest an offering within the ritual itself, or you may choose to go the extra mile and give an offering that takes a bit more time. Sometimes called an exchange, payment, or sacrifice, this special offering keeps the energy flowing, demonstrates your commitment, and puts you in the state of mind that you want to attract (for example, a generous spirit attracts generous opportunities and people). Magick has different interpretations of words, its own mystical language, and it is important to redefine words that have been given negative connotations by misconceptions of Witchcraft, Wiccan, and occult traditions. I want to make it clear that the word *sacrifice* actually means "to make sacred or holy," and you, a unique Divine Essence incarnate in your body, decide what holy, sacred item you want to offer, give, or exchange for what you hope to receive. These sacred offerings are the true Magick of spellwork and will work best when they are of a "like for like" nature. For example, if you want to receive companionship, you must open yourself more to others, and if you desire more money, perhaps a tithe is in order.

If you want to conceive a child, you can volunteer at a children's hospital, school, or charity. If you want to attract a lover, you can shower yourself with fresh flowers, take a warm bath, receive massages, or indulge in other acts of self-love. Or if you want optimum health, you may have to give up dairy or gluten or add more fresh produce to your diet. The sacred offering must match the energy of what you want to *experience*, not what you are trying to be rid of.

Allow me to give you an example. It's mid-December as I am wrapping up this book, and recently I decided to host a tamale-making party during a heavy snowstorm for people who had never made tamales. I asked myself what spell I could cast to give a personal example of a sacred offering. I tapped into my quiet self and noticed money worries, stress over the busyness of the holidays, and a desire to rekindle the joy of the holidays that I felt as a child. As the carne asada simmered, I sprinkled rose petals around a photo of my Mexican ancestors, lit a candle, and asked myself (and them),

"What is the opposite virtue of this anxiety I am feeling?" It took a full day of pondering before I realized that I wanted to feel trust and childlike wonder. I wanted to feel blessed by the Magick of Jupiter, the planet that influences the Sagittarius season from roughly November 20 through December 20 and whose realm is expansion, success, and generosity. I decided that my sacred offering would be to stop doing the adult stuff for a few hours to sit and watch Christmas cartoons and black-and-white classics while stringing popcorn. Paying it forward by indulging my inner child worked like a charm as I felt joy and fun in teaching my neighbors how to make tamales.

Magick is practical even as it is steeped in lore, myth, and fables. The idea of giving an equal exchange of energy for what you want to receive can be found in Greek mythology. In ancient times, the funeral rites included placing a coin under the tongue or on the eyes of the deceased as payment to Charon, the ferryman, for crossing the rivers Styx and Acheron to gain access to Hades, the Underworld, on the other side of the rivers.

There are, however, some spells that do not require sacrifice or sacred offerings. These include self-protection, health, divining, scrying, money (enough for your basic needs), and calling upon the deities or the elementals for help. These things are your divine right. Ultimately, an exchange for your spell's desire should be made and decided upon by you.

If you have some ideas about what your offering could be, but you don't have a clear vision, you can divine by omen with any three of the options I offer below. Regardless of which divination technique you choose, first take a moment to be still and quiet. Envision the experience you want your spell-work to bring you. Begin with an incantation by calling for the assistance of your spirit guide, an ancestor, or familiar animal by name. You can even ask for help from your higher self by calling your own name.

> "Hail and greetings to
> (spirit guide, an ancestor, familiar, or higher self)
> Please assist me as I divine
> For a vision, omen, or sign
> Of the exchange I freely give
> Like for like its nature does live
> By my will so mote it be."

Go outdoors if possible. Being in nature gives the universe and your spirit guides more opportunities to present an obvious omen. Perhaps take a walk. Admire the life in the breeze, sunlight, trees, animals, or whatever crosses your path. Breathe deeply and calmly. Let go of any tension or anxiety. Sometimes, the answers rise to the surface of our clear, relaxed minds.

If you prefer or must stay indoors, go to your bookcase to practice the form of divination known as bibliomancy, which can be practiced with absolutely *any* book. Close your eyes, and run your hands over the books before you. Select that book that makes you feel a tingly sensation, warmth, or a strong knowing that indicates the presence of your intuition. Open the book, inwardly calling your spirit guide by name. Let your eyes fall on the first passage you see for a clue to your sacrifice or sacred offering.

If no images or insights appear in your mind, touch a favorite crystal, amulet, or necklace and repeat the incantation until you feel a thrumming in your heart center. Be as heartfelt as you can about your request to receive a message or omen for the exchange that is the most fitting.

If you are still uncertain after three tries, select a few special offerings for your spell that would fit the requirements, and use a pendulum to determine which, if any, might be acceptable. Pendulums can be bought at a store, or you can simply thread a needle as your pendulum. Hold the pendulum in the palm of your hand to make a connection with it. Next, hold the end of the chain or string with the point of your crystal or needle just an inch or so above your palm. Ask the pendulum to show you the "Yes" answer, which could be either a straight line or circle. Then, say, "Stop!" and wait for the pendulum to stop moving. Next, ask the pendulum to show you "No" as the opposite of the "Yes" answer (if "Yes" was a straight line, "No" would be a circle and vice versa).

✳

"I give people the steps for writing a spell, and now I want them to see how Magick works in their lives by giving real-life examples. I want the last chapter of *The Enchanted Diary* to be about our stories. It's a living tribute to our Goddess herstory. A play on his-story (history), get it?"

"Clever," Connie said, then her smile turned into a grimace as she clutched her lower belly.

"Are you okay?" I leaned forward to rest my hand on her knee.

"A little indigestion is all." Connie wiped beaded sweat from her forehead with the back of her hand. "Go on," she urged.

I paused, unsure what to do next. I glanced over at James and Michael, and they both had stern expressions. Suddenly, I felt a strong instinct that Connie was holding onto everyone's pain like it was her duty. I could sense that through healing and helping others, she had inadvertently taken on their pain. Within my mind's eye, I saw that the poison had settled in toxic pools in the pockets of her body. I went into "fix-the-fixer" mode.

"I just bought *Chinigchinix*, a rare book that includes records written by Gerónimo Boscana, a Franciscan friar," I said, trying to get quickly to my point. "I'm falling further down the rabbit hole in my search for a Native grandmother. Father Boscana was a missionary at Mission San Juan Capistrano from 1812 to 1826 and recorded how California Indigenous healers extracted the sickness from patients through a straw, like pulling out grey, dense smoke."

I paused, wondering if she knew I was saying this because of her. "Are you holding onto our negativity as you help us release our shadow and shine the light of our souls?" I wanted to ask, but it seemed disrespectful, so I asked her silently, without words.

Connie locked eyes with me but seemed unable to speak what was on her mind. This was a first. She winced again.

"I drink peppermint tea when my lactose intolerance kicks in after eating pizza. I will bring you some," I offered. (It would take years before I realized that eating something indigestible and masking the body pain with anything was the opposite of self-care.)

The room became unseasonably warm. I held my ground. The candlelight shot up, and the energy of the room shifted again. The heat and tension abated, and the air tingled with positive electricity.

Connie smiled. "You want to write about Goddess herstory. I like that."

I paused, then asked, "I was wondering if you would write me a story about your earliest magickal education?"

HOW SPELLS WORK

Spells work because of three things: belief in the possibility of manifesting your desire, clarity of intention, and repetition.

One of the most interesting and complex aspects of curating Connie's fifty years of magickal knowledge and practice is learning when to leave the instruction as is and when to adapt it to modern sensitivities. As a wordsmith, I feel it is libelous to assume we can translate a text exactly, since etymology has shown that the meanings of words change depending on culture and context over time. Yet early magickal instruction seemed to purposefully omit some directions, as if our mentors wanted us to figure it out on our own, such as this adage from Connie's treasure trove:

"The spell conditions the mind step by step, forming a focus and catalyst for the portion of the brain which enables one to create changes in the astral substance."

Let's unpack this. Through the casting of a circle, we condition the mind to focus on our desire through a step-by-step process, which builds muscle memory to anticipate Magick and expect miracles that defy the logic of nonbelief. Magick makers and Witches live by a different set of rules. The number one difference is that we believe it is in our personal power to create Magick through engaging in the eternal conversation with our empowered self, nature, and the cosmos. We seek miracles, and they find us.

The astral substance is the physicality of nature's seasons and other universal influences. Examples from nature that symbolize the general themes for the seasons will vary depending upon where you live and may include blooming flowers and (re)birth for spring; hot sun, radiating joy, and life force in summer; falling leaves that remind us to release what doesn't serve us in fall; and colder weather that forces us to rest inside and restore for winter. Universal influences could include the phases of the moon, days of the week, or planetary movements. Your spells will be stronger and work better if you go with the flow of nature rather than fighting against its energetic currents.

However, your intention and need will always supersede any symbolic correlation you try to make. Your focus, belief, and repetition are your strongest, most potent magickal tools. Feed the intention to create a spell that only you could write and manifest. Cultivate trust and acceptance of divine timing and the manifestation of your desire. When you write your first spell, why not start with a magickal incantation that has been repeated for decades and can tap into the collective power of thousands of practicing Witches?

"As above, so below
As the universe, so the soul
As without, so within
Let this Magick rite begin."

12

Coming Out of the
Broom Closet

"There is only one of you in all time, this expression
is unique. And if you block it, it will never exist
through any other medium and it will be lost."

Martha Graham

I t takes courage and pluck to be a Witch in this world. Courage arises
from being true to yourself and accepting that the only opinion that
makes a difference is yours. Repeatedly following your inner guidance
can develop a muscle memory that will allow you to effortlessly follow your
core truth, time and again. It's a matter of releasing your desire to control
how others perceive you. Believe in the Magick around and within you.

When you share your spirituality with others, aim to use the language appropriate for your audience. When people would ask about my books in the early
2000s, I would do a jewelry check to guesstimate their response. If they wore a
gold cross, I would say that I wrote a seasonal cookbook, like farm to table, and
that would be all. If their energy seemed open to learning new information, I
might mention that I wrote about the necessity of sustainability during medieval
times or old Celtic holidays like the solstices. If they wore handmade jewelry or
precious stones, I would tell them I wrote a potluck book for sabbat rituals with
spells. Meet people where they are. It doesn't help to scare them away.

There is a pattern to all breakthroughs in life: the greatest, most enlightened moments of success and happiness are often preceded by bleak

moments of despair. If you are worried about telling others about your spiritual practice, you must hold yourself steady. Try not to lash out at them. This moment of opening up about what you do and believe can be a source of great pride if you act with courage and grace. Believe in yourself. Believe in your Magick.

Remember that there are all kinds of courage—big kinds that take your breath away and little mundane ones. Most importantly, remember that courage is a gift to yourself. It takes courage to walk the path of the Witch and accept the truth of living a cyclical life of birth, death, and rebirth.

Courage Spell

Gather the following supplies:

- Red candle

- Red stones, such as garnet, red jasper, carnelian, ruby (can even be red rocks)

I recommend performing this ritual on a Tuesday at dusk. Tuesday is the day of Mars, the deity of action whom you will be invoking, and dusk is the time when night and day meet and all things seem possible in this liminal space. However, feel free to choose a day or time that feels most powerful to you. Magick is created by your intention. Follow your instincts.

Take several deep breaths. Stand tall as a tree. Imagine that you are in a sacred grove of trees where the wind doesn't blow and nothing moves until you will it. The entire grove is quiet and cannot be disturbed by any outside influence. This is your private wood between the worlds. Standing as a tree, stretch your roots into the soil by imagining your energy descending deep into Mother Earth. Now reach for the sky and the sun with your branches.

Face the east and ask that the Element of air come to your aid and bring its powers of inspiration and fresh ideas. Call upon your favorite flying creature or animal. Face the south and ask that the Element of fire come to your aid and bring its powers of drive and determination. Call upon your favorite power animal or creature. Face the west and ask that the Element of water come to your aid and bring its powers of changeability and heart. Call upon your favorite aquatic creature. Face the north and ask that the Element of earth come to your aid and bring its powers of grounding and security. Call upon your favorite land animal. These animals can be either mythical or practical.

Light a red candle to represent your will and passion to call upon your heart-centered courage and honestly look at your fears. Place red stones, such as garnet, red jasper, carnelian, ruby, or rocks painted red around the candle in a circle. Hold the vision of yourself standing as a tree in a secluded wood, connected to both the earth and sky, and chant the following:

"As above, so below
I call upon this wisdom to know.
In the center of the energies, I stand,
Ready for courage close at hand.
Roots reach deep into Mother Earth
I am strong and know my worth.
I stretch to the protection of Father Sky,
Empowered by a love that will never die.
I call upon Mars, whose power shall start
The flame of courage that fuels my heart."

Imagine light energy pulsating from your heart center and emanating out. Your light makes everything around you more beautiful. Know that you are supported by the Source of all things. Visualize taking this ball of light with you into situations where you need to face your inner demons or work through traumatic situations. Sit with the candle as long as you can, holding onto the light of your courage.

You can choose a small spell candle for this ritual so you can allow the candle to burn all the way out in one sitting. Perhaps this is when you choose to look at the shadow collage you created from the ritual on page 136. Review old diaries or pictures and envision yourself as a tree shining heart light to sustain you if you come across something difficult to process. Journal if you like writing, or create in whatever form that best lets you express what courage feels like inside of your body, mind, and unique spirit.

✳

I didn't want to believe that Connie was sick. She hadn't been out in public in months. Our three-hour visits were punctuated by other students coming and going. She called everyone who came to visit part of her magickal family, but I refused to leave my special seat at her knee. In the last few weeks, I went as often as I could, sneaking away for whatever juicy tidbit of wisdom she might offer. I wanted to spend as much time with her as possible. Time was moving too fast; I could feel it in my bones.

I arrived one day in early December. Connie's birth children were present as well as many of her magickal children, members of the Crimson Dragon coven, so I knew something was up. At least twenty people jammed into the crowded house, as if we were celebrating Yule early and were waiting for our Elder High Priestess to initiate the cabalistic cross. Except Connie wasn't in her usual chair, and the mood was heavy, hushed, and expectant. James held my elbow and ushered me quietly down the hallway to Connie's bedroom.

Connie was in bed, propped up by several pillows. She had a wan look about her. I sat down on the edge of the bed, and she handed me three ribbons for the Yule knot work: silver, black, and grey.

"What's this?" I asked. We were never given the ribbons until the day of the ceremony on the sabbat, which was still two weeks away.

"I've decided we should have a simple Yule ritual," Connie said. "Just the cab cross and the knot work."

"I didn't bring my chalice," I said.

"It's okay," Connie said.

Quietly, people gathered around Connie's bed while some lingered in the hallway. Solemnly we made the arm and hand signals and intoned the invocation for the cabalistic cross. Connie didn't leave the bed for her ritual instructions. I secured the loop of my three ribbons to a perfume bottle on Connie's dresser and tied three knots, praying for clarity in this moment, my mentor's life, and mine. My head was spinning. What was happening? Why were we doing this ritual now? I tried to make eye contact, but the others were either staring ahead or inwardly focused with their eyes closed. Tears streamed down Sariel's face. Nick looked like he was made of granite.

After everyone had cleared out, I returned to Connie's bedside. She looked exhausted but smiled at me and giggled under my penetrating gaze.

"Are you . . . ?" I started to ask.

"Here's the essay I wrote about learning to read the coffee grounds from my grandmother." Connie handed me a couple sheets of paper covered in her beautiful, slanted, cursive handwriting. "For *The Enchanted Diary*."

"Thank you," I said. I felt like she was handing me a piece of her to keep forever, but the cold fear I'd felt earlier again gripped my chest.

"I want to give you a reading," Connie announced with a firmness that silenced me. She shuffled the cards and placed the deck on the bedspread between us. I cut the deck, and she pulled three cards: the Star, the Sun, and the World. Three archetypes to represent a message from my past, present, and future. It's always a big deal to get all Major Arcana in a reading.

Connie exhaled in delight and relief. "Aw, look at that. You're going to be just fine."

"You couldn't ask for a better reading," I said. I stared in awe at the cards and the message I strung together. I whispered, "Through honoring my inner light and accepting happiness, I will achieve the success I want."

Connie placed her hand over mine. Tears welled in our eyes while we drank in each other's spirit through the windows of the soul. The love flowed back and forth between us as a palpable heart energy, a vortex as strong as a tornado. In her eyes she asked me to be brave. She was dying, but the others needed more time to accept the end that was fast approaching. We smiled simultaneously. The tears receded.

I rose from my seat and forced myself to walk away. Pausing to stop at the door, I looked back one last time. I gripped the door frame as if I could stop the world from spinning and death's scythe from falling if I just held on. Eventually, Michael came to bring Connie some medicine, and I turned to go. Part of me wanted to stay and talk with the others. I heard whispers of, "She'll pull through," and there were those who could not stop crying, fearing the worst. I hugged whomever I crossed paths with on my way out.

That night I dreamed of the framed wolf poster that sat like a guardian angel behind Connie's chair. The spirit of the wolf: both a loner and a tribal member, but mostly a teacher. I heard Connie's voice say, "I want you to have this." I woke up in a cold sweat and burst into tears. Connie passed from this world that night as the moon crossed the sky.

THE LOVE LANGUAGE OF SELF-CARE

Energy builds like a muscle, so when you consistently shower yourself with protection and kind deeds, you may eventually remember yourself as the Creative Source—both God and Goddess. Living the life of a Witch who can accept death as part of life requires lots of healthy self-care.

Think of simple moments of joyful self-care, such as taking a nap, getting a massage, drinking a smoothie, oiling your body, drinking plenty of water, journaling, bathing, hiking, sunning, reading, or taking your vitamins. Kindness to the self-spirit reverberates back upon oneself. The more you are accustomed to administering loving care to yourself, the less tolerant you will be of nagging and negative thoughts and discordant situations and people. The habit of placing oneself in the center of a vibration of love, peace, and joy motivates one to actively move out of negativity and into positivity.

This remembering of our Divine nature is the core of Witchcraft and the belief that we can manifest anything and communicate with spirits. Your Magick will be more successful when you believe deep down that you can receive and share in this cycle of goodness.

Witchcraft as a self-care lifestyle includes ritual herbalism as one part of a holistic approach to living attuned with nature. A reciprocal, energetic exchange with the plant world lifts our spirits to levels of consciousness that are higher than those we can reach alone. Plants, crystals, and magickal tools pull us into their vibration, and we are lifted out of the mundane to the magickal. Working with our allies teaches us to see ourselves as Divine. Whether our frayed souls need calm or energy or purification, nature offers a path back to wholeness and a reunion with Oneness.

One of my favorite herbal self-care activities is a facial steam. Water cleanses the skin as much as it does the soul and the heavy heart. The steaming water of this ritual is a way to fill your cup and treat yourself with the tenderness that is needed in the most intense moments of our lives. The steam causes your face to sweat, allowing impurities to be released as it hydrates and promotes circulation. The compounds in herbs such as calendula and chamomile are also incredibly soothing and moisturizing; they're also anti-aging. This is in part due to enhanced blood flow to the face and in part due to the antioxidant activity of some of the herbs and oils. Geranium, sandalwood, and frankincense essential oils promote the renewal of skin cells. Chamomile and lavender calm the nervous system.

If you tend to have dry, mature, sensitive, red, or inflamed skin, then the category of herbs most valuable to you will be those that are slightly cooling, softening, and moistening, such as calendula, chamomile, rose, lavender, and comfrey. If you have oily skin, you'll want to seek out herbs that have an astringent property such as rose, rosemary, red raspberry leaf, and sage. These herbs help tighten and draw the tissues together, shrinking pores in the process. For acne, you'll want herbs that are antiseptic, antibacterial, and cleansing, such as tea tree (or in New Zealand, manuka), eucalyptus, peppermint, and rosemary. If you have combination skin, you can use a mixture of herbs; calendula, chamomile, and rose would be my top picks. Lemon peel is something you can add no matter your skin type. It's energizing and invigorating and makes for a lovely addition.

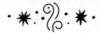

Facial Steam for Self-Care

Gather the following supplies:

- Towel to drape over your head

- Bowl (preferably ceramic)

- One essential oil and/or a handful of dried or fresh herbs

- Timer

- Trivet for your bowl

Make it a goal to get the first steam that releases from your plant allies so you can receive the highest benefit and deeply breathe their medicines into your sinuses and respiratory system.

1. Pour six to eight drops of one essential oil into the bottom of a glass or ceramic bowl. You can add dried herbs or flowers, but they must be pesticide-free.

2. Bring three to four cups of water to a near boil in a small pot. If the water boils, let it cool for thirty seconds.

3. Pour the water into the bowl.

4. Quickly set your bowl on a trivet, set a timer for ten minutes, cover your head with the towel, and lean as close to the steaming water as you can (don't burn yourself!).

5. Breathe as deeply as you comfortably can.

6. Envision the plant, whether lavender, eucalyptus, orange, or your favorite herbal ally, sending its healing energy throughout your body, and your head, throat, and chest lighting up with Divine Essence.

✳

Connie's final rite of passage was held in the park, a large green space at the end of the cul-de-sac between her apartment building and a huge Gothic church. Also known as the Celebration of Life, this ceremony brought the peace our Witch community needed as many covens came to honor Connie. I approached Connie's apartment, my hands trembling as I carried homemade chocolate chip cookies on a red plate inscribed with the words "You are special." I had tried not to cry into the bowl while I mixed the ingredients. I was attempting to be grateful for having known Connie, but I was just too sad—we should have been celebrating Yule, not the life of our beloved Crimson Dragon.

The screen door of Connie's home was propped open, and people crowded in, wall to wall. Merlin the Highlander Cat sat atop the bookshelf, which seemed to be missing something, though I couldn't be certain of what. I added my cookies to the dining room table, which was already overflowing with food, and turned to find myself standing in front of James and Michael. Michael pulled me into a warm embrace.

"You knew," he whispered in my ear. "I saw you yesterday. You knew she was crossing."

"Come on, she goes exactly eight sabbats with these. A full year of her teachings on the Wheel of the Year." I held up my chalice with eight knotted ribbons. "And we're not supposed to notice the Witch is heading for Summerland? It's too perfectly planned. She was a Virgo after all!" I burst out crying at my attempt at a joke.

James leaned his lanky body over to hug me until I could control the crying. I willed myself steady.

"Jamie, we want you to be able to take anything from here that speaks to you. Her family has already taken what they want." I smiled at this couple I had come to know and love so much in three short years. They were like Connie's sentinels, and I would always treasure them for that.

James nodded to a dark-eyed man in his thirties with an impressive beard. The man stepped closer to us.

"Jamie, this is Jason, Connie's son."

"Thank you for being such a comfort to my mother," Jason said as he hugged me. "We want you to have a piece of her with you."

His embrace was warm and filled with such gratitude, I felt overwhelmed.

"It was my honor," I said, fighting back the tears.

Of course, I had wanted to tell them about my dream. I glanced at the wolf poster but hesitated. After Nana Mame died, all her daughters claimed to have dreamed about being bequeathed the china and other treasures. The best family heirlooms went to the one who'd had the dream at the latest hour in the evening, which apparently marked Mame's final decision. Because I loved it so much, I thought the wolf picture would be everyone's most prized possession, and I didn't want to appear greedy.

"It's yours, honey," Michael said. "You don't even have to ask."

"Come back in a few days to get it," Jason suggested.

I agreed to come back and wove through the crowd to get fresh air. The scarf I had given Connie lay folded on her table next to the recliner.

Inspired, I grabbed the scarf, feeling like my knees would collapse underneath me. I couldn't pretend to be strong much longer. I wanted to weep and not stop crying until I had cried a river in Connie's honor. But now I had one important thing left to do—a growing and overwhelming desire to connect with Connie's blood family. I always knew what I had for Connie's granddaughters, but now I had something for Alexa.

Outside, the fresh, cool December air filled my lungs, and I smelled a hint of the sea. I remembered a story Connie had told me about how she once flirted with Poseidon by kicking at small waves as they crashed on the beach. She stepped in ankle deep and called to the god of the sea as a lover—to embrace her, fill her up, and take her away. In my mind's eye, I saw the rogue wave that had come out of nowhere to drench Connie through.

"Jamie!" Alexa, Connie's daughter, caught my elbow, pulling me out of my reverie. "It's Alexa." She'd found me before I could find her.

Although we hadn't met until that moment, Alexa recognized me somehow, and we immediately embraced. Alexa and I were both in our mid-thirties, sisters from the same mother, but different. *I got the Elder High Priestess, she got the Little Mother,* I thought, until another thought quickly entered my head: *But didn't we both get the full package of the human as the Divine Feminine, the Goddess, and the Mentor in the end?*

Alexa and I pulled away from our embrace after a long while and held each other by the forearms, looking into each other's eyes. I sent her as much strength as I could. Then I placed her mother's scarf around Alexa's shoulders.

"I made this for your mama. I want you to have it. I'm new to knitting, though, so there are some holes in it. Spirit Holes of self-compassion."

"I love it." Alexa wrapped the scarf around her neck. She had the same brown eyes as Connie, but softer. "These are my daughters, Kristen and Shayla." She gestured to the two young women behind her.

From my satchel purse, I took out two signed copies of *The Teen Spell Book* that I had inscribed to both of them with the wisdom Connie had always emphasized: "Live your one magickal life in a way that feels right to you. Follow that inner Witch wherever she takes you."

Blonde with blue eyes, Shayla leaned in and gave me the most sincere and comforting hug. She conveyed the cheer and bright light that Connie had brought to my life. She also had a steely kind of strength, tough as nails. She was going to hold it together.

I turned to the more reticent daughter, Kristen. Dark eyeliner rimmed her dark eyes, which were full of spunk and verve.

"You have your yiayia's eyes, mischievous and magickal," I said, using the Greek term for "grandmother" that had been her granddaughters' name for Connie.

When we hugged, something electrical passed between us. I sighed, comforted by the connection.

"Kristen anointed yiayia when we went to the funeral home," Alexa said, proud of her daughter's strength at sixteen. The grief and memories felt thick in the air. It was a lot to process for someone so young yet not without considerable power.

"I got to say goodbye to her in the same way that she'd once welcomed me and my cousin Wynnzdie into her world of Witchcraft and Magick on the day of our 'baptism,'" Kristen said with a hint of sarcasm.

My left eyebrow raised automatically, as if I was invoking Connie, and Kristen quickly modified her answer.

"I mean my Wiccaning," she said with a puckish grin.

A woman approached and told Kristen how much she looked like Connie. She handed Kristen an earring that her daughter had made for Connie. Her daughter had kept the other one, she said. Kristen put it on her left ear, and it looked like it was going to stay there for a long while. These beauties would carry Connie's Magick into the next generations.

Judith, High Priestess and the owner of Eye of the Cat, called us to the start of the ceremony on the park's green. Wearing a black cloak, Judith stood next to a large cauldron and a table piled with bundles of dried herbs, satchels, corn dollies, and knotted ribbons.

The collection of spells that were missing from the bookshelves! I thought.

Slowly, people came to join the circle. I lost track after counting at least one hundred. Dressed in our magickal regalia, we looked like a small Renaissance festival at the corner of Junipero and Fourth in Long Beach—except for the keening. The loud crying shook me to my core, but knowing Connie would live on through her children and granddaughters, who each stood at a cardinal point, filled me with gratitude for knowing such a beautiful soul. Flames flickered from the top of the cauldron, and I marveled at how we could be having this Pagan ceremony in the middle of a city in 2004.

Sariel clasped the hilt of a four-foot silver sword, and the wailing grew to a fevered pitch as the final rite of passage began. She picked up the sword and held it at shoulder's length to draw the circle of protection around the mourners, enfolding us in the sacred boundary that would protect us during the ceremony, separate us from the world of the mundane and its dense consciousness, and bring us into the enlightened magickal realm of ritual. The sniffling and weeping rose as Sariel turned to walk the perimeter of the large gathering of people. At her first steps, the church bells began to toll, the sonorous ringing following Sariel as if on cue.

Immediately I felt the Christian church bells were honoring the passing of a Witch, Elder High Priestess of the Crimson Dragon of the Druidic Craft of the Wise. It was appropriate, ironic, and the greatest piece of Magick I could imagine: the Sunday fundies were honoring the passing of one of the Wise Ones. Tears of hilarity and sheer irony pierced our collective grief like a pin through a bubble. I started to giggle like Connie, the sound of water cascading over rocks in a creek. Sariel winked as she passed me and I laughed even harder. My heart burst open with the oneness and connection of us all.

I turned to look at Judith, certain that daggers were headed my way, but she smiled at me in gratitude and raised her arms high in the air.

"That's right!" Judith called out. "The Crimson Dragon is being welcomed home. Don't cry because she's gone. Laugh because she lives on in us."

Soon laughter won out over crying, and tears turned from sorrow to joy. I watched Nick and Shayla joke with each other like brother and sister. Members of Connie's personal family called in the four directions. This one grand gesture felt like such a harmonious integration of Connie's two families supporting each other as we mourned one Witch who had touched so many people through her brilliant facets, just like a diamond.

Random people started to gather about fifty feet from our circle, curious about everything going on. Did they know they stood among Witches? Did they finally see that Witches are people who love, laugh, and grieve like everyone else? I could feel Connie's presence so strongly, and I hoped these outsiders would feel the Magick of this moment and the power we all have to shift, manifest, and enlighten. I wanted to lift them all up, as Connie had carried me through some of my darkest days. I wanted it so bad, it ached.

"Connie, the Crimson Dragon, is eternal," Judith said as she added Connie's spells to the cauldron. "She lives in the spiral of the smoke, the Magick she crafted in all of us. She wanted you all to be empowered. Honor Connie by honoring your Inner Light and Divine Essence and being true to yourself."

After the ritual, people stayed well after dark, talking about Connie and breathing their love for her into the night air. The pain of losing her was met with the joy of knowing her in a celebration that bordered on controlled chaos that just . . . felt like her. Like the stippling in one of her drawings. Each little dot a memory of her that formed the composition of all of us crying and laughing and loving.

A WITCH'S NAME

A magickal or Witch name allows you to better inhabit the persona of your Divine Essence that you most want to step further up and into. This name you give yourself is the sword on which you will fall because it represents the keenest description of your essence. Your Witch name is also a shield of protection with its own force field that gains power over time. When you repeatedly embody your Witch name in the magickal circle, it builds power that can work like an invisibility cloak in your daily life or a call to action at the next ritual.

When you divine for a Witch name, you are setting out on a journey with a new horizon. You can choose to reserve this name for your special diaries or you can share it with the world and change important documents, like your driver's license. You may choose to create a spell to further bond with your Witch name in ceremony. Or you may decide that sacred ceremony is simply calling yourself your Witch name aloud as you walk upon this earth. Everyday Witch. Everyday Divine. A magickal name brings the sacred into the mundane and blends the two together.

There was no lineage offered for the phonetic origins of this ritual in Connie's notes. I believe it is important to recognize that these traditions and rituals are made up by humans, and we can't always trace everything in a linear way to where they came from—nor should we. Because Spirit comes from within and connects us to all human traditions, anyone may write their own spell or modify the rituals they read in a book.

🔥 Divination for a Witch Name

You will need your tarot or playing cards and a place where you will not be disturbed. Light a white candle and take three deep breaths. Relax into a meditative space while you maintain your concentration. Cut the deck, discard the top seven cards, and place them to the side. Pull three cards from anywhere in the deck. Note the phonetic values in order.

Example:

King of Wands	3 of Wands	9 of Swords
"EL"	"DA"	"RI"

"ELDARI" is the result. However, you can play around with different combinations, such as "DARIEL." You may add more cards one at a time, but do not exceed thirteen total.

TAROT CONVERSION KEY

MAJOR ARCANA

The Magician	shal	Strength	the	Devil	lan
High Priestess	shan	Hermit	kam	Tower	she
Empress	jan	Wheel of Fortune	tan	Star	oma
Emperor	shi	Justice	sher	Moon	aur
Hierophant	ran	Hanged Man	ken	Sun	dia
Lovers	shar	Death	sha	Judgment	mir
Chariot	san	Temperance	nen	World	tho
				Fool	ria

MINOR ARCANA

Wands		Cups		Swords		Pentacles	
Ace	ba	Ace	be	Ace	sa	Ace	co
2	ca	2	ce	2	di	2	do
3	da	3	de	3	ta	3	go
4	fa	4	fe	4	hi	4	lo
5	ga	5	he	5	va	5	no
6	ha	6	je	6	wi	6	po
7	ja	7	ke	7	ni	7	so
8	ka	8	le	8	pi	8	to
9	la	9	me	9	ri	9	vo
10	ma	10	ne	10	si	10	tha
Page	na	Page	te	Page	ti	Page	mam
Knight	pa	Knight	ve	Knight	bi	Knight	thi
Queen	na	Queen	an	Queen	fi	Queen	lyn
King	el	King	mur	King	li	King	ar

It might not be your thing to give yourself a Witch name. Follow your own path. Listen to the wisdom of your soul. Witchcraft is ultimately life craft, so live your best life. Seek the wonder and Magick in every day. Remain open so others can show you the wisdom they have gained, but blaze your own trail. Be true to yourself in this world. Raise your vibration. Speak love. Listen to nature and hug the trees. There is a little Witch in all of us.

EPILOGUE

Over the years I have turned to Connie on numerous occasions to ask for her wisdom. When I'm lucky, I hear her giggle with delight when I'm on the right track, or I feel her penetrating gaze or raised eyebrow that tells me I am avoiding the truth with my silly games. A picture of Connie sits on my ancestor altar that remains up all year. Ancestors don't have to be from your family line; they can also be based on mutual affinity and your deep connection.

Five years after Connie's passing, my children's father and I divorced. The planet of death and rebirth, Pluto, squared my sun in my astrological chart, invoking one ending after another for years. The struggle for survival drained me until finally, like a phoenix, I rose up again. I legally changed my name from Jamie Wood to Jamie Della, dropping the surname that attached me to the patriarchy. This new identity was made in deference to my Nana Della and is a declaration of my devotion to the Divine Feminine. I fell in love with a wild mountain man who accepts and honors my witchy ways and moved to the mountains and the forests so I could live deep in nature. In the calm of the wilderness, I listen to the whispers of the trees, connect with the consciousness of this alive world, and sense the Magick everywhere and in everything. Connie's final reading is proving to be true.

"My yiayia was a very skilled Witch," Kristen wrote to me recently. "I remember people telling me stories about her tarot readings chilling nonbelievers to the core because she would read their soul like she was meant to take its measure."

I am immensely grateful that my mentor's entire family was consulted and entrusted me with the magickal treasure trove of Connie DeMasters, Crimson Dragon. Witchcraft has traditionally been an oral tradition with lessons and tests, so I hope that my gift to you through this book instills in you the precious feeling of sitting with the Wise Ones just like my time at my mentor's knee instilled in me.

This book contains a mere sliver of all the knowledge that has been passed down to me from Connie and many other special Witches over the years. In sharing it with you, it is my inmost intention to inspire you forward on your path, helping you connect with your special and Divine Essence so you may shine as brightly as you were destined to—as a beacon of light for others in your life.

(※) Grandmother's Legacy by Connie DeMasters, from *The Enchanted Diary*

1954: I am seven years old, always under the feet of my yiayia (Greek for "grandmother"), especially in the kitchen. There is the familiar smell of the sweet blend of ingredients cooking on the stove in a small, long-handled, brass pot. Today is different: I've been formally invited to the gathering of women in our family to sit down; drink what comes out of the pot in very small, delicate cups and saucers; and partake in the ritual that follows.

1962: I am fifteen years old, spending the summer learning how to cook Greek food in the kitchen with Yiayia. I would rather go to the beach with my cousin. I came here to play; the last thing I came up here for was to work. Over breakfast, Yiayia gently reminds me that she is in charge. Resigned to my torture, I wash the breakfast dishes. Afterward, she notices my long face and starts making this funny clucking noise as she hands me the familiar long-handled, brass pot.

She says, "It's time to learn a little Greek Magick." For the first time, I notice how tiny and graceful her hands are. "There are two of us, so take two demitasse cups and fill them with water, pour the water out of the cups into the brass pot, and put the pot on the stove." I wonder to myself, *Has Yiayia always been so small?*

"Next, put a teaspoon of sugar per cup in the pot, then put a generous teaspoon of powdered Greek coffee per cup (you can also use Turkish coffee) and turn on the stove," Yiayia says. "Watch, because when it starts to boil, the coffee floating on the water will crack. When it does, remove the pot from the fire, count to three, then put the pot back on the stove. When it cracks again, take the pot off the stove, count to three, and put the pot back on the stove for a third time. As it starts to boil, count to three, throw a kiss at the pot, and take it off the stove."

I do as she says and wait for the next instructions.

"Now, pour the liquid into the cups, making sure they both have the same amount of coffee with equal froth on top. The froth is the start of your fortune and also the hardest to master. The hardest lessons to master are always connected to, and healed by, love, patience, and faith."

December 5, 1986: I am thirty-nine years old and Christmas is in full swing, but a veil of sadness dampens any holiday cheer. My father is dying. My yiayia calls to me. She is now a stunning, graceful woman of almost ninety. I am a yiayia now, standing in the same kitchen, cooking with the same brass pot.

"The coffee is ready," I say. My mood is gray as I sit down in the living room and pass Yiayia her cup. We sip the pleasantly sweet, thick coffee, and as we do, I look into the face of ancient feminine wisdom, her eyes sparkling and so full of mirth that I start laughing. And the ritual begins.

We slowly drink the coffee all the way to the grounds. We swish the cups around three times clockwise, then turn them upside down on the saucers, where they sit for at least five minutes. When we turn the cups back up, the grounds have left patterns in the cup. From this we read our fortunes. We have done this for over thirty years, hundreds of times, but never like this. The hair stands on end all over my body. I hear the crash of thunder in my head, and my ears ring. Looking into the cup is dizzying.

"What do you see?" comes a voice that sounds suddenly tired but also excited.

I reply, "I see a veil of the finest, most delicate lace with a face underneath at rest. I see a seven on one side of the cup, three doves flying up on the opposite side, and only one path out of the top. I see my father's peaceful death in seven days."

Quietly, my yiayia takes the cup and peers inside for what seems to be a long time. When she looks up, she has tears in her eyes.

"You are right," she whispers.

In that moment, our eyes lock. She takes my hands and says, "For many years, I have watched and waited for this time to come. For this power of sight was given to me, and for a while I thought it would die with me. You have proven where this power is to go, so I freely give to you what was freely given to me. Thus, it shall go on as it always has."

Yiayia drank coffee for five more years but refused to read the grounds. My father died on the seventh day. Today, I teach, and I watch, and someday another woman's day will come.

Celebrating the changing circle and going with its flow is at the base of the Witchcraft I practice, an eclectic earth-respecting path inspired by a fae Witch, Crimson Dragon, Celtic queen, shamanic priestess, and plant sisters. We are all our best teachers within the Witchcraft lifestyle. You are the one to determine what it means to honor the turning of the Wheel of the Year and the cosmos and how (or if) this communication will heal the wounds that have separated you from your light, essence, and your belonging in the grand web of life.

Through decades of practicing Witchcraft and ritual herbalism, I have come to believe that we learn much more about ourselves and our path when we have a mentor. Confidence grows when a mentor holds a mirror up so you can see all the wisdom inside yourself. And when you don't have that person to reflect all the beauty that is your Divine Essence, you have a magickal mirror to channel your bright soul. Rewild yourself by believing in the Magick that is within. Accept the invitation.

I learned the Wiccan Way sitting at the knee of a Greek yiayia for three short years, and yet the Crimson Dragon has been with me for well over two decades. She's still teaching me. Now, she's teaching you.

Acknowledgments

I am so grateful for this bonus year with my mentor Connie DeMasters, who has been teaching me how to see the gems in my past and the multilayered gifts from the Goddess that surround me today. It is with deep pleasure that I share that selections of Connie's collection will be preserved at the Adocentyn Research Library in Albany, California.

First, I must thank Alexa Bishop for such profound generosity of spirit to share your mama's magickal wisdom with me. My soul sister, thank you for your faith in me that I could make something beautiful from memories and spells printed in dot matrix. I am eternally grateful to all of Connie's family, specifically Shayla, Jason, and Kristen, for trusting me to depict my version of the Crimson Dragon for the world to know.

Thank you from the bottom of my heart to my superstar early readers who read every single word: Larry and Marianne Russo, Colelea Lea, and Barbara Dretzke. You are my heroes and heroines and I am so blessed to have you in my life. I so appreciate the tarot and divination insight of Tania Pryputniewicz and support from the Women's Ojai Wellness sisterhood (Helena Pasquarella, Annette Ayala, Irasha Moon, Virna Merino). Deep gratitude for the Mount Shasta Goddess Temple sisters and Mandala Priestess Yeshe Matthews, cousin coven of Courtnie Wolfgang and Kelle Smith (who co-wrote the Air Ritual with Willow), and my sweet friend Victoria Seaborn. I am grateful for the consistent encouragement of my Waldorf mamas Gina Illes, Kristen Krofina, and Gina Garrison; ALL of my crazy and wild-hearted Northern California Women's Herbal Symposium sisters but mostly especially Elise Higley, Reem Khalil, Tiffany Casler, Kris Knapp, and Laura Jaeger; the consistency of Chrystic Grizmacher; the always positive cheerleading from Meloney Hudson; the fine editing skills of Barbara Ardinger; ultimate hype-woman Tonya Cooper; writing guidance from Shawna Kenney, Marla Miller, and

Acknowledgments

Cherie Kephart; and my early champions in the publishing world, Windy Dorresteyn, Marcela Landres, and Julie Castiglia.

Thank you, Mom, for editing the shadow chapter. Your courage amazes me. Deep love to all my big, boisterous, and crazy Mexican family, and my children whom I adore with all my heart, Alethia, Skyler, and Kobe, and my sweet baby granddaughter Lucy.

I am so grateful for Katarina Samohin, whose illustrations have brought the Magick to life with images that capture the essence of each chapter. You have captured my words and sentiment with your art with such grace. Many thanks to my agent, Jill Marsal, and editors, Sarah Stanton, Lyric Dodson, and Alan Getto, for ushering this beautiful book forward.

Finally, thank you to my beloved mountain man, Joey Conti, for being there for me through the highs and lows as I wove the threads of this tapestry together to create and share *A Box of Magick* with the world.

Appendix

SUSTAINABILITY

When purchasing or harvesting herbs, consider the energy with which the plants were tended. It is among Witches' best practices to consider the *energy* of where herbs and crystals grow and how they are harvested. This energy, just like our intention, serves as an important ingredient for all rituals. The farm-to-fork movement has educated thousands of people on the importance of fresh produce. Something that was recently plucked from the rich soil has more life force and therefore more potency, higher nutrients, and more Magick. Seek herbs that look vibrant at your farmers' market, find small farms that practice organic, sustainable, and/or regenerative farming, or grow your own herbs. The United Plant Savers lists approximately forty herbs that are currently most sensitive to the impact of human activities. Herbs from this at-risk list that are most often used in magickal practices include palo santo, sandalwood, kava, echinacea, gentian, white sage, and yerba mansa.

It is also important, whenever possible, to consider whether or not the crystals you purchase are sustainably and humanely harvested versus collected by exploitative labor practices. Be wary of stones that have been trademarked, that suggest super-specific, brand-named uses, or those branded with obscure, scientific names. Sometimes these are simply artificially colored quartz crystals, and the higher cost is only because of the marketing. Whether you collect crystals for personal use, to sell, or for crafts that you sell or give as gifts, there are five important questions to ask before you purchase:

1. Were these crystals locally sourced?
Often you can purchase crystals from someone who owns a mine or makes a living of collecting crystals locally. Your knowledge of the crystal's origin fosters the connection between you and the crystal taken from the earth, which then

radiates and transmutes energy within your home, office, or wherever you place your crystals. Since crystals are alive with unique spirits of their own, those that are gathered where you live, like locally made honey, will have a greater ability to help you deal with the stressors of your immediate environment. These adaptogens can be plants, mushrooms, or crystals that energetically help your body respond to stress, anxiety, and fatigue and promote overall well-being. Where I live in the Eastern Sierra, you can collect white crystals, chalcedony, garnet, turquoise, quartz, and obsidian, just to name a few.

2. What is your relationship with the supplier?
You want to know which company or family owns the mine this crystal originated in so you can investigate their practices. We vote with our dollars based on whom we financially support, so consider this truth: you can buy a rose quartz from a family mine just like you can purchase strawberries from a family farm.

3. Are the crystals you are buying abundant and available, or are they rare and potentially endangered?
As of 2023, some of the plentiful crystals include carnelian, quartz, rose quartz, calcite, and amethyst. Some of the rare crystals include moldavite, Afghanistan lapis lazuli, malachite from the Congo, and meteorites from South America. If a crystal forms in a lot of places, you can be assured of its sustainability. If you own crystals that are on the brink of extinction, then be certain you respect and honor them as the last of their kind.

4. What are the labor practices of the countries where your crystals originate?
For example, pietersite is a crystal discovered in only one mine in South Africa, a country notorious for its slave labor practices. Reputable crystal books such as Melody's *Love Is in the Earth* or Judy Hall's *The Crystal Bible* will tell you where crystals are found.

5. Have you considered that the rocks and stones in your neighborhood carry Magick, memory, healing, and the unique spirit of the land?
Terrapsychology is the study of the soul of a place. Wherever you live, it is good enough to pick up a stone, rinse it off, place it under the moon, and ask it a question or for a blessing.

Appendix

COLORS

The natural and supernatural worlds speak in a vibrational language of energy carried on waves, whether by telephone, electricity, in hurricanes, ocean currents, or colors. Each color carries a unique vibration of energy that communicates to us and can affect our emotions and our Magick. You can wear a certain color, decorate an altar with a color theme, burn candles in these hues, or visualize yourself surrounded by a certain color to achieve the desired effect. As with all things magickal, the best results will come when you utilize colors in the way that best resonates with you. Your intuition is your greatest tool.

Red: love, desire, passion, energy, will, vitality, power, strength, confidence, courage, life force, health, and achievement

Orange: spirituality, success, attraction, adaptability, opportunities, motivation, harmony, encouragement, and happiness

Yellow: mental clarity, charm, light-heartedness, friendship, communication, joy, business, and solar energy

Green: money, growth, richness, calmness, nature, balance, employment, luck, prosperity, fertility, love, and healing

Blue: truth, peace, calm, healing, tranquility, understanding, patience, self-awareness, health, dreams, forgiveness, and water

Purple: intuition, power, divinity, royalty, spiritual communication, ambition, and opening to the spiritual world

Pink: unconditional love, nurturing, goodwill, affection, romance, friendship, and protection

White: protection, blessings, purity, truth, healing, meditation, and unity

Silver: meditation, hope, stress relief, clairvoyance, astral and lunar energy, and intuition

Brown: grounding, balance, endurance, stability, home, and security

Black: removal of negativity and blockages, shape-shifting, and banishing

MOON MONTHS

For centuries, the moon has been interpreted in conjunction with the zodiac, which provides guidance for the type of energy that rules or governs each sign. You can search online for which zodiac sign is affecting the full moon or any other moon phase. Different cultures, of course, will have different names for each moon, but these are the names most often used in the practice I follow.

January: Capricorn, Wolf Moon, Element of earth. Focus your Magick on security, financial gain, and comfort. Capricorn is the sign of the initiate, the hard-working sea goat that dives to the depths of the sea and climbs the highest mountain. Capricorn energy is sensible, practical, ambitious, ethical, and reliable.

February: Aquarius, Storm Moon, Element of air. Focus your Magick on humanity, intellect, freedom, and change. Aquarius is the sign of the humanitarian. This is revolutionary energy that is trendsetting, inspirational, individualistic, and exciting.

March: Pisces, Chaste Moon, Element of water. Focus your Magick on justice, growth, and pure intent. Pisces is the sign of the two fish and tends to be fluid and emotional. Pisces energy is steeped in sensitivity, intuition, spirituality, imagination, and compassion.

April: Aries, Seed/Pink Moon, Element of fire. Focus your Magick on manifestation, new growth, and fresh starts. Aries is the initiator of every cycle of manifestation and represents the seeds of your desires. Aries energy is self-motivated, energetic, courageous, impetuous, and inspiring.

May: Taurus, Flower Moon, Element of earth. Focus your Magick on what is blooming and beautiful in your life. Taurus provides us with the drive, energy, and desire to persevere against all obstacles. Its energy is persistent, caring, stubborn, visceral, and enduring.

June: Gemini, Dyad Moon, Element of air. Focus your Magick on communication, balance, and harmony. Gemini energy brings duality to our awareness in a fun-loving and expansive way. This energy is intellectual, conversational, thought-provoking, and aware.

Appendix

July: Cancer, Buck Moon, Element of water. Focus your Magick on gratitude, home, and relationships. Cancer is known for empathy and the womb of time. This energy is nurturing, intuitive, and protective.

August: Leo, Corn Moon, Element of fire. Focus your Magick on wort cunning, magickally connecting with herbs. Leo marks the birth of self-consciousness, and its energy is loving, witty, magnanimous, and radiantly ready for the stage.

September: Virgo, Barley Moon, Element of earth. Focus your Magick on precision of intention, celebration, and sustenance. Virgo represents sovereignty of the virgin. This energy is objective, disciplined, reflective, precise, and discriminating.

October: Libra, Blood Moon, Element of air. Focus your Magick on fairness, insight, and gratitude for those who have crossed over and their gifts. Libra represents balance and harmony. This energy is charming, diplomatic, romantic, creative, and generous.

November: Scorpio, Snow Moon, Element of water. Focus your Magick on transforming negative energy or bad habits. Scorpio is a secretive sign that enjoys deep mysteries. Scorpion energy is sensual, intuitive, and alluring.

December: Sagittarius, Oak Moon, Element of fire. Focus your Magick on conviction, steadfastness, and loyalty to self. Sagittarius is the sign of the archer, seeker, life student, and wanderer, and as such this energy is carefree, enthusiastic, optimistic, and childlike.

Recommended Reading

Andrews, Ted. *Animal-Speak: The Spiritual & Magical Powers of Creatures Great & Small*. St. Paul, MN: Llewellyn Publications, 2002.

Avalon, Annwyn. *Water Witchcraft: Magic and Lore from the Celtic Tradition*. Newburyport, MA: Weiser Books, 2019.

Bennett, Robin Rose. *The Gift of Healing Herbs: Plant Medicines and Home Remedies for a Vibrantly Healthy Life*. Berkeley, CA: North Atlantic Books, 2014.

Bethards, Betty. *The Dream Book: Symbols for Self Understanding*. Dublin: New Century Publishing, 2016.

Beyerl, Paul. *The Master Book of Herbalism*. Blaine, WA: Phoenix Publishing, 1984.

Budapest, Zsuzsanna E. *The Grandmother of Time*. San Francisco: Harper San Francisco, 1989.

Cameron, Julia. *The Artist's Way*. New York: TarcherPerigee, 2016.

Campbell, Joseph. *The Hero's Journey: Joseph Campbell on His Life and Work*. New York: Harper & Row, 1990.

_____. *Myths to Live By*. New York: Penguin, 1993.

Cunningham, Scott. *Cunningham's Encyclopedia of Magical Herbs*. St. Paul, MN: Llewellyn Publications, 1985.

_____. *Wicca: A Guide for the Solitary Practitioner*. St. Paul, MN: Llewellyn Publications, 1989.

Recommended Reading

Emashowski, Lynda. *Whispered Wisdoms of the Moon*. Self-published, 2018.

Della, Jamie. *The Book of Spells: The Magick of Witchcraft*. Emeryville, CA: Ten Speed Press, 2019.

Diamant, Anita. *The Red Tent*. Toronto, ON: Picador, 2007.

Echols, Damien. *High Magick: A Guide to the Spiritual Practices that Saved My Life on Death Row*. Boulder, CO: Sounds True, 2018.

Emoto, Masaru. *The Hidden Messages in Water*. New York: Atria, 2005.

Findhorn Community. *The Findhorn Garden: Pioneering a New Vision of Man and Nature in Cooperation*. New York: HarperCollins, 1975.

Forrest, Steven. *The Inner Sky: How to Make Wise Choices for a More Fulfilling Life*. Borrego Springs, CA: Seven Paws Press, 2012.

Gawain, Shakti. *Creative Visualization: Use the Power of Your Imagination to Create What You Want in Your Life*. San Francisco: New World Library, 2008.

Gilbert, Elizabeth. *Big Magic: Creative Living Beyond Fear*. New York: Riverhead Books, 2015.

Gladstar, Rosemary. *Rosemary Gladstar's Medicinal Herbs: A Beginner's Guide: 33 Healing Herbs to Know, Grow, and Use*. North Adams, MA: Storey Publishing, 2012.

Grimassi, Raven. *Spirit of the Witch: Religion & Spirituality in Contemporary Witchcraft*. St. Paul, MN: Llewellyn Publications, 2003.

Hall, Judy. *The Crystal Bible*. Plano, TX: Walking Stick Press, 2003.

Hay, Louise. *You Can Heal Your Life*. Carlsbad, CA: Hay House, 1984.

Houston, Jean. *The Possible Human: A Course in Enhancing Your Physical, Mental, and Creative Abilities*. New York: Tarcher/Putnam, 1982.

Ingerman, Sandra. *Soul Retrieval: Mending the Fragmented Self*. San Francisco: HarperOne, 2006.

_____. *The Book of Ceremony: Shamanic Wisdom for Invoking the Sacred in Everyday Life.* Boulder, CO: Sounds True, 2018.

Judith, Anodea. *Wheels of Life: A User's Guide to the Chakra System.* St. Paul, MN: Llewellyn Publications, 1997.

Jung, Carl. *Man and His Symbols.* Garden City, NY: Doubleday, 1964.

Kimmerer, Robin Wall. *Braiding Sweetgrass: Indigenous Wisdom, Scientific Knowledge and the Teachings of Plants.* Minneapolis, MN: Milkweed, 2015.

Kyber, Manfred. *The Three Candles of Little Veronica.* New York: Steiner Books, 2003.

Leopold, Aldo. *A Sand County Almanac: And Sketches Here and There.* New York: Ballantine Books, 1986.

McCoy, Edain. *The Sabbats: A New Approach to Living the Old Ways.* St. Paul, MN: Llewellyn Publications, 2002.

_____. *A Witch's Guide to Faery Folk: How to Work with the Elemental World.* St. Paul, MN: Llewellyn Publications, 2002.

Myss, Carolyn. *Sacred Contracts: Awakening Your Divine Potential.* New York: Harmony, 2003.

Noble, Vicki. *Shakti Woman: Feeling Our Fire, Healing Our World—The New Female Shamanism.* San Francisco: Harper San Francisco, 1991.

_____. *The Double Goddess: Women Sharing Power.* Rochester, VT: Bear & Co., 2003.

Pinkola Estés, Clarissa. *Women Who Run with the Wolves: Myths and Stories of the Wild Woman Archetype.* New York: Ballantine Books, 1992.

Redmond, Layne. *When the Drummers Were Women: A Spiritual History of Rhythm.* Brattleboro, VT: Echo Point Books & Media, 2018.

Ruiz, Don Miguel. *The Four Agreements: A Practical Guide to Personal Freedom.* San Rafael, CA: Amber-Allen Publishing, 1997.

SARK. *A Creative Companion: How to Free Your Creative Spirit.* Berkeley, CA: Celestial Arts, 2004.

Starhawk. *Spiral Dance: A Rebirth of the Ancient Religion of the Great Goddess.* San Francisco: Harper San Francisco, 1999.

Starhawk, Diane Baker, and Anne Hill. *Circle Round: Raising Children in Goddess Traditions.* New York: Bantam, 2000.

Teish, Luisah. *Jambalaya: The Natural Woman's Book of Personal Charms and Practical Rituals.* San Francisco: HarperOne, 2021.

Tompkins, Peter. *The Secret Life of Plants: A Fascinating Account of the Physical, Emotional, and Spiritual Relations Between Plants and Man.* New York: Harper & Row, 1989.

Tuttle, Susan Ilka. *Green Witch Magick: Essential Plants and Crafty Spellwork for a Witch's Cupboard.* Beverly, MA: Fair Winds Press, 2021.

Wood, Jamie. *The Wicca Cookbook: Recipes, Ritual, and Lore.* Berkeley, CA: Ten Speed Press, 2000.

Weatherstone, Lunaea. *Tending Brigid's Flame: Awaken to the Celtic Goddess of Hearth, Temple, and Forge.* St. Paul, MN: Llewellyn Publications, 2016.

About the Author

J amie Della is an ordained shamanic priestess, playwright, potter, and author of ten books, including *The Book of Spells* and *The Wicca Cookbook*. She has studied Magick and spirituality from around the world for more than twenty-five years. Jamie writes the "Herbal Journeys" column for *Witches and Pagans* magazine and for the "Writing the Magick" and "Homesteading the Hollows" blogs on her website. A fierce water activist, she launched the newsletter *Every Last Drop: Exposés on the LA Eastern Sierra Water Wars*, the *Keep Long Valley Green* newsletter, and wrote and acted in the murder mystery play, *A Bloody Day in Brawley*, a satire on LA's water steal in the Eastern Sierra.

Jamie offers both in-person and online workshops on creativity, water activism, SoulCollage® and ritual herbalism. Her bimonthly newsletters, published on the esbats, are inspired by rural living under a blanket of stars. Discover more at jamiedella.com or follow her on Facebook and Instagram @jamiedellawrites.

About Sounds True

Sounds True was founded in 1985 by Tami Simon with a clear mission: to disseminate spiritual wisdom. Since starting out as a project with one woman and her tape recorder, we have grown into a multimedia publishing company with a catalog of more than 3,000 titles by some of the leading teachers and visionaries of our time, and an ever-expanding family of beloved customers from across the world.

In more than three decades of evolution, Sounds True has maintained our focus on our overriding purpose and mission: to wake up the world. We offer books, audio programs, online learning experiences, and in-person events to support your personal growth and awakening, and to unlock our greatest human capacities to love and serve.

At SoundsTrue.com you'll find a wealth of resources to enrich your journey, including our weekly *Insights at the Edge* podcast, free downloads, and information about our nonprofit Sounds True Foundation, where we strive to remove financial barriers to the materials we publish through scholarships and donations worldwide.

To learn more, please visit SoundsTrue.com/freegifts or call us toll-free at 800.333.9185.

Together, we can wake up the world.

sounds true
WAKING UP THE WORLD